D1062759

PRESENTATIONAL
SPEAKING for BUSINESS
and the
PROFESSIONS

Under the Advisory Editorship of J. Jeffery Auer

PRESENTATIONAL
SPEAKING for BUSINESS
and the
PROFESSIONS

WILLIAM S. HOWELL
University of Minnesota

ERNEST G. BORMANN
University of Minnesota

HARPER & ROW, PUBLISHERS

New York, Evanston, and London

DISCARDED

WIDENER UNIVERSITY
WOLFGRAM
LIBRARY
CHESTER, PA.

Cover and chapter-opening illustrations
by Jim Spanfeller

Presentational Speaking for Business and the Professions

Copyright © 1971 by William S. Howell and Ernest G. Bormann

Printed in the United States of America. All rights reserved. No part of this book may be used or reproduced in any manner whatsoever without written permission except in the case of brief quotations embodied in critical articles and reviews. For information address Harper & Row, Publishers, Inc., 49 East 33rd Street, New York, N.Y. 10016.

LIBRARY OF CONGRESS CATALOG CARD NUMBER: 78–127343

CONTENTS

Preface   ix

PART I   THE BASES OF PRESENTATIONAL SPEAKING   *1*

1.   The Unique Nature of Presentational Speaking   3

   The Rise of Presentational Speaking   7
   Presentational Speaking Described   9
   Presentations Are Important Speech Events   10
   The Range of Presentations   11
   Presentations and Oral Reports   12
   Intraorganizational Presentations   12
   Interorganizational Presentations   14
   Interpersonal Presentations   15
   The Professional as Manager and Salesman   15
   The Presentational Speaker as Change Agent   16
   The Elements of Presentational Speaking   18

2.   The Environment of the Presentation   22

   The Cultural Context   23
   Formal Aspects of Organizations   23
   Informal Aspects of Organizations   35
   The Informal and Formal Structure of Organizations   35
   Summary   36

3.   The Dynamics of Face-to-Face Communication   38

   The Importance of Interpersonal Communication   38
   The Case of the Hasty Resignation   39
   The Paradigm of Face-to-Face Communication   43
   The Case of the Hasty Resignation Analyzed   53

Planning the Informal Conference   55
The Presentation in Two-Person Conferences   59
Summary   60

4. The Dynamics of the Business Meeting   62

    The Importance of Small-Group Communication   64
    The Complexity of Small-Group Communication   65
    The Tendency to Reject the Complexity of Group Dynamics   68
    The Tendency Toward Unrealistic Expectations   69
    A Realistic Picture of a Good Group Meeting   70
    Adapting the Presentation to the Small Group   75
    The Ad Hoc Meeting   75
    Meetings of Small Task-Oriented Groups   80
    Analyzing the Small Group as an Audience for a Presentation   86
    Summary   87

5. Motive Analysis: Prerequisite to Presentation   90

    Motivation Defined   90
    Emotions and Motives   94
    A System for Motive Analysis   95
    Habits as Motives   96
    Deficit Motives   99
    Other-than-Self Centered Motives   102
    Summary   105

PART II   TECHNIQUES OF PRESENTATIONAL SPEAKING   107

6. Organizing the Presentation   109

    The Earmarks of Sound Organization   111
    Message Preparation   113
    The Process of Organizing Materials for a Specific Audience   115
    Patterns of Organization for Presentational Speaking   120
    Three Basic Patterns for Presentations   122
    The Use of Notes   131
    Summary   132

7. Statistical Forms of Support   134

    Amplification   135
    The Role of Supporting Material   136
    The Case of the Deteriorating Cake Mixes   136
    Using Statistics as Support   139
    Graphic Methods for Presenting Statistical Summaries   156
    Summary   165

8. Nonstatistical Forms of Support   168

    Nonstatistical Evidence   169
    Evidence as Supporting Material   174
    Clarification as Supporting Material   175
    Summary   185

9. Reasoning as a Method of Presentation   187

    The Problem of Identifying and Evaluating Reasoned
        Elements in a Message   188
    The Proposition as a Key Element in Presentation   194
    The Effective Wording of Persuasive Propositions   195
    Planning the Reasoned Content of a Presentation   200
    How to Use the Unit Plan for Rational Presentation   201
    A Pattern for Problem Analysis and Solution   203
    Reasoning and Motivation   207
    Criteria of Reasoned Appeal   208
    Summary   210

10. Suggestion as a Method of Presentation   213

    Suggestion and Reasoning Compared   213
    Nonverbal Techniques of Suggestion   217
    Proxemic Elements in the Presentation   217
    Personal, Nonverbal Techniques of Suggestion   220
    Verbal Techniques of Suggestion   221
    The Use of Suggestion in the Presentation of Self   234
    Summary   241

11. Multimedia Aids to the Presentation   244

    What Audio-Visual Aids Contribute to the Presentation   244
    Participative Involvement Experiences   256
    Passive Involvement Experiences   261
    Still Pictures and Recordings   267
    A Multimedia Setting for Effective Presentations   276
    Summary   278

12. Responding to the Presentation   281

    Interdependence of Speaker and Listener   282
    Listening to Learn   288
    Critical Listening   295
    Recurring Fallacies of Presentation   299
    Creative Listening   303
    Summary   306
    Index   308

PREFACE

In our communication-oriented consultation with businessmen and women in many corporations, as well as with members of various professions, we have discovered that today's experts and managers need an understanding of and ability to make presentations, rather than training in public speaking per se. We find that skill in presentational speaking serves as a foundation for the study and development of other communication skills required of today's executives and leaders of professions.

It is true that managers and leaders give speeches to large and small groups within their organizations for inspirational purposes, or to audiences outside their organizations for public relations purposes. They are often aided in the preparation of such speeches by writers in their public relations and/or publicity departments in order that their remarks may be appropriate to the specific occasion.

A *presentation*, however, differs considerably from such a public speech. Its basic purpose is to secure a favorable response from those who have the decision-making power to accept or reject the proposal being presented. The proposal may offer an innovation, it may present a revised budget, the speaker may be "selling himself"—whatever it may be, the speech communication situation is significant and crucial because the communicator has a vital stake in the outcome. He knows he must make and defend his proposal in the give and take of a decision-making conference; that his success or failure depends on his ability to effectively inform and convince his peers or superiors and win them over to his point of view.

It is essential, therefore, that presentations be prepared with great care. In the process of such preparation executives become increasingly aware of difficulties in communication and of the need for overcoming these obstacles in order to achieve their desired goals. Training in making effective presentations is often what is needed when they request help with their communication problems.

A presentation carefully prepared, given under controlled conditions that exact a performance of professional quality, provides an excellent prototype for training in communication theory and skills for technical experts, organizational leaders, members of the professions and managers in business and industry. Anyone wishing to improve in organizing and developing ideas, exploiting visual and electronic aids, phrasing and delivering oral messages effectively can practice and study these elements in the context of the presentation. The very same skills will be found indispensable in less formal organizational communication situations, e.g., telephone conversations, interviews, the conference, and group discussion.

Presentational Speaking for Business and the Professions is based on an approach formulated to meet the needs of today's managers, executives, and members of professions who frequently must submit proposals to the scrutiny of their customers, peers, and higher management. The book is divided into two parts. The first portion examines the bases of presentational speech with emphasis on the unique nature of presentational speaking, the presentation of self, and the environment of the presentation. It also treats in detail one of the most important settings for intraorganizational speaking: the small-group meeting. The role of motives in the speaker–audience relationship is examined, and a system of motive analysis is proposed. The second section develops the organizational principles necessary to effectiveness in developing and delivering spoken messages. Throughout Part II the reader will find detailed discussion of the many techniques of presentational speaking, including the use of multimedia aids and elements involved in responding to the presentation.

The book is suited to undergraduate and graduate courses in business and professional speech communication which are designed to do more than present another course in "public speaking." The authors have for many years served varied business and professional organizations as consultants in communication. The present concept of presentational speaking grew out of current practices within the professional and managerial community, interpreted in the context of modern communication theory. All theories and applications have been tested repeatedly by on-the-job use. Consequently the reader can expect to find in this book materials that will help him meet present and future demands in his business or profession.

The authors thank the organizations and individuals who provided the photographs used in Chapter 11.

William S. Howell
Ernest G. Bormann

PART I

THE BASES OF PRESENTATIONAL SPEAKING

Presentational speaking in modern organizations has assumed an importance that requires study as a specialized form of communication. Very nearly all up-and-coming leaders and managers find it necessary, occasionally or frequently, to present proposals to groups with decision-making power. Part I treats the central concepts that are involved in the interpersonal interaction of the presentation so vital to the progress of both individuals and their enterprises.

Basic to our study are an understanding of the unique nature of the presentation as it occurs in an environment and knowledge of the ways in which that environment contributes to or detracts from the communication process. Certain fundamentals of face-to-face communication are crucial, as are particular dynamic relationships in task-oriented meetings. Finally, motives of the individuals involved shape their responses to the message presented. Part I of this book attempts to supply the reader with basic facts and theories on these fundamental matters to build a firm foundation upon which the techniques in Part II may rest.

CHAPTER ONE

THE UNIQUE NATURE OF PRESENTATIONAL SPEAKING

John Jamison finds himself confronting a problem in communication that seems incapable of satisfactory solution. For two years he has supervised the development of a new product, an off-the-beaten-track breakfast cereal which John is convinced can be promoted and sold profitably by his company. Now the time has come to take the next step toward that goal. Manufacturing processes and techniques are reasonably well worked out and tested. Cost estimates of production are firm. A market test of the new cereal involving saturation advertising and marketing in two large cities, St. Louis and Minneapolis, has been readied.

To proceed, John Jamison must have the approval of the Board of Control of his company, a group of seven representatives of top management. He has been allotted twenty minutes for his presentation, and has two weeks to prepare. His mission on P-Day: to persuade the board to approve manufacture of the new product and authorize the expenditure of $740,000 to ascertain its sales potential.

John considers his mission impossible because of the amount of information he feels obliged to transmit to the board and the absurdly brief time limitation of twenty minutes. A quick calculation shows him that if he tells the board what they really should know concerning the new product, about eight hours of lecture with visual aids would be required. To say that John is frustrated as he tilts back in his chair and contemplates the immediate future would be the understatement of the year.

With a nagging sensation of time running out, John has exhausted his conventional alternatives and is seeking frantically for *some* off-beat long shot, a last refuge, a final desperate expedient. He remembers a memo from The Training Division of a month or two ago that offered individual consultation to managers who are preparing presentations. Luckily, the one-page memo found its way into the bulging, dusty "Training" file instead of landing in the wastebasket. In a few minutes John has Paul Osterhus, an instructor in speech communication, on the phone, and Paul has agreed to join John at lunch in the company cafeteria.

Luncheon conversation between Paul and John takes several surprising turns, from John's point of view. He finds that his predicament of eight hours of material to present and twenty minutes to do it in is not exceptional, in fact it is the norm. He learns that success in coping with this problem has come, not from a masterly condensation of information into well-organized essentials, but from meeting the expectations of individual members of the decision-making group. For the first time he is made sensitive to the "pitfall of projection," the tendency we all have to design a presentation that would satisfy *us*, disregarding the preferences and prejudices of the people we will talk to. And he is led to appreciate that his first step in preparing his presentation is to analyze the motivations of the people who are to receive it. When he knows the priority of interests each board member has in any new product, he is ready to select from his mass of information what will be most persuasive to that person. This strategy of selection, rather than logical briefing, is the organizing principle recommended by Paul for one reason: in the past it has produced better results than any other procedure.

Back in the office, with a new set of guidelines, John sets about analysis of his persuasion problem, person by person. He has observed the board in action for several years, so when he begins to list statements about the dynamics of decision-making within the board, he has considerable information. He recalls that interaction among board members has been dominated by the three senior members, each with a vigorous and aggressive approach to group deliberation. John decides he will make his pitch to these men. The other four he sees as lieutenants of the big three. Hence, he need only convince his selected opinion leaders and his success is assured.

John begins motive analysis with Joe Perkins, president of the Company and the moderator at board meetings. Joe is "top status" man on the board in every way. He has the highest rank, the longest service with the company (he was one of the founders), and is older than the others. Joe Perkins' training for his present responsibilities was "in plant," on the job, totally. As the company grew and expanded into new product lines, Joe was solving associated problems of production. His particular talent was improvement of production techniques. Everyone knew that Joe could figure out how to produce any product more efficiently, for less cost. Now in his mid-60s, Joe has settled comfortably into thinking about the business operation in terms of the criterion that has served him so well throughout his career, "How can we keep costs down?" When previous new products had been presented to the board, John could remember how Joe kept harping at his one recurrent theme, costs. "O.K." he would say, "show me how soon we can pass the crossover point!" the "crossover" being that point in time when a new product starts showing a profit.

Next John turns his thoughts to Homer Lydgate, head of the company's marketing operation. Homer is in his late 40s, a hot-shot up-and-coming executive who had become an influential member of the inner group through several breakthroughs in advertising and distribution. Homer was pirated from a rival milling company some six years before. His advertising caught the fancy of millions, and the decision to create a new salary bracket for Homer and start him near the top has paid rich dividends. Under his direction, company merchandising evolved from the dullest in the industry to perhaps its most novel and exciting. Naturally, Homer perceives each new product in terms of its advertising potential. Novelty is his hang-up. Sound but run-of-the-mill proposals have little attraction for him.

The third member of the influential trio is Marshall Everding, known throughout the company as the theory-happy character on the top-management team. As company comptroller, he manages the financial operation with high competence. He enjoys keeping up with new developments in data processing and computer technology. His ideal is to run the company according to the most modern financial, engineering, and management theories, for only then, Marshall is convinced, can his company compete successfully.

One of Marshall Everding's favorite theories is that the company with the most complete product line, but one that is free of internal duplication, has a real competitive advantage that will build substantial profits over the long pull. Consequently, he fusses continuously about modifying manufacturing in the direction of making each product distinctive and, in the aggregate, covering the range of the market comprehensively. When a new product is being evaluated he has two questions: Does it overlap anything we are now producing? Is there a gap in our present line that this product can fill? If the person presenting the innovation answers the first question negatively and the second in the affirmative, to the satisfaction of Marshall Everding's informed and inquiring mind, then Marshall's initial apparent obstructionism usually changes to hearty support.

Already, John's presentation is taking shape. He devises a five-part strategy that serves as the organizing principle of his talk. Phase 1 is brief, a two-minute, rather technical, description of the new cereal he has developed. Parts 2, 3, and 4 are of approximately equal length, none to exceed five minutes. One of these sections deals with the cost picture, with particular emphasis upon evidence that the crossover point should occur in less than average time. Another section develops the novel advertising possibilities of this unique and extraordinary cereal. The third part of the presentation shows that the company, with the addition of the new cereal to its already extensive product line, can meet every known market better than can any single competitor. The time remaining, perhaps three or four minutes of the allotted twenty, John will leave for questions and comments, for he has learned the hard way that not every doubt can be anticipated, and unanswered questions block favorable response. The question period then becomes the last step in his five-part plan.

Implementation of the strategy is relatively easy. From his eight hours or so of material John can select impressive evidence to drive home his three-pronged attack. He enlists the help of the audio-visual section of his company to prepare eight or ten simple, colorful visuals to be used with the overhead projector. He rehearses before a sympathetic and knowledgeable associate who comments frankly and suggests changes. When the production has "jelled," with all visuals and major content items in approximately final form, he rehearses some more, always before the video tape camera. His notes are discarded, and his timing is practiced until he knows that with only an occasional glance at the clock at certain checkpoints he can finish "on the button."

John does not memorize his talk, because he understands that only a professional actor can make memorized lines sound fresh and spontaneous. To be sensitive to his listeners, and particularly to the influential three, he must react to them continuously. So he practices in an informal, direct, and conversational style. Many words and phrases that seem to be effective are retained as the talk gains in ease and smoothness. But no paragraph is ever literally reproduced in a subsequent rehearsal. To communicate effectively in the small-group situation, John knows that he must preserve the extemporaneous character of his speaking.

When the appointed hour came for the man to whom we have given the pseudonym of John Jamison, he was relaxed and ready. He felt that he had equipped himself to meet the needs of the occasion and more pertinently, to supply the facts of the case that would be most vital to his audience. In the actual instance acceptance of the proposal came quickly.

When John Jamison and his colleagues discuss his performance before the Board of Control, they do not refer to it as a "public speech." Business and professional speaking today is no longer public speaking in the sense of a speaker addressing a political rally or giving a college lecture or an after-luncheon talk. Men and women who work with and lead others in business and presentational situations seldom need training in public speaking. What the leadership community needs is to learn how to deal with communication problems like the one faced by John Jamison—that is, they need to learn to make *presentations.*

THE RISE OF PRESENTATIONAL SPEAKING

David Woods, whose first job title in an electronics firm was "Presentations Manager," and who spent two subsequent years working with about one hundred writers, editors, printers, typists, librarians, photographers, and visual specialists in the "Presentations Department" of a large aerospace firm, suggests that the use of the term *presentation* to refer to a business-related speech activity has been common since at least 1950.[1] The trend toward presentational speaking in business and industry has gained momentum since that time. Even the Dale Carnegie course has shifted its emphasis as evidenced by the slogan used in the late 1960s: "stamp out public speaking." By 1970, more and more important business decisions were made on the basis of face-to-face communication situations where the theory and techniques of public speaking were no longer adequate. The concept of presentational speaking as we develop it in this book represents theory that is evolving to meet the needs of business and the professions.

The development since World War II of the modern industrial state is one important factor in the rise of presentational speaking. Organizations within the highly developed countries have become more elaborate and complex. As a result, personnel in positions of leadership are frequently called upon to develop proposals, make explanations, and provide justification for past and future action and policy. These spoken communications take place both within and outside organizations. Usually, these ventures are of major significance both to the communicator and to the group which the speaker represents.

The complexity of organizational structure has been accompanied

[1] David Woods, "Presentations: A Semantic Illusion?" mimeographed paper presented to Speech Communication Association (formerly Speech Association of America) Convention, 1967, p. 2.

by an equally complex proliferation of goods and services. Even such a common necessity as the family automobile has become so intricate that a host of specialists must tend to its welfare. In addition, each automobile firm markets a bewildering variety of model lines and provides so many combinations of extra accessories that selling a car is no longer the simple matter that it once was. Many salesmen today must explain and sell a series of product lines requiring involved explanations of material, design, and function and intricate refinements of production and structure. Often selling a major product or service requires a careful and clear exposition of complicated matters that justify terming the interaction a "presentation."

The situation involving a salesman selling a car or new siding for the home is complicated enough, but much selling is even more elaborate. For example, representatives from a highly specialized electronics firm not infrequently find themselves selling a million-dollar contract for space-age components to a governmental agency or a military service.

We have mentioned only a few of today's representative speech-communication situations resulting from technological and organizational changes that have taken place in highly developed countries in the last few decades. Although history furnishes striking examples of diplomatic negotiations, military strategy sessions, and meetings among various representatives of civilian centers of influence, until recently such communications situations were unusual. North American society, however, finds such confrontations a routine chore undertaken frequently by top managers and public administrators. In short, we have witnessed in recent years a proliferation of speech occasions in which important issues are negotiated, compromised, or decided by representatives of corporations and other organizations.

Concomitant with developments in organizational speech communication was the rise of an audio-visual technology to support and enhance crucial messages. The evolution of radio, commercial and industrial films, and the recording industry in the 1920s, the development of cheap and dependable audio-tape-recording devices in the 1940s, the refinements and innovations in photography in the last few decades, and the rise of the television industry in the 1950s contributed to audio-visual technology. One illustration makes the point. Many millions of dollars are invested yearly in the production of television commercials. As a result, the art of preparing brief, effective audio-visual persuasive messages has been brought to a high degree of perfection.

Just as specialists appeared in the advertising agencies to work on various audio and visual support for the commercial message, so specialists in audio-visual presentations emerged to support the crucial persuasive messages of the organization. The major difference was that the television commercial was usually delivered by an announcer while most salesmen, managers, engineers, doctors, nurses, teachers, dentists, architects, city planners, hospital administrators, city managers, and so forth, had to give their own messages although they could often call upon specialists to prepare charts, slides, film clips, and other audio-visual aids to support their efforts. The above trends contributed to the evolution of the new format that is labeled *the presentation.*

Is the new format worthy of special treatment? David Woods, speaking from fifteen years' experience in government, military, and industrial organizations, suggested to the Speech Association of America that it "must insure that all speech students understand the theories and possess the necessary techniques to prepare and present presentations skillfully when called upon. And all students who enter a profession within business, industry, government, or the military *will* be called upon to assist with presentations."[2]

PRESENTATIONAL SPEAKING DESCRIBED

Why have the older terms gone out of style, and what is the referent for the new term, *presentation?* Perhaps, the best way to begin is to distinguish the referent for *presentation* from the activities that have traditionally been called *talks* and *public speeches.*

A talk is a relatively informal speech situation. Today a manager or member of a profession gives talks to small groups or audiences in the community. Generally, the speaker is asked to provide informative and authoritative insights into something related to his specialty. He may make a few remarks (seldom supported by audio-visual materials) and then throw the meeting open for questions. Talks are gratifying to the ego of the speaker (if the meeting goes well) and are useful and enjoyable for the audience (if the question period has been lively) but they seldom play an important part in decision-making.

Increasingly, the leadership community gives public speeches to large groups within the organization for inspirational purposes or to groups outside the organization for public relations purposes. The inspirational, public relations, or public service speeches are usually ghostwritten to a greater or lesser degree and they typically do not use audio-visual devices to support them.[3] (Even such an elementary aid as the blackboard is seldom used on such occasions.) The fact that an important person typically relies on someone else to write his speech indicates that the emphasis is upon giving a good impression to the

---

[2] *Ibid.,* p. 8.

[3] See, for example, "Ghostwriters Give Boss the Word," *Business Week* (January 21, 1967), pp. 72–74.

audience of both the speaker and the organization he represents rather than upon achieving change, justifying an action, or making a decision. The leadership community tends to give public speeches as representatives of their organizations for the same reason that firms invest money in institutional advertising.

When the individual who can read a speech written by his public relations department for the public speaking occasion and can speak informally to a community group needs to make a presentation, the situation changes. He must face the challenge of communicating where failure is damaging and success important to his own personal career, to his divisional unit, and, on occasion, to his entire organization. Usually, a person gets organizational help in preparing a presentation, but he cannot often rely on a ghostwritten effort. He cannot adapt to listener response moment by moment and handle questions competently with second-hand information and ideas. Delegation to a professional announcer or reader sacrifices prestige and in most instances the "pro" lacks the depth of information needed to interact with knowledgeable cross-examiners. Meeting the important communication situation of advancing a proposal may well be an instance of a key assignment that cannot be satisfactorily delegated. To state it plainly, to be maximally effective the top man has to prepare and deliver his own presentations.

What follows is a description of *presentational speaking*, derived from a detailed analysis of the realities of today and the demands of tomorrow in the career of a successful member of business, government, or the professions.

PRESENTATIONS ARE IMPORTANT SPEECH EVENTS

The term *presentation* implies an important speech situation. When someone presents something, he does so with a flourish that connotes importance. "May I present . . ." is an introduction that suggests the person being introduced is someone of substance and the occasion is important when contrasted with the simple "I would like to have you meet. . . ." A person gives a presentation to offer himself or herself, a sales proposal, a program, or a budget of some magnitude to others who usually have the power to accept or reject the substance of the message. Typically, the entire proposal is accepted or rejected in the sessions initiated by the presentation. It sinks or swims in the form in which it is presented. Almost always, stakes are high. Consequences to the people making the decision, and particularly to the person with the proposal, are substantial. The results of the presentation are immediate and measurable. Decision often comes in a few minutes, nearly always in a day or so, and it is typically a "yes" or a "no," categorically and finally. In a sense, feedback from the presentation is definite, concrete, and unmistakable.

Presentations are often made to peers or superiors in crucial situations. Presentations are given in a context where the individual is judged as to skill, understanding, and competence on the basis of the presentation. Much important organizational work is done via presentations at the highest decision-making levels. Lower management echelons work up proposals and make presentations to higher levels for final decisions. The typical presentation is prepared by the person who gives it in consultation with and aided by content specialists and audio-visual experts. Hence, one need not be an artist to have good charts and diagrams. But one does need to know what information is required and how to recognize a good visual when an artist presents one for approval.

Typically, presentations are developed upon request of a supervisor or employer who has the power to authorize them. One reason for the assignment of presentations is that they require audio or visual support or both and thus are expensive. On some occasions presentations may be given repeatedly to different groups but the most common situation is one in which a presentation is prepared with a definite persuasive purpose for a specific audience. Audiences for presentations may be a single individual, usually are a small group (five to twenty, occasionally as large as a hundred), and seldom multiple listeners and viewers via mass media.

Presentations are the most carefully prepared, structured, developed, tested, and rehearsed speech messages given by a member of an industry, a unit of government, or a profession. Quite often, the organization's higher-level specialists and managers become involved in reviewing presentations in advance of their delivery. The "dry run" is the rule rather than the exception. Only advertisements receive a higher ranking from top management in terms of inspection and approval. Frequently, a presentation is prepared in a way that resembles a professional theatrical production or a motion picture. Within the trade such elaborate presentations are sometimes characterized as a "dog and pony" show.[4]

THE RANGE OF PRESENTATIONS

As with most speech forms, presentational speaking encompasses a wide variety of practices. Presentations fall along a continuum. At one end is the presentation developed by one person to be given once and

---

[4] C. R. Gould, "Philosophy on Oral Presentations," mimeographed paper presented to Speech Communication Association Convention, 1967, p. 3.

at the other end is the message packaged by a team to be given by a group of people to many different audiences. Along the continuum fall presentations developed by one person to be given several times, those developed by several persons for delivery by one person, those developed by several people for delivery by several, those developed in a package designed for delivery by almost anyone, those rare presentations complete in themselves that may be presented by simply turning on the audio-visual equipment and to which a live spokesman may be added for additional effect, and finally those that employ a team of spokesmen.

PRESENTATIONS AND ORAL REPORTS

Presentations should be distinguished from oral reports that are not as significant as a presentation and that do not utilize the audio-visual resources of the organization as extensively. Audio-visual materials are optional for some routine speech situations; they are necessary for and characteristic of the presentation. Audio-visual materials play such an important role in the presentation that one might well think of them as central to the message. The situation is such that only carefully prepared audio-visual materials can do the job that needs to be done in the time allotted. The less elaborate talk required by a traditional meeting or training session is commonly called an *oral report*. Presentations and oral reports constitute the most frequent set speech situations in today's society. Other numerous forms of communication are the group discussion meeting and written materials such as reports, articles, proposals, and brochures. Quite often, a written report will be available to supplement a presentation.

Our emphasis in this book is upon presentational speaking. We do, to be sure, discuss oral reports as we proceed. We emphasize presentational speaking, however, because learning the principles of preparing and delivering the important messages amounts to learning thoroughly the same skills and knowledge that are required for the less complicated, less important, and more informal oral reports.

INTRAORGANIZATIONAL PRESENTATIONS

For illustrative purposes we will examine the typical presentations delivered in a business organization, recognizing that analogous situations occur in all organizations. In the modern corporation the need for presentational speaking stems from the fact that all important decisions require information and technical skill beyond the capabilities of any one individual. Decisions require the collection and organization of vast amounts of data, the accumulated wisdom of many people, and the artistic and intuitive talents of many others. All of this technical skill, talent, and information must be assembled and focused upon the problem in question to yield a policy, a decision, or a proposal for action. The final decisions of an organization will be wise and useful only insofar as they are based upon the systematic examination, testing, and understanding of each professional's contribution to the total decision.

The real accomplishment of the modern corporation is the fact that it provides talented individuals with an opportunity to become deeply, if narrowly, specialized. It enables each to relate his professional skills and specialized knowledge to those of the others. John Kenneth Galbraith asserts that the ability of the modern industrial corporation to combine the specialized abilities and knowledge of many people on one project "dispenses with the need for genius." He goes on to say that "the resulting performance, though less inspiring, is far more predictable."[5]

Similarly, members of professions find themselves delivering presentations and oral reports that are the product of a group. Where before, a medical doctor might have served in general practice as the diagnostician, laboratory technician, surgeon, pediatrician, and psychiatrist for a patient, today's medical specialist works with a group of other highly trained doctors and their skills and information must be coordinated. The electrical engineer, the certified public accountant, the marketing research analyst, the registered nurse, and the university professor also find themselves coordinating their work with many specialists within the modern organization.

The basic task of coordination requires that knowledge be brought to bear on the common purpose with efficiency and that the total organizational resources be mobilized. Coordination consists in extracting information from specialists, testing its reliability and relevance, and making decisions and plans. The part of the modern organization that guides and directs the enterprise consists, therefore, of individuals whose daily routine is dedicated to obtaining, testing, exchanging, and digesting information. Much of the exchange is by word of mouth. An important part, to be sure, is in committee meetings with the give-and-take that characterizes a good group session. On many occasions, however, the exchange is instigated and facilitated by a presentation or presentations.

One of the more important and widespread occasions for a presentation within the organization, therefore, is the managerial situation. Here a presentation leads to a decision by a higher level of

[5] John Kenneth Galbraith, *The New Industrial State* (Boston, 1967), p. 62.

authority. Here the organization selects a member to whom it assigns the responsibility for preparing a presentation for the next level of management. The presentation is delivered to a small group of relevant specialists and managers. The case of John Jamison is illustrative.

Another important managerial circumstance in which presentations are useful is a meeting of executives devoted to the regular review process leading to approval or disapproval of past actions or to the location and definition of current problems. The yearly evaluative session of profit-loss figures, product lines, and personnel performance at Minnesota Mills features presentations.

Presentations within the organization may also serve an educational function. Orientation presentations given to new employees explain the nature of a business or industry: explanations of how to do a particular operation within the company; or a review of policies. Such presentations as "General Research Corporation and You," or "How to Test for Weaknesses in the T18 Assembly," or "Our Retirement Program at General Biscuit Company," are examples of such situations.

We should note that much of the presentational speaking within the organization has a direct or implied persuasive intent. A presentation to higher management concerning past performance or a departmental budget for the next fiscal year usually implies that the person making the presentation wishes a certain kind of decision. Even such an educational presentation as "How to Test for Weakness in the T18 Assembly" intends that the target audience for the presentation will become motivated to utilize the information as recommended.

INTERORGANIZATIONAL PRESENTATIONS

When representatives from several organizations meet in joint endeavor, one or more presentations may be needed to facilitate business. When one corporation seeks to sell another a part, a program, or a product, the stakes are high for both organizations and the problems are often extremely technical. For example, if Information Systems, Incorporated, a manufacturer of computers, needs to subcontract a component to another firm, the contract is not let without considerable negotiation. If William's Tool and Die wishes the contract, they will usually send a team to meet with a similar team from Information Systems. The representatives will include not only salesmen and buyers but also electrical and/or mechanical engineers and experts in production. Efficient transmission of essential information is prerequisite to a productive negotiation. In this setting presentations are helpful.

INTERPERSONAL PRESENTATIONS

One important class of presentation is "organization sponsored" but the actual participants are salesmen and consumers. One does not expect a presentation when buying a hat or a toaster, but when a salesman is dealing in products and services requiring a major outlay of capital he may give a sales presentation. Some typical examples are an insurance salesman selling a comprehensive investment program, a salesman for a building contractor selling homes, a salesman selling new siding for a house, combination windows, and so on. In such situations the salesman often has a presentation supplemented by models, demonstrations, sample kits, filmstrips, or slide projectors.

Although the practice of using presentations in a professional-client relationship is less widespread at the moment, the time is coming when such presentations will be utilized to a greater extent. Recently, the dental school of the University of Minnesota added a faculty member with the title of Director of Communication and Behavioral Research whose duties it is to increase the communicative skills of dental students and to work with graduate dentists in developing better communication with their patients. Some orthodontists are using slide projectors, before-and-after pictures of patients, and other audio-visual devices in presentations to patients as they consider or embark on a program of orthodonture. Certainly other professions will come to more careful use of the techniques of presentational speaking to improve professional-client communication. Think of the improvement in doctor-patient understanding that would occur if medical doctors routinely gave a brief presentation about the patient's disease, tumor, broken bone, and so on. A significant proportion of presentations evolves out of the need of specialists and professionals to communicate with nonspecialists. As the professions become more and more specialized the need for professional-client understanding increases, as does the difficulty of communication. Presentational speaking is one avenue to the common ground of understanding.

THE PROFESSIONAL AS MANAGER AND SALESMAN

One of the concomitants of modern science and technology is the emergence of the professional (the narrowly and thoroughly specialized individual) as manager. Thus, the electrical engineer leaves the laboratory to become the departmental head, the experimental psychologist becomes dean, and the lawyer becomes governor. The specialized training and knowledge such an individual brings to his new job as manager is useful but must be supplemented with an ability to coordinate the efforts of others. Thus, the specialist-become-manager needs the ability to develop, present, and listen to presentations.

The manager needs the persuasive abilities required for presentations in order to function effectively. Frequently, he finds himself seeking to persuade people both in meetings within his organization and in meetings with representatives from outside agencies. In a very real sense professionals are becoming salesmen. In some of the most important negotiations in contemporary society the parties need to be technically trained as well as skilled in persuasion. For example, many engineers are influential in gaining acceptance for those large inter-organizational contracts that sustain our highly developed society. Professional training *and* persuasive ability are both prerequisite for many positions of leadership in our twentieth-century urban culture.

THE PRESENTATIONAL SPEAKER AS CHANGE AGENT

The case of John Jamison suggests many characteristics of the unique form of verbal communication called presentational speaking. The major generalization we can make about its successful application is in itself a guiding principle: *presentational speaking is proposal-oriented and audience-centered.* Everything that is planned and done supports the proposal that is being advanced. Yet all lines of reasoning, evidence, and illustrations are selected through analysis of the receivers of the message. One might envision this reciprocal duality as a transportation logistics model where the recommendation dictates the destination, the goal to be attained, while the receivers of the message determine the route, the means of transportation, and the speed with which the distance from starting point to trip's end can be traversed. ETA, the estimated time of arrival, is computed by combining the factors of destination, including distance and terrain, and characteristics of appropriate devices of known ability to convey a given load through time and space.

The goal of presentational speaking is almost invariably change; hence, with few exceptions, the presentational speaker is an innovator. A universal characteristic of people is resistance to change. The status quo seems preferable to rearranging the world because of our inertia, which is another way of saying that we are naturally lazy. The person who would initiate significant changes can expect to encounter resistance; hence, the innovator must be prepared to shoulder a burden of proof. This means he has a double job to do. He must satisfy the critical judgment of his listeners to the point where they will concede the soundness of his proposal. Then he must get them involved, personally, with his project to the point where inertia yields to positive response. The pitfall for the innovator is doing half a job. He produces conviction and stops there, not realizing that only agreement PLUS wholehearted involvement can precipitate the adoption process.

Above all else, the communication that occurs in successful presentational speaking is *interactional*. The X-factor that tips the balance most often in the critical presentation is not the quality of the information involved; rather it is the quality of the interaction between speaker and listeners. Typically, a trend sets in as communication continues. Either the audience and speaker grow closer together, or they drift apart. When the sender engages the interest of the receivers to the point that they are "caught up" in his message and are thinking their way through the presentation within him, even, forgetting that it *is* a presentation, the speaker has a kind of interaction that guarantees involvement. In the case of John Jamison we noted that he carefully avoided memorization, not only because he wanted to remain flexible and ready to adapt to developing interaction, but also because it is difficult to achieve joint reflective thinking with a message that is predetermined, word for word.

To the skilled and thoughtful innovator, the name of the game is interaction, but the foundation element, the ultimate and most rewarding talent, is the *ability to predict response*. When we single out an individual for excellence in interpersonal communication, what do we mean? We are not thinking about voice, vocabulary, or fluency. We are impressed by the person's sensitivity to people and situations, his high batting average in saying the right thing at the right time, his ability to avoid making foolish and inappropriate comments. Because he understands response tendencies of people, he knows what and what not to do. The reason he does not utter the tactless slur is because he knows how the recipient will react, something that does not enter the mind of his more self-centered associate. The only explanation of his consistently superior use of the spoken word to achieve his ends is that, to a degree greater than possessed by others, he has the ability to look at an individual *in context*, understand his reaction potentials and priorities, and come to sensible conclusions about the actions of that individual sufficiently accurate that unpleasant surprises are usually avoided.

We suggest that the self-centered person is less able to predict response. This is a subjective judgment, reasoned from the assumption that time spent thinking about one's self will not be devoted to picking up clues that might reveal the feelings of others. Research is needed to correlate personality traits with this central talent for interpersonal relations. To the present time we have established only that equally intelligent adults differ widely and reliably in this predictive skill. We are not certain that ability to predict response is responsive to training, and if it is, we as yet would not know how to set about helping an individual or a group work toward improvement. Truly, much remains to be learned about this dimension of sensitivity that is so extremely necessary to effective communication. But we can use the over-all concept "necessity to predict response" as a frame of reference in which to analyze and develop a methodology of presentational speaking. On a common-sense basis we can be selective about techniques and procedures, using the criterion of their probable utility in helping us predict the response of those with whom we interact.

Before we leave our examination of the presentational speaker in the role of innovator, we should note some factors in the presentational-speaking situation that limit and structure its format. Expectations are tuned to an occasion that may produce a vital decision, so participants are prepared to pay close attention. The factors of significance and high stakes restrict the range of persuasive methods that are suitable. Pressure-persuasion is inappropriate, typically. A "hard sell" is ineffective, because emotional responses are acknowledged to be misleading and hence are sternly controlled. There are few impulse decisions. The decision-making group checks on each other's thinking. As a result, "facts of the case" persuasion tends to dominate presentational speaking.

THE ELEMENTS OF PRESENTATIONAL SPEAKING

In the remainder of this introductory chapter we will overview the major factors of concern to the preparation and execution of presentations. These basic elements of presentational speaking are five in number; two of them are *central* and three we classify as *situational*.

Central elements.   Most elementary and fundamental is *presentation of the recommendation*, a determination of minimum essentials. In terms of the ability of specific receivers to understand and interpret the message, the proposal can be inspected and evaluated for clarity, meaningfulness, and efficiency. Organization and coherence are necessary, as is evidence used for clarification and support. These basic materials can be isolated and manipulated until an optimum arrangement is attained, but this must always be done *in context*, in terms of the people and circumstances of the actual presentation.

The second central element in the interaction is *presentation of self*. The history of interpersonal relations between the individual presenting and the persons receiving sets the stage for the reception of the speaker as a human being. At the moment he begins to communicate, forces in the thinking of his audience, and in his own mind, are operating for and against him. To some degree, he is a "nice guy" or a "stinker," a personal rating independent of professional competence. He is reacted to as he is located on the continuum from "highly competent" to "incompetent" by his listeners, and the score they assign to him influences their reactions to his materials. Both these initial judgments are revised, upward or downward, by the quality of the interaction between source and receivers as the presentation progresses.

The self-concept of the source can be a help or a handicap. Self-confidence—up to a point—enhances effectiveness. Fear, always based upon feelings of personal inadequacy, is invariably destructive. If the speaker feels quietly confident, thoroughly prepared, and can anticipate the interaction of the presentation with pleasure, he is certain to be more favorably received than would otherwise be the case.

Presentation of self is a major contributing factor to success or failure. Fortunately, it is the result of variables that yield to analysis and can be controlled.

Situational elements. The most predictable of the situational elements in presentational speaking is *adaptation to standard human obstacles.* We have mentioned rigidity, resistance to change, which is omnipresent. Usually, jealousy causes some opposition to a recommendation, in the form of reluctance to aid the advancement of an associate. In a group of a half-dozen professionals, no matter how intelligent, secure, and cooperative they may be, we can be sure that among the forces influencing their judgment are prejudice, vanity, timidity, pride, and ignorance. Presentations are too often prepared without conscious compensation for these universal human attributes. A part of motive analysis is to identify the standard obstacles in a particular group and adjust the presentation to minimize them.

Another situational element is *adaptation to particular circumstances.* In a sense every presentation is unique. Events preceding it have never happened before, and will never occur again. To some degree a room is suited or unsuited to the nature of the particular presentation to be made therein. The subject of the proposal lends itself to or makes difficult the use of audio and visual devices. The human and physical environments must be adjusted to *in the individual instance,* never by formula, if the potential effectiveness of the presentation is to be at all realized.

The final situational element is *adaptation to the motives of individual receivers.* Some low-level motive analysis can identify the standard obstacles, but effective adaptation to a variety of listeners is more complicated and difficult. Here the person planning the presentation must hypothesize what personal interest each key (highly influential) individual in the group has in the recommendation. What does each man see as important, what does he want as an outcome of the occasion? When John Jamison answered these questions of motivation for the three most influential board members, an appropriate operating principle became obvious and the strategy of his entire presentation evolved effortlessly.

This book attempts to expand and clarify the two central and three situational elements in presentational speaking in the context of modern business, professional, governmental, or educational organizations. We deal with these realistically as variables to be defined, understood, and controlled. For our reader we play the role of consultant, supplying counsel as Paul Osterhus did for John Jamison. If we are successful, the reader will find new and better answers to his problems of presentation, with, we trust, the success that rewarded John's thoughtful preparation and implementation.

QUESTIONS FOR DISCUSSION AND REVIEW

1. What are some of the factors in modern business, industry, and the professions that account for the rise of presentational speaking?
2. What are the differences and similarities between oral reports and public speeches?
3. What are some of the important features of presentational speaking within the organizational context?
4. What are some of the important features of presentational speaking in situations attended by representatives from several organizations?
5. What are some representative situations in which you foresee you will soon be required to make presentations?
6. What are the implications of the concept of presentational speaker as change agent?
7. What are the central elements of presentational speaking?

REFERENCES AND SUGGESTED READINGS

BORMANN, ERNEST G., RALPH G. NICHOLS, WILLIAM S. HOWELL, and GEORGE L. SHAPIRO. *Interpersonal Communication in the Modern Organization.* Englewood Cliffs, N.J.: Prentice-Hall, 1969.

DANCE, FRANK E. X. "Speech Education for Physicians and Dentists," *Today's Speech,* 5 (January, 1957), 23–25.

McBATH, JAMES H. "Speech and the Legal Profession," *The Speech Teacher,* 10 (January, 1961), 44–47.

MERRIHUE, WILLARD V. *Managing by Communication.* New York: McGraw-Hill, 1960.

THOMPSON, WAYNE N., and S. J. INSALATA. "Communication from Attorney to Client," *The Journal of Communication,* 14 (March, 1964).

CHAPTER TWO

THE ENVIRONMENT
OF THE
PRESENTATION

Every presentation takes place in an environment that significantly influences the development, delivery, and interpretation of the message. Among the most important elements in the environment of the presentation are the organizations which provide speaker, audience, and occasion.

In our discussion we will use the term *organization as* interchangeable with *institution* in the sense that an institution is "an organization, establishment, foundation, society, or the like, devoted to the promotion of a particular object."[1] Organizations include business and industrial firms, hospitals, charitable institutions, local, state, and federal governmental agencies, as well as legal, educational, administrative, and legislative bodies both public and private. We will not

[1] *The Random House Dictionary of the English Language* (New York, 1967), p. 737.

include crowds, mobs, audiences, public meetings, or other collections of people that have no officers, formal positions, bylaws, articles of incorporation, constitutions, or other rules of procedure established either in writing or by custom.

While ecclesiastical bodies differ from military establishments and while a manufacturing corporation contrasts in some respects with an educational institution, all organizations have much in common. Our purpose in this chapter will be to examine those common features of organizations that shape and restrict the presentation.

THE CULTURAL CONTEXT

Organizations reflect the cultural context of a given time and place. The organization of the Methodist Church in the early nineteenth century in the United States was a reflection of the westward migration, the frontier living conditions, the optimism of the times, and the zealous desire of the leaders of Methodism to save the great heartland of the Ohio and Mississippi valleys for Christianity. The organization of the Ford Motor Company in the early part of the twentieth century in the United States both shaped and was shaped by the industrialization and affluence of post–World War I America.

As organizational forms developed in one culture (for example, North American business organizations) are transferred to others (for example, joint ventures of Minnesota Mining and Manufacturing Company and Sumi Tomo in Japan), the structures modify and are modified by the culture. Thus, we say that Japan is becoming Westernized even as we observe that American business practices must be changed in order to succeed in the Japanese culture.

What is happening around an organization, its cultural environment, reaches into the organizational structure to influence the nature and flow of communication. A person planning a presentation ought not limit his analysis to the situation within a given organization and assume it to be isolated from the larger community.

FORMAL ASPECTS OF ORGANIZATIONS

Some communication within the organization is official and follows the formal channels, while other messages are informal and unofficial. The presentation is a major technique for *official* communication and therefore flows through *formal* channels. One seldom prepares a presentation for the grapevine. The *formal* characteristics of corporate structure, therefore, play a vital part in the shaping of presentational speeches. By *formal* we mean those structures that are indicated by tables of organization, job descriptions, position titles, lines of author-ity, and formal channels of communication. For example, the organiza-tion of the College of Liberal Arts includes a dean, several associate deans, departments, departmental chairmen, and numerous commit-tees with their chairmen. One can diagram the way all of the discrete elements of the college fit together on a chart which reveals the formal structure. An organizational chart implies levels of authority, division of tasks and responsibilities, and jurisdictional boundaries for various divisions.

Whenever people work together to do some common task or reach a shared goal, they discover, as they continue to work, that certain persons do some of the tasks better than others. Thus, over a period of time people tend to specialize and do more of those things they do well. The basketball coach plays his best men in a close game and he plays them in the positions in which they are most competent. Special-ization is a natural outgrowth of group effort and a key to successful accomplishment.

The management of an organization must solve two main problems in order to successfully mobilize its human resources to achieve re-sults. First, the managers must get the employees to do specialized tasks, and, second, they must coordinate and integrate the efforts of the various specialists. The typical solution to the problem of achieving rapid and efficient specialization despite employee turnover is to develop a formal structure. If the requirements of each position are clearly spelled out and if they are widely understood, individuals can be trained to develop the necessary skills in other organizations, by educational institutions, or on the job. Once trained, a person can readily assume a similar position in another organization. For example, the requirements of a relief pitcher for a professional baseball team are clearly spelled out and widely understood among baseball profes-sionals. If a team needs a relief pitcher, it can trade for one with confidence that as soon as the player arrives he can begin his job without a period of indoctrination.

Newly established organizations tend to start with a formal struc-ture based upon those developed by similar organizations. A new governmental agency will be organized along the lines of similar established firms; a new hockey team will be organized along the lines of the older hockey teams.

Formal structure and specialization. The demands of specializa-tion require that various tasks be divided among the personnel and that a given job be described in such a way that it justifies full-time effort of a capable individual but does not require so much that one trained person cannot perform the specified tasks. Quite often, of course, the formal structure that evolves over the years contains much wisdom. A successful organization's formal structure and traditions may be compared to an evolving computer program. As computer programs may be developed and shaped over a number of years by many different programmers facing many variations of the same problem, so may the design of an institution be shaped gradually by many people.

The computer program carries with it the accumulated wisdom of all the past programmers, and each new programmer can build upon that body of knowledge without having to start anew. Since the computer software has the power to store knowledge about data processing in a form that can be quickly assimilated by a neophyte, it accumulates knowledge so each generation of programmers can build on past achievements. In somewhat analogous fashion the formal structure of an organization contains the accumulated knowledge of the experience of many individuals. For example, the form of the organization may result from the knowledge that certain tasks can be assigned to one person because past experience indicates that people of a certain level of training, education, and experience have often performed these jobs. Frequently, a given formal position developed because another position was overloaded and additional help was required to do the work satisfactorily. Thus, trial and error in dividing up the amount and kind of work often produce the basic pattern of an organization. As a result, an appropriate organizational arrangement contributes to the efficiency with which people can be assigned to specialized functions. With the aid of the formal structure the very complicated work of many organizations continues despite their frequent changes in personnel.

Subtle distinctions among the various specializations soon appear. For example, some of the work may require exceptional skills, training, or commitment for its accomplishment and the number of people able to do the job may be small. Recruiting personnel for such specialized tasks may be difficult. The organization values most highly those specialists who are doing difficult jobs for which replacements are in short supply.

Typically, the formal structure indicates the difference in value to the organization of a given job by a status ladder. The basic organizational metaphors include climbing or descending, upper levels or lower levels, upper, middle and lower management, moving up or dropping down, achieving the peak or pinnacle or slipping into the depths.

Notice that we are discussing the *form* of the organization without reference to individual differences in the people who comprise it. We make no ethical judgments at this point about the question of whether some people *ought* to be considered better than others or if the pyramid and ladder metaphors are wise or useful in structuring human relationships. The fact of the matter is that for organizations task specialization inevitably leads to such evaluations.

Formal structure and coordination.   A second problem of organization facing any conglomerate of people trying to work together is that of coordination of effort. The formal structure of every organization should provide for one or more positions devoted largely to setting goals, dividing up work, integrating work, establishing schedules, and evaluating progress. Because the position of coordinator requires an overview of the way the specialties interact, it is typically placed above the task specialists in the structure. Often, observers of the organization rightly infer that the integrative positions are necessarily of higher status than the technical specialists. Frequently, people within an organization perceive the work coordinators (managers, supervisors, chiefs, officers, heads, chairmen, leaders, presidents, deans, etc.) as of greatest value to the organization. But not always.

The work of the organization may be such that some of the specialists themselves are of greater value to the organization and thus are awarded higher status. For example, the surgeons of a hospital may be more highly regarded than the hospital administrator even though the latter sets the date and time the surgeon may use the operating room. In like manner, the faculty of a college may feel certain professors to be of higher status than the dean.

The managers of any organization divide and integrate specialized tasks, set goals, and evaluate achievement largely by means of communication. The formal organizational structure, therefore, includes channels through which messages are to go to achieve the necessary coordination of effort. The formal channels are of particular importance for presentations designed as internal communication since they are official messages designed to flow through channels. People seldom prepare a presentation for an informal luncheon meeting, a talk about organizational matters on the golf course, over coffee in the cafeteria, or at a bar. However, one does not skip levels of structure or bypass or ignore positions that are part of the formal structure when giving a presentation.

As large numbers of specialized task functions are coordinated to meet the requirements of building a bridge, meeting a mass market, teaching thousands of students, ministering to hundreds of patients, or providing a postal service for several hundred million people, the organization must be able to identify successful and unsuccessful performance. The usual answer to the problem of finding job breakdowns and correcting them or of finding and rewarding unusually good work is to make a given formal position the locus for praise or blame. The person holding a key position relating to praise or blame has the responsibility for the success or failure of the work within the span of his command.

With responsibility the person has sanctions to punish and the ability to reward people within his jurisdiction. We will refer to the right to punish and reward as authority. One should not confuse the organizational meaning of authority with the use of the term to characterize an individual who, because of background and training, can do a particular job or can give sound advice on technical problems. A person might be an authority on diseases of the heart without having organizational authority within the hospital. The doctor's expertness goes with him wherever he goes. The formal position has a certain amount of authority associated with it no matter who assumes it. *Authority*, as we use the term in the present context, refers to an organizational assignment of the right to impose sanctions, offer rewards, make decisions, and commit organizational resources (money, manpower, etc.) to certain projects. "Only the supervisor has the authority to fire him," illustrates authority in the organizational sense.

Since an organization is composed of formal positions, arranged to indicate importance to the total enterprise, with formal channels of communication connecting positions, the basic structure can be represented pictorially. One can study the functions of every organization and make a graphic representation of the various specialized positions, their relationships in terms of higher or lower status, and the channels of communication among them. We shall refer to such a visual representation as the *table* of organization.

Figure 2.1 presents a table of organization. Positions A, B, C, D, $\cdots$ J are managerial. The other unlabeled positions are of specialists of various sorts providing work and services to be integrated into the total effort. Some of the specialists, for example those whose work is integrated by supervisor B, are of higher status in the organization than

Figure 2.1   Table of Organization

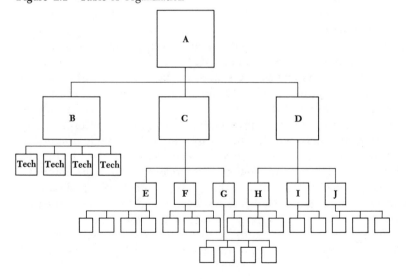

others (indeed, of higher status than some managers at the level of positions F and G). The lines connecting the positions indicate the formal communication channels that characterize the organization. Position E is connected by a formal channel to position C. Position E is not connected by a formal channel to position A. Thus, communications aimed at position A from position E must first be transmitted to position C and then sent on to position A.

Let us say that managers must make some important decisions about a very large project that requires the resources of the total organization. They must bring the work of the units managed by positions B, C, and D into coordination. Position A is able to use formal channels to send messages to B, C, and D, and they in turn may send messages back to A and to one another. Should the decision-making of the four individuals in positions A, B, C, and D require communication with the person in position E, the formal channels require that the messages for E be first sent to C and then on to E. (A large organization may have formal channels such that the individual in position A may send some messages directly to every other position. Even so, however, important messages for E from position A usually go first to position C.) Clearly, the transmission of messages through formal channels under these circumstances can become extremely cumbersome. Informal communications can get around the problems of using formal channels but they are unofficial. Decisions and other integrative efforts must eventually go through proper forms.

The official meeting provides a way for individuals of varying status whose positions are not ordinarily connected by formal channels of communication to communicate directly. People in positions A, B, C, and D may meet with the person in position E and thus establish direct interpersonal communication. The meeting supplements the *formal* communication systems effectively. Often, when the person in position E must present vital information to upper management in a meeting, he will use a presentation.

Position status related to the source of the message. Members of the organization who have little opportunity to communicate with persons within other divisions seldom know firsthand the people to whom they sometimes give presentations. (Again the informal communication channels such as the grapevine may provide rumors or gossip about a given person.) John Jamison was fortunate in that he could develop his presentation with some insight into the interests, abilities, and motivations of the three key members of the Board of Control in his company. Had Jamison been asked to make a presentaton on the new product to upper management at the Beaumont, Texas, plant where the product was to be manufactured, he could not have made so thorough an analysis of the audience and he would have had to rely upon cues from their formal positions. Of course, Jamison should adapt to the cues the audience in a branch plant provides him during the speech.

Further, the source of a message influences the perception of the message. That is, the same presentation made by a person in position C on Figure 2.1 to people in positions E, F, and G will probably have a different effect than if given to members in positions H, I, and J. The same message delivered to the same audiences by the person in position A would have a different impact than if C delivered it. The prestige and credibility of the source of a message is a factor in the persuasiveness of the communication.[2]

One must carefully discriminate between two elements of source credibility. The source of a message may influence a target audience because of the formal organizational position of the speaker. Thus, having a presentation given by the chairman of the board, by the president, or by an assistant vice-president makes much difference in its impact on an audience. The presentation may also have an impact because the speaker is charming, believable, trustworthy, and competent regardless of his formal position.

When the presentation represents a given unit within the organization rather than the personal position of the individual who makes it, the choice of the proper source for the presentation becomes an important part of the persuasive strategy. People planning the presentation should ask questions such as, would it be wiser for the manufacturing manager in position C in Figure 2.1 to give the presentation himself (although it was largely worked out by the assembly manager in position E) or would it be better to have the person in position E do it?

The decision as to which person in what position should deliver the presentation ought to result from careful evaluation of the audience and the purposes of the message. The first basic principle relating to source status and the presentation is: *all other things being equal, the higher the organizational status of the speaker the higher his credibility and the greater the effect upon the audience.*

The first corollary of the above principle is: *all other things being equal, the organizational status of a message source has a greater influence on internal organizational communication than on external communication.*

[2] Source credibility experiments abound in both psychological and speech journals. See, for example, K. Andersen and T. Clevenger, Jr., "A Summary of Experimental Research in Ethos," *Speech Monographs,* 30 (1963), 59–78, and C. Hovland and W. Weiss, "The Influence of Source Credibility on Communication Effectiveness," *Public Opinion Quarterly,* 15 (1951), 635–650.

Position status related to the receiver of the message. Equally important to the persuasive impact derived from the status of the source is the effect of the formal position of the members of the audience upon *their* perception and interpretation of a presentation.

The first basic principle relating to receiver status and the presentation is: *the presentation will have greatest impact if its preparation, context, and delivery recognize the formal status, authority, and responsibility of the listeners.*

One can hardly overestimate the importance of according each member of the audience the status, authority, and responsibility provided by his position in the formal organizational structure. People seldom like to be treated as though they had less status and prestige than they think they have. If a speaker treats someone as though he has less status than his organizational position implies, the typical response is a bristling "Do you know who I am?" Interestingly enough, if one behaves toward others as though their position has more status than is the case, they also become irritated. If we treat the lieutenant as we would a colonel, he becomes uncomfortable. Perhaps, the lieutenant detects the irony, intentional or not, or he may be reminded in a painful way that his position is not as important as he would like to think. Often, of course, the lieutenant may really think that he ought to be a colonel. Lacking sound evidence to the contrary, a speaker ought to accord each member of the audience the respect due the prestige and status of the person's position.

Even the decision as to which members of the organization are to attend the presentation is important to its ultimate success. If a person feels left out because he was not invited to the meeting, if he feels that his position was not recognized as having the status and authority he feels that it has, that very fact may cause him to oppose the change recommended by the speaker.

If the receiver of the presentation is of higher organizational status than the speaker, it affects the preparation, language, and delivery of the speech. When one speaks to a superior, these tendencies can be noted in the care with which messages are prepared (the higher the status of the audience the greater the tendency to make careful preparation), the candor with which one speaks (the higher the status of the audience the greater the tendency to make more guarded pronouncements and phrase commitments carefully), and the formality of the delivery (the higher the status of the audience the greater the tendency to adopt a more formal style of delivery). The status differential is important to presentations within and without the organization. John Jamison talking to his Board of Control had to adjust to the status differential. Likewise, a salesman making a presentation to the president of another corporation needs to be sensitive to reactions stemming from his listener's high status.

Position status and barriers to understanding. Low-status persons making presentations to high-status individuals tend to emphasize the positive and send on only the "good news," filtering out information that the speaker feels will be disturbing to his audience. The speaker's tendency to tell only good news is strongest when the listener has *fate control* over him.

Fate control is illustrated by the supervisor-subordinate relationship. When the subordinate talks to the "boss," he is usually conscious of the fact that the latter controls his salary, working conditions, job security, and promotions. The dangers of succumbing to the "good news" barrier are clear. If the subordinate does not pass on the pertinent bad news, he may suppress relatively minor difficulties until they become major crises.

When the speaker has higher formal status than the receiver, another set of barriers to communication appears. A speaker addressing listeners of lesser status tends to assume that his audience will interpret his message as he intends to have it deciphered. The high-status speaker tends to concentrate upon the content of his speech and neglect the audience. Generally, one finds it easier to be concerned about adjusting to the peculiarities of our superiors than to remember to be considerate of the habits and interest of those who work in positions over which we have fate control.

When the speaker has higher formal status than the listeners, he can predict that the audience will carefully search his presentation for hidden meanings and that they often will draw unwarranted inferences from slightly ambiguous remarks about matters of particular interest to them. For example, if Milt Brewer, sales manager of Minnesota Mills, makes a presentation to his salesmen to introduce a new method of evaluating selling practices, he may intend only to explain procedures. Arnie Swenson, however, who is disgruntled with his territory may infer that Milt is planning a sweeping reorganization of the division. Swenson may anticipate a different and better assignment. Should Milt make the evaluation but not change the territories, Arnie may accuse him of having made promises he did not keep. Generally, therefore, when Milt or any manager makes a presentation to people over whom he has fate control, he should be careful to protect against his listeners making wish-fulfilling speculations or interpretations from his message.

Communication among peers is usually the most comfortable. Peers seldom have clear and direct fate control over one another and thus are not as threatening. One can predict a less formal, more candid, and freer climate for the give-and-take following a presentation. Nevertheless, peers who meet and work together frequently develop differing amounts of respect and esteem for one another, and an informal pecking order often emerges. The resulting informal structure will exhibit the same specialization of function and the same arrangements of status as do formal positions. This is true even though it may be unique to the people forming the group. (That is, it may be unique in the sense that a change in personnel will change the entire pattern of roles and status within the group.) If informal groups spring up among peers, the status differential that arises will affect communications in a way analogous to that affecting the formal status arrangements.

Position authority related to the source.   When the members of a division of an organization plan a presentation, they must examine the authority as well as the credibility of the source when picking a person to make the presentation.

At this point we must carefully distinguish official organizational communication from the presentations of individuals. Often, the presentation is meant to be, and is clearly perceived to be, a presentation of the thinking and policy of an organizational unit or of the entire institution. Such official presentations contain the composite wisdom (or folly) of the group and the person delivering the presentation is not speaking for himself but for the entire group. On other occasions, however, a person may prepare a presentation which is his own personal approach to the question under discussion. The listeners all understand that the speaker is solely responsible for the content of the speech, he takes personal responsibility for it, and he in no way commits the organization to ideas within it. (Of course, even if the presentation is an individual matter, the person's organizational status and position cannot be eliminated as a factor in its interpretation. Nonetheless, when the president of an organization makes a personal, off-the-record presentation, it is a different matter than when he speaks officially for the entire group.)

To illustrate the various factors involved in selecting a source with high organizational status as opposed to a source with less authority, consider the following situation. The question under discussion is whether or not Systems Dynamatic, Incorporated, will build a plant in the ghetto area of the inner city. The public will interpret the very same message differently if it is attributed to different sources and with varying amounts of official sanction. For example, the president of Systems Dynamatic may give the presentation as official spokesman for the company. He may give it unofficially as his personal opinion. A vice-president in charge of investigating the project might give it as the official conclusions of his task force or as his personal opinion.

Official presentations by sources with the authority to take action are often drafted with great care and the language is searched for legal, technical, and public relations implications. Under such circumstances presentations may be partially or totally scripted. Often, too, while the presentation is made by the individual in the position of authority, a group of supporting resource people will attend the meeting and be prepared to deal with specific and technical questions relating to parts of the presentation. Official presentations by authoritative (in the organizational sense) people are designed to legitimatize and finalize the contents of the message.

A person with the authority to take action may wish to present material in an unofficial and personal way to get a reading on the response of others within or without the organization. The frequency with which high officials publicly suggest important programs of the federal government for the first time in university commencement speeches and campus lectures testifies to the importance of the "trial balloon" function of such presentations.

Position authority related to the receiver.   The authority of the people who will hear the presentation is a factor in its preparation and development. John Jamison was making his presentation to a group that had the ability to accept and implement his recommendation or to reject it. When listeners have this amount of authority, the persuasive elements of presentational speaking are most critical. The speaker having fate control over his listeners might succumb to the temptation simply to order them to accept his recommendation. Succumbing to such temptation is very unwise for any manager. It is true that giving orders is much easier and requires less discipline and understanding than developing persuasive presentations; hence, the threat of punishment is often used to force compliance. But the manager who resorts to "ordering" cooperation sacrifices the resources within the group. The employees' resentment at being deceived, apparently being consulted when actually they were dictated to, will prevent them from contributing their critical thinking and good ideas in the future.

The authority of the receiver of the message is a factor in presentations made by representatives of one organization to another. In today's corporate society a frequent setting for interorganizational presentations is a conference involving representatives from two large enterprises. For example, Systems Dynamatic, Incorporated, may have embarked on a three-year development program aimed at ultimate sale of something to the Defense Department of the federal government. The project is speculative until the company can demonstrate a workable prototype. At that point, the investment of time and effort by Systems Dynamatic may be translated into profit or loss by the outcome of a series of sales meetings in which a team of people from Systems Dynamatic confer with a group representing the Defense Department. The salesmen make presentations explaining the software and hardware of the system and its capabilities. They may demonstrate the prototype, discuss potential delivery dates, costs, and so on.

The authority (or lack of it) of the Defense Department group to commit the government to a contract is critical in shaping the content and the conduct of the entire exchange.

INFORMAL ASPECTS OF ORGANIZATIONS

Our discussion to this point has considered the influence of the formal characteristics of organizations on the development of and responses to presentations. If people were, indeed, interchangeable as the standardized parts of mass produced products like automobiles or washing machines, our discussion would be complete. However, individuals do differ in ways that affect their organizational behavior. The new manager does not do things in the same way as his predecessor. Although the new manager inherits the authority and prestige associated with the status of his position, he does not necessarily exercise his authority in the same way nor is he liked or disliked, respected or discounted, as was the other person. Thus, the formal hierarchy of status, authority, and responsibility is reinforced, discounted, and changed by the informal relationships that develop among people as they work together in the various task-oriented small groups that compose the organization.

In the course of working together some people demonstrate unusual competence in their specialties, so a person becomes not only a design engineer as predicted by the formal structure, job description, and so on, but he is perceived as an extremely responsible, hard-working, and gifted design engineer named Henry Walker. Others may exhibit unusual skills at working together with groups; they are able to initiate group projects, build cohesiveness and *esprit de corps,* mobilize group resources, and guide the group to successful completion of its tasks. As people demonstrate these various abilities, the others in the organization come to rely upon them to perform their specialties, particularly in times of stress or crises, *regardless of the formal structure of the organization.* Thus, an individual may come to perform tasks that the table of organization would assign to someone else.

Power. When "sizing up" the audience before a presentation, therefore, one should always examine both the formal and informal working arrangements of the people within the organization. To keep the two features separate for the purpose of analysis we will use the concept of power for the informal counterpart of the formal concept of authority. *Power* refers to the ability to make and implement decisions and changes. Power may be a function of the effective exercise of authority. Thus, the person in authority may make and implement the decisions and changes for which his position is responsible. On occasion, however, power may be exercised by a person without commensurate organizational authority. The latter circumstance generally results from an ability to command the necessary material resources and personal support of the members of the organization. Power differentials commonly emerge when people with varying amounts of authority interact closely in task-oriented small groups within the organization. The informal roles that emerge through interpersonal interaction may thus give an individual power disproportionate to his authority.

The earning of *esteem*, which is the counterpart of prestige, proceeds in much the same fashion as the accumulation of personal power. As people get to know one another by working together over a period of time, some demonstrate more commendable talents, personal characteristics, and accomplishments than others. The formal position of a person will limit to some extent the range of task behaviors that the individual can exhibit, but even so, a person can always earn greater or lesser amounts of esteem from his colleagues no matter what position he holds.

THE INFORMAL AND FORMAL STRUCTURE OF ORGANIZATIONS

In a sense the informal departures from formal structures of the organization represent a blurring of the lines of control, of the communication channels, and of the specializations established to increase the efficiency of the institution. From a theoretical point of view the organization would be much more efficient if the formal map matched the actual operations. When power and authority coincide, when prestige and esteem approximate each other, then those unfamiliar with the internal dynamics of the organization will be able to cooperate in a joint effort with less tension and waste motion. Learning the ins and outs, including skeletons in closets, feuds and attachments, requires time, effort, and tact. The energy devoted to such study could be invested in other activities if the organizational map fits the territory.

The student of presentational speaking, therefore, ought to begin with a thorough analysis of the formal context of the communication as outlined above. On occasion, one may have time for no more than that. Whenever possible, the next step is to examine the informal matters of power and esteem related to the personalities involved. For example, when John Jamison began his analysis of his audience person by person, he recalled the dynamics of group interaction on the board and the fact that the board was dominated by three powerful and prestigious members. He, therefore, aimed his presentation specifically at the big three. Because he was an insider, he knew that although all members of the board had equal status as board members some (like Joe Perkins, the president of the company) had higher organizational status and others (like Homer Lydgate) had earned power and prestige beyond their years and formal status.

Even more specifically, Jamison knew some of the hobbies, interests, and preoccupations of each individual in the big three. He could plan to accommodate his presentation to the individual directly. Fully exploring the adaptation of a message to a given individual takes us from the realm of larger context to direct person-to-person speech. The next chapter treats in greater detail the nature of interpersonal communication and how the student of presentational speaking can make concrete and detailed analysis of the individuals within the audience after having examined the organizational context and its influence.

SUMMARY

Organizations are formally structured conglomerates of people devoted to the achievement of a common goal. Organizations are shaped to some extent by the larger cultural context but most share some common formal characteristics, including positions with defined task responsibilities arranged in a status hierarchy and connected by lines of command or control and channels of communication.

The formal organizational structure affects such important elements of communication as the credibility of the source, the responses of the receivers, the perception of the surface or the deeper meaning of the message, the difficulty of achieving high-fidelity communication across status barriers, and so on.

As people work together within an organizational context, they often achieve working arrangements that depart from those one would derive from the formal table of organization. Within the restrictions imposed by the formal structure and the geography of the physical environment people get to know one another, become friends or enemies, learn to esteem one another as good people and good workers, and some earn extra power and esteem. Power and esteem affect the context of presentational speaking as much, on occasion, as do the formal considerations of status, authority, and responsibility.

QUESTIONS FOR DISCUSSION AND REVIEW

1. What is meant by the concept *organization?* By *institution?*
2. How can a formal organizational structure aid the leadership in getting the members to learn to do specialized tasks rapidly and

efficiently? How can the formal organizational structure hinder such effective specialization?

3. How can the formal organizational structure aid the leadership in coordinating the efforts of the various specialists? How can it hinder such integration?
4. How do the formal channels of communication within an organization compare and contrast with the informal?
5. What is meant by the concept *power?* By *authority?* By *esteem?*
6. What are the advantages and disadvantages of an official meeting as a formal setting for a presentational speaker?
7. What effect does the formal organizational position of a speaker have upon the way people perceive the presentation?
8. What effect do the formal positions of the listeners have upon the way they perceive the presentation?
9. What is meant by the concept of the *good news* barrier to communication?
10. What is the effect of organizational status on the presentational-speaking situation?

REFERENCES AND SUGGESTED READINGS

Argyris, Chris. *Integrating the Individual and the Organization.* New York: Wiley, 1964.

Bass, Bernard M. *Leadership, Psychology, and Organizational Behavior.* New York: Harper & Row, 1960.

Berlo, David K. *The Process of Communication.* New York: Holt, Rinehart and Winston, 1960.

Bormann, Ernest G., Ralph G. Nichols, William S. Howell, and George L. Shapiro. *Interpersonal Communication in the Modern Organization.* Englewood Cliffs, N.J.: Prentice-Hall, 1969.

Etzioni, Amitai. *Modern Organizations.* Englewood Cliffs, N.J.: Prentice-Hall, 1967.

CHAPTER THREE

THE DYNAMICS OF FACE-TO-FACE COMMUNICATION

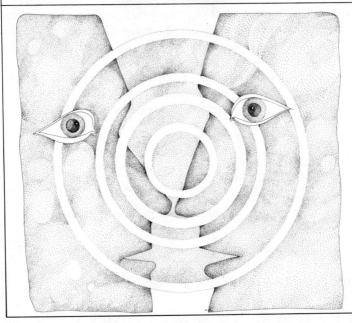

Having presented the organizational context for much business and professional speaking in Chapter 2, we turn in this chapter to the dynamics of the most basic communicative unit, two people talking together. The dynamics of face-to-face communication serves as a theoretical basis for our analysis of small-group communication in Chapter 4 and of the presentational speech in the remainder of the book.

THE IMPORTANCE OF INTERPERSONAL COMMUNICATION

Busy executives and professionals often dash from one conference to another. The doctor may see a steady stream of patients during his office hours. A lawyer may have a calendar filled with conferences with clients. A teacher may have counseling sessions with a number of students each day. A manager may move from a conference with his boss to a telephone conversation with a salesman from another company to a discussion of a problem with one of his subordinates to a briefing conference with his secretary. Often, the person under pressure feels that the communication events are coming so fast that all that can be done is to improvise on the spot. He may try to keep abreast of developments by relying primarily on instinct to keep going. Nothing could be more disastrous than to succumb to the temptation to improvise each conference, interview, or counseling session. Certainly, such casual improvisations contribute much to the poor quality of business and professional communication.

Another reason that the quality of communication within the informal two-person conference tends to be low is that it resembles the social interactions of passing the time of day. If a person can chat with a colleague about the play they both saw the evening before while having morning coffee, why not talk about a business or professional matter of considerable importance in the same informal, aimless, and casual way? The answer is that even the most casual dialogue is a complicated enterprise and that for two people to talk something over efficiently is more difficult than for two people to dance well, to sing a duet, or to play bridge together. To create misunderstanding in a discussion of a play is perhaps unimportant but to fail to communicate on important business or professional matters is serious. A sense of proportion about communication situations is required if the risks of poor communication are to be minimized when much is at stake.

The importance of the business conference and the disastrous consequences of poor-quality informal communication are graphically illustrated by the case of the hasty resignation.

THE CASE OF THE HASTY RESIGNATION

Cass Carlyle was a dedicated and able television station manager. Under his guidance WKDR-TV had grown into the most powerful and prestigious channel in the metropolitan area and had achieved national distinction. He was a former newsman who had risen to an executive position from his job in the news department. Carlyle took particular pride in his news programming. WKDR-TV had developed a unique, recognized reputation for providing distinguished, objective, and vital reporting of important news and in-depth treatment of important issues and stories. WKDR-TV under Carlyle's direction avoided emphasizing the sensational and stressed the careful preparation of its news analyses to assure absolute accuracy and fairness.

Carlyle hired Albert Johnson when he needed a new young man to groom for the position as top newscaster and analyst because of the failing health and approaching retirement of William Dawes. Hiring a replacement for Dawes was difficult. Distinguished, poised, an able performer, Dawes personified WKDR-TV news for the people in the market area. His personal following was large and loyal and included the most substantial and influential people in the community. Media time buyers fought for the chance to place commercials on Dawes's newscasts. Carlyle had searched, with the aid of his top people, for six months before they decided to bring Albert Johnson into the operation. Although Johnson was in his early 30s, he had already risen to a position as a reporter for a national television network. Well educated, with a bachelor's degree from an Ivy League school and a master's degree in broadcasting from a leading graduate school, Johnson seemed to be the best candidate.

Johnson had a compelling television personality, was a topnotch newsman, and seemed to have a quick and facile grasp of the deeper implications of events. Johnson would have been hired sooner had it not been for his flamboyance, which some of the news staff believed might be dangerous to the station's image. The news department was divided in its discussions prior to hiring Johnson. One faction argued that WKDR-TV was solid but in danger of becoming stodgy and that Johnson would be good for the department because of his flair. The other, headed by Winston Longacre who had some ambitions of his own about taking over Dawes's position, argued that Johnson was a bit superficial as well as flamboyant and that he might do something impetuous and unwise. In the end, Johnson's favorable qualities placed him ahead of the other applicants and he was hired.

Johnson had been with WKDR-TV for six months on the morning of the fateful conference with Carlyle. Johnson had started with a brief by-line spot of news analysis on the six o'clock and ten o'clock evening news. He also did the late news on Sunday evening. In many respects he proved to be a good employee. Everyone agreed that he had talent and that he was easy to work with except for a certain tendency to overreact in a crisis situation and for a certain professional arrogance. He had added a touch of excitement and an air of crisis, on occasion, to what had previously been a relatively low-key operation. Gradually, even those who had been against hiring Johnson were won over and the highly cohesive news department came to respect him and be pleased with his work.

Things were moving along very well when a crisis developed in the Middle East and Johnson gave a series of in-depth analyses of the situation on both the six o'clock and ten o'clock news. Carlyle thought they were brilliant. He was pleased by them. He was, therefore, upset when Winston Longacre asked for an appointment and told him that Johnson's analysis of the Middle East had disturbed several of the senior men in the department. Longacre himself was an expert on the

Middle East, having been sent to the region a number of times on fact-finding missions for the station. He assured Carlyle that Johnson had made several substantive errors on two of the newscasts. Carlyle probed gently to discover if, indeed, Longacre's complaint was related to his original position on hiring Johnson. Longacre assured Carlyle that he had changed his mind about Johnson and that he thought the younger man was an extremely able person, that WKDR-TV was very lucky to have him, but that in this instance he felt they owed it to the station and, indeed, to Johnson, to have the matter brought to his attention. Johnson could do a better job if he were a bit more patient, did his homework more carefully, and did not rely quite so much on his charm and talent, according to Longacre.

Carlyle discussed the matter with several other newsmen and decided that Longacre was right and that something should be said to Johnson about the way he had done his background preparation for the Middle East spots.

The next day, Carlyle was in his outer office discussing a problem relating to the cancellation of the Talbott Agency account with his secretary when Johnson stepped into the doorway with a cheerful greeting. Carlyle looked up with a frown. Seeing Johnson, he was forcibly reminded of the unpleasant task he must attend to and in characteristic fashion decided to do so immediately. "Hello, Al," he said, "Could you step in a minute?"

Johnson caught something of Carlyle's discomfort from his voice and noticed the frown on his face. He felt a moment of panic. Something serious apparently had happened. "Sure, Cass," he said, "I've got a minute."

The two men went into the office and Carlyle closed the door. Johnson noticed the move, which was somewhat unusual, and again he thought, "Something is up for sure." He searched for a problem or crisis that might have upset Carlyle but he could think of nothing.

Carlyle took a deep breath and cast about for some way to begin. If only Johnson had not caught him in the middle of that irritating business about the Talbott cancellation. Carlyle toyed with the idea of passing the time of day in some innocuous fashion and postponing the issue. But he had been station manager long enough to recognize the tendency of managers to postpone difficult conferences. Carlyle had a firm rule about not putting off painful decisions so he took a deep breath and plunged ahead.

Johnson, in the meantime, was watching with some apprehension as Carlyle sat back in his chair looking off at the corner of the office. To Carlyle the pause seemed short, while to Johnson it seemed very long.

"Al, I've been viewing those backgrounds of the news spots you have been doing on the Middle East with a lot of interest."

Johnson felt a wave of relief and relaxed. He felt very good about the Middle East spots. He had received some flattering mail, confirming his belief that the programs were very solid accomplishments. The old man was going to hand him a bouquet and he had been worried that something was wrong.

"Thank you very much, Cass."

"They've aroused a lot of interest. It's not always easy to interest people in the Middle East. That problem has been with us so many years."

"That's true," Johnson said, somewhat puzzled because Carlyle was still noncommittal.

"Sometimes I think that we in public affairs broadcasting get so involved in interesting the audience that we don't keep, ah . . ." Carlyle was proceeding slowly trying to find precisely the right words.

Suddenly Johnson was aware that something was going wrong. He was not going to get a compliment. Carlyle did not like his Middle East analysis.

"We don't . . . we aren't always as careful of the basic information . . . the foundation of facts as it were . . . not as careful as we should be."

"What do you mean?" Johnson asked, standing up and putting his hands flat on Carlyle's desk. Carlyle felt uncomfortable looking up at Johnson, yet he did not want to stand. The temperature of the meeting was rising too fast for Carlyle.

"Well, it's just that some of the boys feel you plunged ahead a little too fast without checking on certain basic background information."

"Are they questioning my competence as a news analyst?"

"No, no, it's nothing like that. They just note, for example, that your treatment of the Suez Crisis was not historically accurate."

Johnson leaned over the desk and raised his voice. "They're saying I did a bad job of research, is that it?"

"Well, no, I wouldn't say that precisely."

"What would you say then? Dammit, Cass, I like to have the cards all out on the table."

"All right," Carlyle stood up. "You did do a bad job of research. You jumped into it a little too fast. You're still a little too impetuous to be a good news analyst. You're going to have to learn . . ."

"If you think I'm incompetent why don't you fire me?"

"I didn't say you were incompetent."

"You said I was too impetuous to be a good newsman."

"Now, wait a minute. Don't take that tone with me."

"Either I'm incompetent and you ought to fire me or I'm not and you have no right to take pot shots at my series which I thought was pretty damn good."

"Just a minute . . ."

"If you don't think that series was a good one, you can have my resignation. If we can't agree on that, there isn't any point in my working here."

"Just a minute . . ."

"Do you think it was good or not?"

Carlyle lost his temper. "No, I think it was bad."

"All right, you have my resignation as of right now."

"Good, I accept it."

Johnson threw the door open and left the room. Cass Carlyle had some sober second thoughts. He was surprised and nonplused. It had never occurred to him that the end result of the conference would be Johnson's resignation. Johnson was also sorry about his hasty decision but both were proud men and neither would back down, so Johnson was terminated. Carlyle had lost an extremely valuable man, one that he might be unable to replace adequately. Certainly, the search for a new man would be time-consuming and frustrating. Johnson had lost an excellent position with a fine chance for promotion to a place of distinction in his profession. Neither man anticipated or wanted the outcome that resulted from their dialogue.

What had gone wrong? To fully understand the complicated dynamics of the case of the hasty resignation we need a paradigm of the process of face-to-face communication. Our paradigm of the interpersonal communicative process can serve as a basic frame of reference for the analysis of business and professional communication. It can be adapted to the two-person conference, interview, or counseling session, to the small task-oriented group and to the presentational speaking situation. We will now describe the paradigm, show how it provides the student with a set of useful concepts with which to analyze communicative situations, and then apply our paradigm to the case of the hasty resignation.

THE PARADIGM OF FACE-TO-FACE COMMUNICATION

A *paradigm* is an example or pattern that is a perfectly clear and complete illustration of the phenomenon under study. A paradigm contains all of the elements of a given class of events in ideal or standard form, exhibiting their distinguishing earmarks clearly, and in typical interrelationship. Synonyms for paradigm include terms like *model, ideal, standard, paragon,* and *touchstone.*

The standard anatomical descriptions of the human body contained in a text on anatomy would be analogous to a *paradigm* of the dynamics of communication. The standard anatomical diagrams include all of the normal organs arranged in the typical structures. The anatomical descriptions stem from observations and dissections of a number of cadavers but may not be a description of any one individual. A pathologist performing an autopsy might discover organs that are atypical in shape and location. Nonetheless, the doctor profits from a knowledge of the standard or ideal structure of the human body. The textbook descriptions serve as a guide to and a touchstone for the discovery, description, and evaluation of details of human anatomy.

In a similar way the paradigm of face-to-face communication results from the study and analysis of many communication events. The paradigm includes all essential elements in standard or typical form arranged in the standard or ideal structure. When a student applies the paradigm to an actual communication event, he may discover the pattern is truncated (some elements missing, some features of the process absent), underdeveloped (some elements in rudimentary form, some features of the process incomplete), or distorted (elements fully developed but out of place or proportion, some features of process exaggerated). Nonetheless, the paradigm serves as a guide and touchstone to the discovery of vital elements and important processes and to their description and evaluation. To lay the groundwork for the paradigm of face-to-face human communication we will make a preliminary analysis of a more elementary communication paradigm and then build our touchstone of human communication on that foundation.

The paradigm of man-to-machine communication.   Man may well learn more about the dynamics of interpersonal communication from his attempts to talk to computers than in any other way. We begin our discussion of face-to-face communication, therefore, with an analysis of man to machine communication.

An unprogrammed computer is a large conglomerate of independent electronic loci that can accept an electrical charge. At any given moment, therefore, a particular locus may be loaded with a charge or not. Out of a large number of such electrical plus or minus charges a complicated pattern of meaning evolves when the machine is properly programmed.

Let us assume that we wish to carry on a conversation with a computer. To begin with, the computer is more helpless in a communication situation than a newborn infant, for the latter can cry and move and express some internal states. The first step is to teach the computer a language. The most basic machine language is expressed in statements of the order, "at point x, y place an electrical charge." The computer can then be taught concepts built up out of patterns of electrical charges such as the Arabic numerals 0, 1, 2, $\cdots$ N.

We must next provide the computer with a set of rules about proper sentences and their grammatical forms and about the possible range of nouns and verbs that will be used in our language. We then tell the computer about the data we wish to discuss and where we would like to have it stored. The computer accepts the information encoded on punch cards or magnetic tape, decodes it into electrical charges, and transfers the electrical patterns to the locations indicated in its memory storage. Being careful to phrase our statements in precisely the right form, we tell the computer to process the information and print out the results. The computer then takes the electrical charge pattern from memory storage and translates it into impulses that strike typewriter keys which hit a ribbon and encode a message we can read.

If the messages we sent the computer are properly encoded (the machine *always* understands a properly phrased message and *always* misunderstands improperly encoded messages), then the computer will dutifully follow the directions outlined above and print out an answer which will always be right. We have succeeded in talking to the computer, and the man and the machine understand one another.

While talking to a computer may seem to be a relatively cut-and-dried matter with little artistry involved, in actuality, writing and "debugging" a computer program is a long, arduous, and often frustrating experience. An aid in the process of communicating with the computer is the fact that the machine is completely dependable and predictable. The computer always responds to the same words and sentences in precisely the same way. Programmers often tell a computer to take two values, to test if they are equal, and if equal, to go to a particular location and get the next direction, or if not, to go to a different location for directions. The computer will dutifully and reliably move in the path outlined, never veering one way or another. When one talks to people rather than a computer, they respond to the same words and statements in different ways and often take off in directions of their own choosing even when given definite instructions.

The main difficulty with talking to a computer is that the machine demands absolute high-fidelity communication. The computer never partially understands. It either understands completely or it stops and asks for more information or it just stops.

If the programmer develops a new set of directions for the computer, the computer accepts the orders without challenge. Again, the problem of ordering or giving directions to another human being is aggravated because unrelated factors may inhibit acceptance and compliance. A person may balk at orders because of the way they are given, because he does not like the person giving the directions, or because he does not approve of the objective they are designed to achieve.

If we define *process* as a series of progressive and interrelated steps by which some end is achieved, then the linking between man and machine represented by our discussion above can be called a communication *process*. Notice that the programmer initiates the communication and proceeds without interruption in step-by-step fashion

until the computer indicates trouble. At that point, the interrelationship that characterizes a process becomes apparent. The programmer
will have to do things the way the computer specifies if he is to
succeed. The end to which the process moves is selected by the
programmer. Success or failure of the process is thus a function of the
man achieving *his* objective through the messages he sends to and
receives from the computer.

The basic elements of the process are indicated in Figure 3.1. The
first step is for the programmer to decide upon some objective that can

Figure 3.1   Paradigm of Man-to-Machine Communication

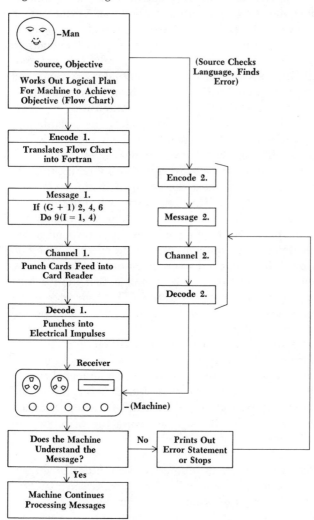

be achieved by the use of the computer. How much FORTRAN does the machine know?[1] How does the machine think (how has it been wired)? How large is its memory capacity? What logical computations can the machine make? Some machines make comparisons of equality and of greater than or less than. When the programmer has studied the machine and knows its language capabilities and its logical capacity, he can plan his presentation to achieve his objective. To do so he makes a step-by-step analysis of the logic of his problem and the way the computer can solve it. He may outline, brief, or diagram his plan in the form of a flow chart. Next, he translates his plan into FORTRAN statements, being careful that each statement is correct and that no crucial information is left out. When he takes his basic message and puts it into machine language, he *encodes* his message. The programmer may select several *channels* to reach the computer with his encoded message. The most common channels include punching the message on cards and having a card reader transmit the information to the central data processor or placing the message on a magnetic tape. (Computer technology has reached a level where typewritten messages and spoken messages may be transmitted to central processing. These form other channels to reach the machine.)

Assume for the moment, however, that in the process of telling the computer what to do the programmer made a grammatical error and omitted a comma. The computer hums along until it comes to the bad grammar. It stops and prints out a curt statement to the effect that the programmer has made an error of a certain type in a given sentence. The programmer checks the message at the point indicated, puzzles about the problem, and finding his error inserts the comma. He tells the computer the message again, this time in proper grammatical form, and the computer buzzes along until it comes across a word that is not in its vocabulary. Again it stops and prints out an error statement. Again the programmer studies the message, discovers his error, and rephrases the direction by either adding another statement to the message defining the new word before he uses it or by using only words already within the machine's vocabulary.

Conceivably somewhere along the way the machine stops. The programmer hopefully awaits information about the statement that has confused the machine but none is forthcoming. The computer only tells the programmer what has gone wrong if the error is one that the programmer foresaw and gave the computer directions on how to indicate the trouble. The current confusion is one for which the machine has no vocabulary. Often, the most trying time for a person trying to debug a new program comes under these circumstances. The

[1] FORTRAN is one of the more common computer programming languages. It was formed from the words *for*(*mula*) *tran*(*slation*).

programmer must search for the error without a hint as to where it can be found. He may try several times without success. But it is necessary to correct every error, for only when the machine understands completely does it proceed with the processing of data. Thus, the two of them, the man and the machine, work together to achieve absolute understanding.

Several features of the process of man communicating with machines are worth emphasizing. First, the machine does not initiate the communication. The computer remains inert until the programmer furnishes it with electrical energy and tells it to begin to do something. The flow of information is from man to machine. The machine talks back to the man primarily to clear up misunderstandings so it will understand what it is supposed to do. Second, the machine *always* indicates by a message or by total noncompliance that it has been unable to process some information or to understand some direction. Third, the machine will not tolerate bad grammar, faulty analysis of its vocabulary, or demands for logical computations beyond its capacity. Fourth, when the computer indicates a breakdown in control, it feeds back messages to aid the programmer to debug the process. *Feedback* has come to be one of the most important concepts in communication with the rise of cybernetics, automation, and computers. Feedback consists of information about errors in the message that the computer provides the programmer so the latter can achieve a state of complete understanding on the part of the machine. Complete understanding (i.e., the programmed machine) is a necessary means to the objective for which the programmer initiated communication with the computer. Fifth, the programmer is the *source* of the communication, he develops the objective, works out the logic, frames the message, and starts the machine. The computer is the *receiver*. The machine does not have an objective and would not process data if it were not for the initiative of the source. Once involved in the process, the receiver does not remain inert, however. The computer goes to work to absorb and understand the messages. When it decodes a message that breaks the internal rules of its wiring, it sends back an error statement that shifts the attention of the source from the over-all objective to the instrumental objective of solving the error. Thus, the interdependence of the process is clear. The programmer must play the game according to the common rules he shares with the computer.

If we abstract out the main elements in the paradigm, we are left with the *source* (the programmer), the *encoding* process (writing the program in FORTRAN), the *channel* (punch cards fed into a card reader), the *message* (the FORTRAN statements), and the *receiver* (the data processing system). The main process features of the paradigm include a complex, reciprocal, interdependent, give-and-take. The process exhibits a step-by-step approach to a clear objective, interdependent in that both source and receiver must cooperate to achieve the objective, and a corrective loop that includes a sensing mechanism to monitor failure and a sending device to indicate error and guide the source as he debugs the messages. The corrective loop is called *feedback*.

The paradigm of man-to-man communication. In many respects man exhibits the same behaviors when processing data as does a computer. Neural patterns are formed by basic all-or-nothing units; the neuron fires or it does not fire just as an electrical charge is present or absent at a given location in memory storage. At a given point in time, an individual's central nervous system contains patterns of information and like the computer the person's memories are fed into consciousness and there juxtaposed with patterns from other memory storage areas to form new combinations. The new combinations may then be spoken or written or simply read off internally from the display panel of consciousness by a person who is daydreaming or talking to himself.

Like the computer, man as a receiver of messages must have sentences in suitable form and expressed in words within his vocabulary before he can understand them. The grammatical rules used in interpersonal communication are much more loosely specified than those required by computers. People will tolerate and attempt to decode elliptical references, ambiguous statements, poetic flights, and sentences that violate the forms of good grammatical manners.

Like the computer, man as a receiver of messages can feed back error statements and indicate difficulty in understanding the message. Indeed, people are potentially much more efficient at furnishing feedback than machines and often much less efficient in practice. Man is potentially more efficient because of his ability to provide a much wider and more descriptive range of error statements spontaneously. The computer can only indicate a misunderstanding from the fund of error statements anticipated and provided by the programmer. A human being can indicate misunderstanding stemming from difficulties that never occurred to the source of the message. Man is less efficient on many occasions because unlike the computer, which will not continue the process until it understands every bit of the message, man as a receiver will often think he understands or pretend to understand a message when he does not. Hence, a person will not always ask for more explanation or proof at a point in a message where the computer inevitably would.

In the final analysis the major difference between man talking to a machine and man talking to a man concerns objectives. The source of the message in our paradigm has an objective and thus initiates communication with the receiver. The source's focus is upon that objective. When the receiver is a machine, the computer is compliant and accepts the source's objective without question. The computer enters into the relationship of interdependence and accepts control from the source as it is led to an understanding of what it is to do and it then does it. In short, the machine always accepts the interdependent role of being a receiver in the communication event. When the target for a message is another human being, the person often is not compliant, does not accept the source's objective without question, does not enter into the relationship of interdependence docilely, and does not accept control from the source. In short, the person initiating a communication event with another human is somewhat in the same position as a man asking a woman to dance. The potential receiver, like the potential dance partner, must agree to take part in the conference (or the dance) and must then accept the tacit rules that govern the dance or the communication. The woman must let the man lead, must follow the lead, and so on. If she does not accept the invitation, if she begins to lead, or if she fails to follow, the dance will fail. If the target for a communication event does not accept the role of receiver, then we often see a conference like the one that culminated with Al Johnson's hasty resignation.

On occasion, of course, a woman may feel that rejecting an offer to dance is to her advantage, just as potential receivers may feel that disrupting and aborting the communication event is to their advantage.

What frequently happens to complicate our paradigm of interpersonal communication is that after the initial attempt of an individual to assume the role of source with another person as receiver a contest ensues over whose objective will be achieved, over who will control the situation, and the interdependent relationship required for understanding may change to an interdependent relationship of conflict.

To examine the practical implications of the contest for control in a two-person communication situation, refer to Figure 3.2, which presents the paradigm of man-to-man communication. The source begins a communication in much the same fashion that a programmer begins to prepare the computer for data processing. The person has an objective in mind and develops the logic of his message to achieve that objective. He encodes the message into suitable language, keeping in mind the internal wiring of his potential receiver. In the case of another person the speaker must evaluate motives, interests, vocabulary, knowledge, habits, physical capacity, and so on.[2] Next, the person selects a channel or channels (sight, sound, touch, smell, taste) and transmits the message to the potential receiver. The message may or

---

[2] Much of the material in the remainder of the book will aid the student in the process of evaluating potential message receivers as to their habits, motives, interests, etc. See particularly Chapter 5 and Chapter 10.

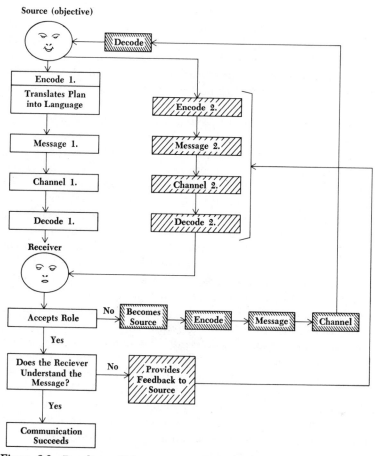

Figure 3.2 Paradigm of Man-to-Man Communication

may not be perceived and decoded by the target audience. If the audience is not reached by the first message, the speaker may transmit others until the listener decodes the message. If the listener accepts the role of receiver and agrees to allow the speaker to play the role of source, the communication can continue in a way very like the programming of a computer. The success or failure of the source in achieving his objective and of gaining a meeting of the minds with the receiver is primarily a function of the communicative skills the two bring to the task. Just as a couple may agree to and want very much to dance together without dancing well, so may two people agree to participate in a conference without doing it very well because they are inept at such things as developing the logic of a message, encoding it into appropriate language for the receiver, selecting channels wisely, and providing and interpreting feedback.

Often, however, the listener does not accept the role of receiver. Rather, the listener develops the logic of a message of his own designed to achieve *his* objective, which is incompatible with the first speaker's. The listener has initiated a new communication event in which he would play the role of source and the other must now decide whether to become a receiver or not. In short, the listener is trying to turn the tables on the speaker and wrest the initiative from him.

The listener's response is not *feedback* in the sense of information related to debugging a program to achieve understanding but is a message in its own right suggesting that if you wish to talk with me we must begin with agreement upon the rules, the objectives, and of our relationship. The person who initiated the event and sought to assume the role of source ought not interpret the message as feedback indicating misunderstanding that can be remedied by more careful encoding and decoding of messages but as a preliminary move much like the response to the question "May I have this dance?" that goes "Maybe and maybe not but if I do agree will you take me to dinner?" Unless common objectives can be discovered and a suitable interdependent relationship established, the other person is serving warning that he will not participate in a communication event that is reciprocal, cooperative, and aimed at achieving a specific objective.

If the first speaker fails to interpret the message of the second properly, he may continue to encode messages and transmit them to the other person doggedly trying to achieve his original objective and assuming that he simply has not managed to penetrate the thick skull of his listener. The second person may follow the same pattern and the result is the common spectacle of two people talking past one another, both functioning as sources in a truncated communication process with no one playing the role of receiver.

On the other hand, the paradigm of man talking to a machine or one man talking to another man represents the basic unit of communication. The more global events such as conferences and meetings may consist of a number of the basic units chained together in a productive pattern. First one then another of the participants may play the role of source for purposes of achieving several instrumental goals that are steps to the reaching of an over-all objective of one or more of the participants. Participant A initiates a communication to achieve an objective and participant B accepts the role of receiver, feeds back cues to facilitate understanding, and then, in effect, says, "Now, let me talk for a while." Participant A then accepts the role of receiver and so they proceed shifting from the role of source to that of receiver and back, but always playing the role in a cooperative interdependent way, providing feedback and achieving understanding in each basic unit of communication. The oft-deplored lack of good listening is frequently not a matter of lack of skill so much as it is an unwillingness of one of the partners in an interpersonal communication situation to play the role of receiver in the paradigm of interpersonal communication. (Which is not to say that good listening skills are to be neglected. Chapter 12 discusses the techniques of good listening and their importance to successful communication. Our point here is that until a person accepts the role of receiver, his behavior is often interpreted by the person who initiated the message as the result of a misunderstanding caused by poor listening. In fact, the behavior may have resulted from an unwillingness to accept the role of receiver in a communication game devoted to achieving the source's objective.)

THE CASE OF THE HASTY RESIGNATION ANALYZED

We have now laid the groundwork for the analysis of the disastrous conference at WKDR-TV. Let us see how the meeting between Carlyle and Johnson fits into the paradigm of face-to-face communication.

Carlyle began the meeting as source. His objective was to change Johnson's future behavior in preparing and delivering newscasts. Carlyle viewed the meeting as a coaching-counseling session in which he would discuss Johnson's performance and attempt to improve it. Johnson was never clear as to the objectives of the meeting. Carlyle encoded the first message and transmitted it by talking directly to Johnson. Before the verbal message was transmitted, however, Johnson was busy decoding Carlyle's random and unintentional actions. Johnson noticed Carlyle's facial expression when the latter looked up at him. Johnson perceived the way Carlyle closed the door, noticed the long pause before Carlyle made his opening statement. Because Carlyle was preoccupied with another matter and his own dilemma as a participant in a tension-producing situation, he did not perceive how these contextual cues and gestures affected his listener.

The first purposeful verbal message was, "Al, I've been viewing those backgrounds of the news spots you have been doing on the Middle East with a lot of interest." Carlyle wanted an opening wedge and intentionally phrased the message in ambiguous terms. He was not ready to raise the real point of the meeting until he had established some rapport with Johnson and had some indication of how Johnson would respond to a criticism of his work. Johnson, on the other hand, felt good about his work and was expecting and hoping for some recognition from his superiors about how well he was doing in his new position. He felt particularly well satisfied with the spots on the Middle East. He therefore read into the ambiguous message the meaning he wanted to have it convey. The old man was going to give him a deserved compliment. Johnson responded with a "Thank you very much, Cass." Carlyle was encouraged by the response to get down to business. Johnson was apparently going to be congenial and easy to talk with. He could get his little unpleasantness out of the way and get on with solving the problem of the canceled account.

Carlyle's next statement brought the issue out into the open. Johnson discovered he was not to get a compliment. At that crucial point in the session, he rejected the role of receiver asking for clarification and achieving understanding so the objective of the source could be attained. Instead, Johnson leaped to his feet and began encoding a series of messages designed to achieve an objective of his own. Just what did they think of him as a news analyst around here? Johnson felt he had been at WKDR long enough to start getting some indication of where he stood. Now he plunged ahead to find out. Carlyle for a time was off-guard and responded as a receiver, providing information and trying to help Johnson achieve his objective. But well before Johnson could discover that he was highly regarded by Carlyle and his colleagues in the news department and that the matter of the Middle East spots was viewed as a relatively unimportant and easily remedied matter, Carlyle rose to his feet and tried to reassert himself as source to achieve understanding and control and reach his objective. In short order both men lost their tempers in the clash of wills and the result was disastrous for both of them.

The post-mortem of the case of the hasty resignation reveals a truncated communication event when compared to our touchstone of the paradigm of face-to-face communication. Neither man accepted the role of receiver, neither provided feedback of a useful sort, and the necessary interdependent relationship was not established.

The session need not have gone in the direction that it did. Carlyle and Johnson never understood one another's objectives in the session. They may not have agreed even if they had come to an understanding but they would have been in a much better position to disagree productively if they had been aware of the dynamics of communication and taken turns playing the role of receiver, actively debugging the messages to discover their content. Instead, they simultaneously asserted themselves as sources of messages designed to achieve their own objectives. If Johnson had asked questions, sought clarifications, waited for a full explanation, he would have discovered that his work was appreciated and that he was doing well. If Carlyle had accepted the role of receiver and discovered Johnson's needs and hopes and provided clarification, the meeting could have been productive. After a preliminary meeting of minds about the over-all objective, which might well have been possible, the two men could have alternated as source and receiver to achieve understanding on lesser issues relating to the over-all problem.

Although ultimately both men must take the responsibility for the unfortunate session, Carlyle as the initiator of the meeting must assume the primary burden for the failure. The person who calls the meeting and transmits the first substantive messages, thereby assuming the role of source, has the burden of preparing and planning for the conference, interview, or counseling session. Although Carlyle would never think of going on the air without preparation, he was willing to initiate an extremely important business session without adequate planning.

PLANNING THE INFORMAL CONFERENCE

Actually, a good deal more can be planned for an informal conference than most people believe. We will not make an exhaustive list of the details to be planned but major items would include the place, the time, and the environmental details of the meeting.

Finding a suitable place. One of the first questions to ask in thinking through the plans for a conference is where would be a good place for the meeting? Carlyle asked Johnson into his office without thinking about the question. One of our colleagues once returned from a visit to the men's room during the intermission at a faculty dance to report that he had met the dean and that before the dean could escape he had been forced to conduct four business conferences. The tendency to broach important matters with another person when one happens to bump into him no matter how casually is widespread and unfortunate. Important communication events ought not to be undertaken in parking lots, in bars, in the car pool, on the drive home, or at the water cooler, at least not without some careful deliberation and conscious choice. We are not arguing against holding a conference outside the formal organizational environment. After carefully weighing the pros and cons an executive might decide to arrange for a luncheon meeting to discuss an important topic. What we are arguing against is the thoughtless discussion of important subjects in an inappropriate place.

For face-to-face dialogues between people who are part of the same organization the context as described in Chapter 2 becomes an important part of the planning. The status relationship between the two participants will be important, the interpersonal relationships developed in previous encounters will be important, and the organizational units that the two people represent will be a factor in their meeting. Carlyle, for example, could choose to have his conference with Johnson as he did in his office. He could have gone to Johnson's desk for the meeting. He could have invited Johnson to lunch or for a drink at a bar. Carlyle could have suggested a round of golf or invited Johnson to his home. If he wished to stress the supervisor-subordinate relationship, Carlyle could choose his office where all the symbols of his authority were on display including the large desk, the thick carpet, and the framed awards for excellence in public affairs broadcasting that adorned the wall. If he wished to play down the status relationship, he might go to Johnson's office or move the conference out of the WKDR building completely.

Finding a suitable time. Carlyle ought to have asked when would be a good time to talk with Johnson. If the person who is arranging the conference takes a moment to think of the other person's temperament, daily schedule, and current workload, a time most suitable for both participants can often be scheduled. To be sure, busy people have great difficulty finding time to meet, but even within the normal scheduling restrictions a good time is often available. According to legend, clever wives soon learn when their husbands are likely to be in a good mood for discussion of certain key marital topics and even then they do not begin talking about them until the signs are propitious.

Arranging the environmental details. For an important conference, a person should plan the details of both the surrounding environmental context and the nonverbal preliminaries that contribute to the social climate of the meeting. Chapter 10 deals with suggestive influences of the communication environment in some detail. Carlyle should have thought about closing the door of his office and what his response should be if Johnson were to stand during the course of the meeting. One cannot take every detail into account but the major ones should be planned. Even such a simple matter as the arrangement of furniture in the office can play an important part in the way the meeting evolves. If Carlyle sits behind his desk and Johnson is shown to a chair across the desk from him, the status difference is emphasized. If Carlyle comes from behind his desk and seats himself in another chair beside Johnson's, the move is likely to suggest a playing down of organizational status and it tends to place the discussion on a person-to-person basis.

If the person who arranges the meeting has taken pains with details like serving fresh coffee, clearing his calendar for the meeting so there are no interruptions from the secretary or from the telephone, if he has apparently spent some time in planning the meeting so everything appears well organized, the general suggestion is one of efficiency. A well-planned conference flatters the recipient because it communicates to him that the person thinks he is important. On the other hand, if the person arranging the conference cannot clear his calendar in order to be on time, cannot seem to get away from more important matters, is constantly interrupted by matters that take precedence over the conference, the nonverbal communication is anything but flattering for the other person.

Should a luncheon meeting seem advisable, the person planning a conference must take into account the possibility that the service will be slow, that the room may be crowded and noisy, and other incidental details of the environment so distracting that whatever advantages there were to the social informality and pleasantness of a luncheon meeting might be overbalanced by the unfavorable aspects.

Planning the conduct of the conference.   In planning the conduct of the conference the first step is to determine the objective. What would be the most desirable outcome of the meeting? The least desirable? What would be an acceptable outcome? Would pushing for the most desirable outcome force a decision that might bring about the least desirable outcome? For example, would pushing for a definite answer in a sales conference raise the possibility of a no-sale decision? Perhaps, planning the conference with the objective of getting the buyer to give serious consideration to the purchase might avoid a rejection and be instrumental to a subsequent sale.

With the objective clearly in mind, a person can develop a plan for the meeting. While one cannot outline a two-person conference as carefully as an extemporaneous speech, somewhat the same approach will be useful. How should I begin the meeting to develop rapport and create a climate in which the work of the conference can get underway? What major points do I hope to make? What is the best order in which to take up the main topics? How can the conference best be concluded? What follow-ups should be planned during the meeting? How is the other person likely to respond to the main objective I have for the meeting? What resistance can I anticipate? Do we have common ground that can serve as a starting place? What do I know about his personality, his motivations, his knowledge, interests, attitudes, habits?

Conducting the conference.   The person planning a conference can select one of two general strategies, the directive or nondirective approach to the meeting. For some purposes the directive strategy that finds the individual making strong moves to assume the role of message source and taking control of the channels of communication if at all possible is a good one. In the directive strategy the person initiating the meeting decides what topics to introduce, in what order, and attempts to keep the discussion to his plan. Certain purposes are well adapted to the directive approach. Among the ones most commonly achieved in directive terms are those of the briefing conference, the negotiation conference, the news and entertainment interview, the research interview, and disciplinary counseling sessions.

The second main strategy is the nondirective one popularized by the psychologist Carl R. Rogers.[3] In the nondirective approach the individual who initiates the meeting makes only minimal moves to

[3] See, for example, Carl R. Rogers, *Client-Centered Therapy* (Boston, 1951).

assume the role of source in the communication paradigm and is alert to cues from the other person as to which role relationship to assume. The nondirective strategy calls for an emphasis on listening, encouraging, being permissive, and seeking the role of receiver whenever it seems appropriate. The nondirective strategy is well adapted to certain therapeutic sessions and may be useful in the hands of a skilled person in such situations as the consultative conference, the problem-solving conference, the sales conference, the employment interview, and doctor-patient, professional-client and evaluative and corrective counseling sessions.

For many situations some balance between a directive and nondirective strategy is advisable, as is usually the case in negotiation sessions, sales conferences, consultative sessions, and the research interview.

In any case, no matter how directive the situation may seem to be, a good communicator will always be willing to play the role of receiver in order to achieve understanding. For some situations, of course, understanding does not assure agreement and success, but at least understanding is a minimal prerequisite for success.

Feedback is such an important component of the communication process that without it understanding is difficult to achieve. One cannot transmit the meaning from his mind to the mind of another any more than one can send the meaning from a human mind to the memory storage of a computer. What can be done is to stimulate the receiver and arouse meanings from the store of potential meanings available. Thus, a computer that has the concept of testing for equality taped into its memory can have that meaning aroused by the decoding of a suitable FORTRAN statement. The programmer, however, can only talk to the machine in hopes of arousing meanings that are within the machine's experience (previously taped directions and data). In similar fashion the source cannot hope to arouse meanings within the receiver unless they have been programmed into the person by his past experience. For two people to understand one another, therefore, feedback becomes a virtual necessity. Unless the source gets information about the meanings he has aroused in the receiver, he has no way of knowing how successful he has been.

Feedback should be planned into the conference. Since the two-person communication situation is often informal, it allows for both verbal and nonverbal cues as to the nature and extent of understanding. Nonetheless, conscious attention to feedback can increase both its quality and quantity.

Nonverbal cues to understanding or lack of it include shaking the head negatively, frowns, puzzled looks, interrogatory grunts or vocalizations, nods, smiles, and sounds of agreement.

Verbal feedback is primarily a function of questions. A questioning attitude, ability to listen, and skill in asking questions are the primary communication skills required to play the role of receiver. Questions take three basic forms, depending upon how pointed (specific) or how general they are. The most general questions are the open-ended ones, which simply ask for a response of some sort from the other person. The question may include some cue as to the general topic under discussion but otherwise leaves the nature and extent of the response up to the respondent. An open-ended question Carlyle might have asked Johnson is "What do you think of the current crisis in the Middle East?"

The most specific questions are those asking for a yes or no response, such as, "Did you discuss the Suez Crisis with Longacre when you were preparing your analysis?"

Between the general open-ended query and the yes or no response a wide range of questions is possible, each focusing the answer more sharply. The either-or question is one that poses two alternatives and by its form suggests there are no other possibilities. The saleslady who asks "Would you like the dress in blue or green?" is using an either-or question.

Questions can be phrased in such a way that they limit the range of possible answers and the field of discussion. To be more specific, "What do you think the role of Israeli air power will be in the current situation?" is an example of a probe that focuses the response more sharply.

Often, an interviewer can use sequences of questions to move from the more open-ended to the specific probes and achieve clarity and understanding. A person may begin by asking a general question and getting a vague answer that leads to a sharper question and a clearer answer that provides the basis for a still more penetrating question and clarification that ultimately leads to an acceptable level of understanding.

THE PRESENTATION IN TWO-PERSON CONFERENCES

The general principles discussed above as they relate to the less well planned and informal conference and counseling session apply to the situation in which one of the participants prepares and gives a presentation to begin the session. The very fact that a presentation is given implies that considerable time, care, and effort have been put into the preparation for the meeting by at least one of the members.

Presentations of every kind can be given to an audience of one. Sales presentations to the general public often are given to one potential buyer. The salesman selling aluminum house siding may bring his materials to the home and make a sales presentation to one individual. The salesman for a line of toys may visit a retail buyer and make a sales presentation in the buyer's office. Certainly, presentations relating to orthodontics, the use of prosthetic devices, the prognosis for serious illness, or procedures for surgery are sometimes given by doctors and dentists to their patients and might well become more common in the future.

In general, the audience of one creates an informal and intimate setting. The person making the presentation may choose to accept questions at any time during the presentation. The speaker can often get continuous verbal and nonverbal feedback. The fact that the speaker has carefully developed a message and supplemented his work with visual aids gives the person making a presentation a considerable advantage in assuming the role of message source.

SUMMARY

The main elements in our paradigm of communication include the *source,* the *encoding* process, the *channel,* the *message, decoding,* and the *receiver.* The process of communication includes a complex, reciprocal, interdependent give-and-take. The process exhibits a step-by-step approach to a clear objective, which both source and receiver must cooperate to achieve, and a corrective loop called *feedback. Feedback* includes a sensing mechanism to monitor failure and a sending device to indicate error and guide the source to develop new messages to achieve understanding.

Among the major items to be taken into account when planning an informal conference are determining a suitable place, a good time, and arranging the environmental details for maximum success.

The person conducting a conference, interview, or counseling session may adopt one of two general strategies, the directive or the nondirective approach. In the directive approach the person conducting the meeting tries to control the topics, the agenda, and the direction of the meeting. In the nondirective session the person who initiates the meeting or the high-status individual is alert to cues from the client, subordinate, or other person as to the role relationship to assume.

Feedback is such a vital component in the meeting that it should be planned for and worked for during the conference. Verbal feedback results primarily from questions. Every skillful interviewer is good at asking questions. The three basic forms of questions are the open-ended, the yes-no response, and the either-or questions. Often, the more sophisticated questioner will plan a series of questions that serve to probe basic issues and attitudes step by step and illuminate the topics under discussion.

Presentations of every kind can be given in two-person meetings. The audience of one creates an informal and intimate setting that makes appropriate an informal and low-pressure delivery of the presentation. Here it is usually possible for the speaker to get continuous verbal as well as nonverbal feedback.

QUESTIONS FOR DISCUSSION AND REVIEW

1. What are some of the reasons for the low quality of communication within the informal two-person conference?
2. What is meant by the concept of a *paradigm?*
3. What are the essential elements of the communication paradigm?
4. What is meant by the *process* of communication?
5. What is meant by *feedback* in terms of man communicating with machine? Of man communicating with man?
6. What is the major difference between man programming a computer and man communicating? What effect does this difference have upon achieving understanding?
7. What is the nature of conflict? Why is it an interdependent relationship? What effect does conflict have upon the process of communication?
8. What are some details to keep in mind when planning the time and place for a two-person conference?
9. What are the general features of a nondirective approach to a meeting? Of the directive approach?
10. What are the implications of interpersonal communication for the presentational speaker?

REFERENCES AND SUGGESTED READINGS

BERLO, DAVID K. *The Process of Communication.* New York: Holt, Rinehart and Winston, 1960.

BORMANN, ERNEST G., WILLIAM S. HOWELL, RALPH G. NICHOLS, and GEORGE L. SHAPIRO. *Interpersonal Communication in the Modern Organization.* Englewood Cliffs, N.J.: Prentice-Hall, 1969.

DANCE, FRANK E. X., ed. *Human Communication Theory: A Book of Readings.* New York: Holt, Rinehart and Winston, 1966.

MILLER, GERALD R. *Speech Communication: A Behavioral Approach.* Indianapolis: Bobbs-Merrill, 1966.

SCHRAMM, WILBUR, ed. *The Science of Human Communication.* New York: Basic Books, 1963.

CHAPTER FOUR

THE DYNAMICS
OF THE BUSINESS
MEETING

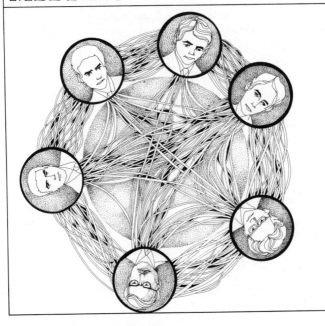

Two people talking together are influenced by the context of ever-changing things, events, and people. All of the formal and informal elements of institutions and organizations discussed in Chapter 2 impinge upon the two-person conference. When Cass Carlyle talked with Albert Johnson, the organization of the television station was an important factor in their communication. Included among relevant things, events, and people were the formal status of Carlyle, the tenure and position of Longacre, and the approaching retirement of Dawes. When we turn to examine the meeting of more than two people, we find the immediate social field becomes an even more powerful influence than the general organizational and cultural environment.

In this chapter we consider business meetings that are small task-oriented group sessions. We do so because the addition of a third person to the social field of a conference introduces a completely new dimension. We restrict the discussion to small groups because much research data provide useful information to apply to meetings of small groups of people.[1] For our purposes we will define the small task-oriented group as one consisting of from three to twelve people. The upper limits to the concept of small group are not as clearly defined as the lower. Nonetheless, certain qualitative changes that take place in the dynamics of communication as groups get larger justify restricting our analysis at this point to meetings of twelve or fewer people.

Research in small groups indicates that five is an excellent number for a work group.[2] Members of groups with fewer than five people complain that their groups are too small. Groups composed of an even number of people are not as efficient as groups totaling an odd number. Hence, five or seven is often a better size for a committee than four, six, or eight. In groups of five or less all participants speak to one another. Even those who speak very little communicate non-verbally with every other person in the group. In groups of more than seven or so the quiet members cease to talk to one another and talk only to the natural leaders and those who have high organizational or professional status. As groups get even larger, the talk centralizes more and more around a few people. Group interaction falls off. In groups of twelve or more a subgroup of five to seven usually holds the discussion, while the others simply watch and listen.[3]

The presence of peripheral observers who have a reason to be present at the meeting and who may vote on decisions does, however, affect the dynamics of the situation. An adequate concept of *audience* for the presentational speech must take into account the effect that the larger number has upon others in the meeting as well as upon the speaker. In this chapter we examine in detail the dynamics of the small

---

[1] For an integrated description of small-group process based upon the research, see Ernest G. Bormann, *Discussion and Group Methods: Theory and Practice* (New York, 1969). For surveys of research, see Barry E. Collins and Harold Guetzkow, *A Social Psychology of Group Processes for Decision Making* (New York, 1964); A. Paul Hare, *Handbook of Small Group Research* (New York, 1962); Joseph E. McGrath and Irwin Altman, *Small Group Research: A Synthesis of the Field* (New York, 1966); Dorwin Cartwright and Alvin Zander, eds., *Group Dynamics: Research and Theory* (New York, 1968).

[2] For a survey of research into optimum group size, see Hare, *op. cit.*, chap. 8.

[3] A study by Forston of sixteen simulated juries containing twelve members discovered that the "Central Work Group" composed of jurors preceived by their peers as being the most active and influential participants in the decision-making process averaged six members with a range of from five to seven. The Central Work Group accounted for about 82 percent of the communication in the deliberations. Robert F. Forston, "The Decision-Making Process in the American Civil Jury: A Comparative Methodological Investigation," Ph.D. Dissertation, University of Minnesota, 1968.

group as they affect the listeners. For the remainder of the book we treat the concept of *audience* in a generalized fashion to include groups of more than twelve.

THE IMPORTANCE OF SMALL-GROUP COMMUNICATION

"One can do worse," writes John Kenneth Galbraith, "than think of a business organization as a hierarchy of committees."[4] Indeed, the most important decisions in the professions as well as in business are often made by groups rather than by individuals. More and more frequently, for example, important medical decisions are made by a group of doctors and technicians consulting about a patient rather than by one doctor alone.

A larger and larger percentage of the time of leaders in businesses and professions is devoted to meetings each year. The trend will undoubtedly continue because, as we noted in Chapter 2, the members of a corporation or organization often wish to talk things over directly. When they are inhibited from doing so by the formal structure of the organization they have two main alternatives: (1) utilize the grape-vine or some informal channel, or (2) discuss the matter in an official business meeting where binding decisions can be made.

The committee session and the business meeting are among the most important forms of communication in any organization. The small task-oriented group discussion can inform personnel directly about important matters in a setting where they can ask questions and make comments. No form of written or pictorial communication can make this claim. In addition, meetings of small task-oriented groups can build a feeling of commitment and involvement, a sense of group and organizational loyalty that is vital to the successful functioning of organizations.

In the years since World War II modern management theory has been influenced by the discovery of the vital importance of small task-oriented groups to the successful functioning of corporations and other organizations. The result is that today's manager needs to understand how to manage a team as well as how to work with individual subordi-

---

[4] Galbraith also writes: "Nor should it be supposed that this is an inefficient procedure. On the contrary it is, normally, the only efficient procedure. Association in a committee enables each member to come to know the intellectual resources and the reliability of his colleagues. Committee discussion enable members to pool information under circumstances which allow, also, of immediate probing to assess the relevance and reliability of the information offered." John Kenneth Galbraith, *The New Industrial State* (Boston, 1967), p. 64.

nates. He recognizes that people are heavily influenced by the small groups to which they belong.[5]

Just as a manager must understand the dynamics of groups in order to manage his unit, so must the presentational speaker understand the nature of group meetings in order to prepare and deliver successful presentations. In Chapter 3 we presented the paradigm of face-to-face communication in a two-person communication situation. In this chapter we examine the additional variables in the small group and their influence upon the attitudes, expectations, and behaviors of participants.

THE COMPLEXITY OF SMALL-GROUP COMMUNICATION

Quite often, people who have not studied science since junior high school view the theories of the physical sciences as difficult to understand. Many engineers who have moved into managerial positions have the notion that physics, chemistry, and electronics are much more complicated and difficult than are presentational speaking or small-group communication.

To compare the levels of complexity of the natural sciences with the study of small-group communication we will compare Newton's law of gravity to our paradigm of man-to-man communication. We urge the reader who feels that Newtonian physics is an exceedingly difficult subject to study the next few paragraphs carefully for we propose to demonstrate that understanding and applying Newton's law of gravity to the study of planetary motion is less difficult than understanding and applying the paradigm of man-to-man communication to the small group.

Newton discovered that there is a tendency for every body in the universe to move toward every other body. Every particle of matter behaves as though it were attracted to and attracted by every other particle, with a directional force working on a line joining the particles. The force with which the bodies attract one another is related to their mass. The force of attraction between the sun and the earth causes the earth to fall toward the sun and describe an orbit around it. The same attraction that pulls the earth and sun together also draws our bodies toward the surface of the earth and is commonly referred to as the force of gravity. In addition to the size of the bodies, Newton discovered that one other factor affected the strength with which the

---

[5] For representative works dealing with the concept of managing a group as well as individuals, see Rensis Likert, *The Human Organization: Its Management and Value* (New York, 1967), and Douglas McGregor, *The Professional Manager* (New York, 1967).

force drew two objects together, namely, the distance between their centers. The force of attraction between two spherical bodies of any size, according to Newton, is proportional to the sum of their masses multiplied and inversely proportional to the square of the distance between their centers. A person might have to consciously recall the technical meanings of *proportional* and *inversely proportional* but the concepts are no more difficult than those of *feedback* and *meaning*. To say that the force is proportional to the size of the bodies means simply that the greater the mass of the objects the stronger their pull. To state that the force is inversely proportional to the square of the distance is simply to say that the further apart the objects the less pull they exert on one another and that with increased distance the pull diminishes rapidly.

If we think of the pull of gravity as a process, a reciprocal relationship in which the two bodies try to achieve an objective, which seems to be to come together (depending on one's optimism or pessimism, a unification or a collision), then we can compare the pull of gravity to the process of interpersonal communication.

The process of gravity is linear, steady, dependable, and predictable. The process of communication is much more complex. Instead of depending upon two factors such as mass and distance, communication involves a multitude of factors within the source, the receiver, the encoding process, the decoding process, and the message itself. Gravity proceeds in a steady state of linearity. Communication may be linear for a bit, may loop into circularity because of feedback, may leap in almost quantum fashion to high moments of insight and communion, may proceed slowly, then rapidly, may halt completely. In every respect the process itself is more complicated than the process of gravitation.

Newton discovered that he could apply his law of gravity to three or more bodies by using the concept of *vector*. He could add a third body to his basic paradigm of two objects and compute accurately the resultant forces that would act upon all three.

For example, Figure 4.1 indicates how the paradigm of two heavenly bodies can be expanded to explain the gravitational effect of a third. Each force is represented by a straight line and the pull on an object at point A will be related in magnitude to line AC in the geometric figure ABCD. Like a computer program, statements in plane geometry can be completely understood. Perhaps a reader will need to peruse the above description of vector and resultant forces several times to clearly grasp the diagrammed relationships. Even so, the principle of vector and resultant forces, while requiring attention to detail, remains a relatively simple matter. We deal with only two variables, mass and distance, and with forces that are linear and steady.

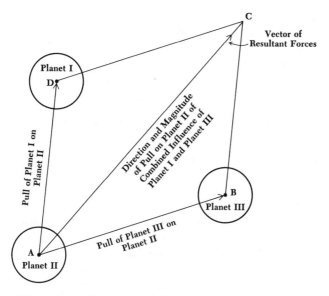

Figure 4.1 Adding a Third Planet to a Two-Planet Paradigm

Turn now to the communication that takes place in a decision-making business meeting of five people.[6] We already know that among the important factors will be the organizational status and authority of each of the participants. The status relationships can be mapped in a fashion analogous to the pulls of gravity. Thus, we might assert that credibility of a message source is directly proportional to magnitude of the status differential and inversely proportional to the organizational distance between source and receiver. The credibility of a message source two status levels superior to the receiver is usually greater than that of an immediate superior. We could further assert that if the message source has direct fate control over the listener the source will have greater credibility than one in a remote division having no direct fate control. However, our metaphor becomes unconvincing because the relationship between status and credibility is not linear, dependable, or steady. But even more important, having examined the status of and relationships among the participants and their effect on the communication, we must then incorporate another variable that is even more central, more complex, and exhibits greater fluctuations than does status. The power and esteem of the individual within the group must

[6] Kurt Lewin developed a field theory of social behavior that is a somewhat sophisticated application of vectors to the small group. See Kurt Lewin, *Field Theory in Social Science* (New York, 1951); also Dorwin Cartwright, "Lewinian Theory as a Contemporary Systematic Framework," in S. Koch, ed., *Psychology: A Study of Science* (New York, 1959), vol. 2.

be analyzed. We might attempt a vector analysis of esteem and power but the paradigm of these interpersonal relationships is less predictable that that of formal status. We need to continue to pile up other crucial factors such as the liking-disliking interaction, the attraction of the group, the feedback patterns, the drive for structure, and the development of a unique group culture including role relationships and norms. Clearly, the addition of a third person to a communication setting introduces resultant forces that cannot be diagrammed in terms of plane geometry, not even in terms of solid geometry. We simply do not have a geometry with sufficient dimensions to begin a graphic representation of the multitude of forces working at any given moment in a committee meeting.

If, indeed, a small-group meeting is such a complicated phenomenon, why is it the common perception that it is a relatively simple matter to gather a half-dozen people together and in an hour or two consider a series of important topics, make several vital decisions, and adjourn in time for lunch?

THE TENDENCY TO REJECT THE COMPLEXITY
OF GROUP DYNAMICS

The common simplistic view of group meetings sometimes results from taking flight from painful realities. For many business and professional leaders a recognition of the complexities of group dynamics is inherently a threat to their self-image. Having spent years of study and work to become experts in electronic engineering, or in marketing research, or in internal medicine, they may find themselves in a managerial position, attending many conferences and meetings. To be told that despite their expertness in their areas of specialization they must now implement their knowledge through small-group communication and that competence in that area is as complicated as expertness in electronics, marketing research, or internal medicine suggests that they are untrained, unaware, and by implication, incompetent for their duties. A typical way to save one's self-image under such stresses is to reject the fact of the complexity of small-group communication.

The rejection pattern often takes the form of denouncing the whole procedure of group meetings as unnecessary, time-wasting, and in other ways inefficient. After all, one can be incompetent in the privacy of his own office less conspicuously than in the more public forum of a meeting. Another way to reject the complexity of the small-group-communication setting is to attribute failure to some external force beyond the control of the participants. The meeting failed because it was doomed by impossible demands, inadequate information or resources, or lack of time. Finally, the participants often attribute their difficulties not to the complexities of the situation and the gap between their simplistic view and the reality of the group meeting but to some innate and irredeemable personality flaw in one or more of the members. If Joe were not so bullheaded, if Sam was less rigid, if the old man would just listen a little, if the others were not so self-serving and bigoted, if the bulk of the members were not so stupid, if Bill was less disagreeable, if there was less apathy, if more people would be willing to do something, the meeting would have been much more productive.

THE TENDENCY TOWARD UNREALISTIC EXPECTATIONS

Another factor in the faulty analysis of group dynamics is that a common and vivid picture of what a meeting ought to be like acts as a surrogate for reality. A business meeting, it is commonly supposed, ought to be an efficient no-nonsense matter. The meeting should be well planned, the agenda should be adhered to, and the contributions ought to be to the point, clear, and relevant. All members should contribute equally and their comments ought to be productive—aiding the group in its careful step-by-step deliberations. The members ought to be involved, eager to participate, people who express themselves clearly, listen carefully, and never contribute to confusion.

In general the meeting ought not to exhibit moments of confusion, departure from the planned agenda, and irrelevancies. The participants ought not talk too much or too little and they ought not be apathetic, dull, or confused. But this ideal business meeting is a fiction found primarily in handbooks on how to conduct a meeting. Committees and small-group meetings rarely fall into the pattern outlined above and if they did they would be useful only on rare occasions for unusual purposes.

Certainly one of the most important purposes for a meeting is to make a decision, and decision-making deliberations cannot exhibit the earmarks of the ideal meeting. Briskly conducted meetings in which the group marches through the agenda with little discussion and rapid votes of approval are simply rubber-stamping pseudo-conferences. The decisions they endorse have been previously hammered out in meetings that were much noisier, less directed, and filled with irrelevancies, departures from plans, and moments of confusion.

Many business and professional people would be more productive and happier in the business meeting if they replaced the impossible ideal picture of what a meeting ought to be like with expectations based on the realities of small-group communication. We do not mean to say that some meetings are not better than others but we do say that to judge all meetings, the good as well as the bad, against an ideal that cannot and ought not be approximated leads to dissatisfaction and guilt.

A REALISTIC PICTURE OF A GOOD GROUP MEETING

Group work requires considerable time. What can one realistically expect of a good meeting? One criterion is the amount of work per unit of time that can be demanded of a group of, say, five persons. Given the complicated network of interrelationships that must be developed and sustained in such a work meeting, one ought not expect the group to cover more topics in a two-hour meeting than an individual could study, deliberate, and decide in one hour of working alone. Yet the temptation is often very great to load up the agenda of a meeting with work that would keep one man busy all day and expect five people working together to handle it in an hour or two. The inevitable happens, and the group fails to cover the agenda adequately. They either get bogged down in the first part of it and leave some important topics untouched or they race through it without dealing with any topic satisfactorily. As a result, the participants come away feeling the meeting was a failure.

Groups have short attention spans. Another unrealistic expectation about working committees is the idea that a group can organize its discussion and focus its attention on important topics, keeping the thread of the deliberations clearly before the members, and move in a logical step-by-step progression through a series of topics. Individuals have attention spans measured in minutes and sometimes in seconds. When individuals read, listen, or think about something, their attention is intermittent and erratic. A person may read a paragraph with good comprehension and be halfway through another before he realizes that he is only going through the motions of reading and that he is thinking about getting a drink of water or about what he plans to do that evening. People listening to a speech may attend closely to what the speaker is saying for a minute or so and then begin to daydream about something else. Even when people are puzzling about an important problem or decision, they often find their attention drifting to other topics.

Groups like individuals have extremely short attention spans. Extensive research by the small-group-communication seminar at the University of Minnesota included measuring with a stopwatch the length of time groups discussed a topic before drifting to another. We now have data collected from student discussion groups in the United States and in Lebanon, Japanese students at the University of Minnesota, business and professional committee meetings, and community discussion groups. The remarkable feature of these data is their stability. Whether the groups were composed of Lebanese co-eds, Japanese graduate students deliberating in Japanese, first-line managers at IBM, University of Minnesota undergraduate students, or educators in public health nursing, the average attention span of the groups was about one minute. In all the groups studied the longest average attention spans were focused upon topics dealing with the subject under discussion, the next longest spans were devoted to procedural topics related to how to best deal with the subject, the shortest bursts of attention were to topics unrelated to substance or procedure. These patterns were found to be stable in a wide variety of group deliberations.[7]

In part, a group's attention span is a function of the messages competing for the group's attention. During any given period of the meeting, of course, individual listeners may or may not be attending to what is being said. Thus, the task of focusing the entire group's attention on an idea is probably even more difficult than the above evidence suggests.

Factors accounting for failure to attend.   Some attending or failing to attend in a meeting is probably a matter of individual habits, training, motives, and interests, and understanding of these is important. Chapters 5 and 12 deal with these topics in detail. Our concern here is with those factors associated with the group that results in failures to attend to deliberations. For example, the status of the speaker will affect attention. A high-status person will be listened to more carefully than a person with little organizational status. A person who has earned esteem by the quality of his ideas and the excellence of his character in past meetings will be listened to more carefully than someone who has little esteem.

When several people are fighting for control of the channels of communication, attempting to assert themselves and assume the role of message source, they often fail to attend to what others say. Early in a meeting when people are busy structuring their social field and forming impressions of the others, members may wish to put their "best foot forward" and, thus, strive to make a brilliant comment. When they have to relinquish the limelight, they often do not listen to subsequent speakers. Instead, they cast about for something suitable to say so they may again impress their colleagues.

[7] David M. Berg, "A Descriptive Analysis of the Distribution and Duration of Themes Discussed by Task-Oriented Small Groups," *Speech Monographs*, 34 (1967), 172–175; Charles U. Larson, "Leadership Emergence and Attention Span: A Content Analysis of the Time Devoted to Themes in the Task-Oriented Small Group," Ph.D. Dissertation, University of Minnesota, 1968.

Realistic and productive structuring of group work. Clearly, focusing a group's attention upon an idea so all members can understand it is a difficult task. Members have trouble chaining together several related ideas to form a progression because of the group's short attention span. Yet the group with an important decision to make will feel pressure and want to get on with the job. Participants in business meetings will seldom tolerate the aimless free-associative pattern that characterizes conversation. If the group has an agenda, written or implied, it forms a standard against which to judge performance. Often, the agenda becomes a liability because members keep commenting on the fact that the discussion has departed from the agenda or that much still remains to be covered even though satisfactory progress is being made.

Participants will vary as to their tolerance for ambiguity and an unstructured meeting. Some will be uncomfortable unless the agenda is clear and strong efforts are made to adhere to it. They resent apparent digressions or departures from the planned outline. Others will feel restricted by a slavish devotion to the prearranged order. They will have what seems to them to be good and important ideas that they wish to express while they are still new and exciting. Many times they will ask for a relaxation of the rules of order and urge more of a "brainstorming" approach.[8]

How to obtain a realistic and productive structuring of a small task-oriented group meeting is one of the most important problems for the student of decision-making discussion. At times, the participants will want and need the freedom to "kick ideas around" without much concern about the order of topics or the coherence of the discussion. At other times, a group will need and demand structure. The members will feel that they now know what they want to do and they would like to get on with it. While all groups have something of a rhythm relating to the desire for relaxed and freewheeling discussion alternating with structured and efficient marshaling of ideas and resources, the specific details of the rhythm tend to vary from group to group. The student of the business meeting must observe, experiment with, and be sensitive to the pulse of a given committee. A sense of timing in these matters is vital. Careful attention should be given to the verbal and nonverbal cues that indicate restlessness with the structure. Often, the members

---

[8] We use the term *brainstorming* in its more general sense of a creative process in which people try to inspire one another to new and novel ideas and solutions. *Brainstorming* is also a specific label for a particular kind of group meeting developed by an advertising executive. The rules for a brainstorming session as developed by Alex Osborn in his book *Applied Imagination* (New York, 1963) include: (1) criticism is ruled out, (2) freewheeling of ideas is welcomed, (3) quantity of ideas rather than quality is emphasized, and (4) hitchhiking or modification of ideas is encouraged.

of the group will react in a way that shows frustration when the chairman reminds them of the agenda. A participant might accept the suggestion that his comment is out of order in a grumpy fashion, sitting back in his chair with a frown. Another person may express confusion about the meaning of an agenda item or about what the group is supposed to be doing now. Someone may suggest that he does not want to make a motion or express a position yet, but that he would like to talk about a few things first. These items are important cues that tell the leader to deemphasize structure for the time being.

Other verbal and nonverbal cues will indicate that a group has reached a point where it wishes structure. A member may suggest, "Let's cut out the talk and get down to business. What do we still have to do?" Participants may begin to look at their watches, shift in their seats, let their attention wander. At such a point, the chairman or someone else in the meeting may suggest that they proceed in a more systematic way and the group will accept the suggestion and move through the agenda. When they wish to follow the agenda, their attention span as a group will continue to be short but they will welcome any attempt by the chairman or by someone else to bring them back to the business at hand. When they are in a mood to "kick the ideas around," they will resent the demand for structure.

Group decision-making. One's expectation of a good meeting must be realistic. Our first step, therefore, is to replace the picture of how groups ought to work with a realistic description of how they, in fact, do work. Extensive observations of a wide variety of school and real-life groups in a number of different decision-making situations reveal the following paradigm of group decision-making.[9]

One basic truth is that decisions emerge from group interaction by a process of elimination. Groups do not pick the best solution from an array of possibilities but rather tend to eliminate the worst, the not so good, and the fair until they are left with a solution or decision, which they then affirm, confirm, and implement. The process of decision emergence is as follows: The group approaches a problem in a revolving, circular manner rather than in a straight line. Thus, the realistic agenda might well suggest a quick run at topics A, B, and C in about thirty minutes and then a return to topic A for a more penetrating discussion, then to B again, and so on. They must find the areas of agreement, the points of conflict.

The group tends to approach a total problem, grabbing hold of it almost any place to get started, no matter what the agenda might

[9] Fisher in his study of group decision-making discovered a four-phase progression from orientation, to conflict, to decision emergence, to confirmation. B. Aubrey Fisher, "Decision Emergence: A Process Model of Verbal Task Behavior for Decision-Making Groups," Ph.D. Dissertation, University of Minnesota, 1968.

suggest. Their first pass at the topic will result in a rather superficial analysis. They will return to the problem again and dig more deeply, begin to cut close to the important issues on which they differ, until disagreement and conflict cause social tension to become so uncomfortable that they pull back and turn to a less painful matter. After a time, they will return to the central issue and drive still closer to a solution. The approach-withdrawal behavior is typical of groups making difficult decisions that are crucial to an organization.

Early in their deliberations, people may display a number of solutions and discover that some are clearly unsuitable, that several are possibilities, and that one of the latter has strong support from a few participants. At that point, they often drop consideration of possible solutions and turn to a discussion of the problem. The proponent of one of the possible solutions might take the opportunity to relate his solution to the problem as it is being discussed. As he does so, some others may attack the proposed solution. During the conflict feelings run high and social tension grows uncomfortable. When things get very tense, someone may crack a joke or make a comment that causes laughter and serves to release the tension. This turns attention away from the disagreement. After a bit someone may ask for some orientation to the big picture. What are we trying to do? What should our goal be? Other members respond by talking about goals and when they seem to be in agreement on objectives the proponent may suggest his solution again and indicate how it would facilitate achieving the goals. Others now emerge as proponents of some of the remaining viable solutions. As the various solutions are defended and attacked, the group swings from problem to solution to goals and back again. At some point during this process the group will discover that a solution has emerged. Often the decision is reached without a formal vote. Somehow the group members discover that for the past few minutes, although the discussion has continued, everyone more or less has come to the same conclusion and all that remains is for the decision to be voiced. After the decision is announced, groups typically spend a few minutes in commenting about the wisdom of the decision and confirming it publicly so there will be little doubt that the deliberations are concluded.

Quite often, groups appreciate a relatively free and unstructured period early in the process to allow for a quick survey of the entire question and to get some preliminary orientation as to the attitudes and positions of important people in the meeting. The group will often need some prodding to get down to the important divisive topics because the typical group resists talking about tension-producing material. Thus, some structuring by a leader or chairman that forces the group to face up to the tough questions may be helpful. Once a decision has emerged and the group needs to formally state, confirm,

and plan details to implement the decision, they are ready for structure and an agenda. They will often march through these items with
little digression during the last stages of the problem-solving process.

If a person understands the difficulty of focusing the group's
attention on the messages being transmitted to the group and the
process of group decision-making, he can participate in and lead the
business meetings more successfully. People will not experience the
feeling of failure so often if the planning of the meeting is realistic and
expectations are based on an understanding of group process rather
than some unrealistic, machinelike pattern of efficiency.

ADAPTING THE PRESENTATION TO THE SMALL GROUP

The person who is to give a presentation to a small task-oriented
group should analyze the audience as a group in addition to his analysis of individuals. The speaker ought not expect the group to absorb,
discuss, and act on more than they can in the time available. The
speaker must take into account such questions as: Is the decision-
making group in the beginning stages of its work? Is it in the midst of
a conflict phase, hammering out basic positions and lining up in
opposition to or in support of solutions? Is it in the confirming stage,
having made the decision and now meeting only to rubber-stamp that
decision? One's objective for a presentation to a group beginning
meetings on an important problem might well be different than the
objective when the presentation comes at the height of the controversy
and still different if the meeting needs a presentation to set up the
confirmation of decision.

In addition to analyzing the audience for a presentation to a small
task-oriented group in terms of the realities of group process, a person
making plans for a presentational speech should examine the characteristics of the listeners, as they are influenced by circumstances in which
the group operates. Although not all meetings fall neatly into one of
the two major categories of business and professional small-group
meetings, the basic principles necessary for audience analysis are
revealed by the *ad hoc* committee meeting for only one session and by
the work group meeting for a number of sessions with essentially the
same membership.

THE *AD HOC* MEETING

The Latin term *ad hoc* means "for this special purpose." An *ad hoc*
meeting is usually set up on a one-time basis. The participants have
not met before in a group meeting and are not likely to meet again, at

least not for the purpose under discussion. Some of the members may have participated in other *ad hoc* meetings and some may know one another socially or at work, but the particular complement of people attending the meeting is unique.

The *ad hoc* meeting is to be distinguished from an *ad hoc committee*. Some organizations, such as universities, have many *ad hoc* committees formed for a special purpose of sufficient importance that they may meet and deliberate for a period of months or even years before they make their report and disband. In an organization an *ad hoc* committee is in contrast to the standing (permanent) committee. Some industries organize project teams much like the university *ad hoc* committee. The project team may work together for a considerable period of time and when the project is completed they break up and the individuals move on to different assignments.

In contrast, the *ad hoc meeting* is held by people who anticipate achieving their purposes at a single meeting. Since the composition of the *ad hoc* meeting is unique, it is a zero-history group. The fact that a group has no history means that the members have no past experience upon which to base expectations of present and future actions. A zero-history group has no feeling of cohesiveness, no culture, no norms to guide the trivial details of communication and social interaction. A zero-history group has no purpose, no direction for the future, no idea of what sort of group it is or where it is going. In short, both the social field and the task objectives are unstructured and ambiguous.

The *ad hoc* group is not only without history but it is without a future. Some meetings start with a zero-history group but the members anticipate that the group will continue for a considerable length of time and hold many more meetings. The *ad hoc* committee studying the restructuring of the university may be told at its first meeting that the goal is to complete its work and make its report in eighteen months. Although the first session of the university committee resembles an *ad hoc* meeting in that the group has no history, the committee does have a considerable future, something that is important to the dynamics of the first session.

The zero-history group with a future is under considerable pressure to test potential leaders and influentials, to develop norms and other features of group culture carefully, to take nothing at face value and check reputation, formal status, and assigned structures before accepting them. Much is at stake, hence the members search and evaluate the social realities of the group with more rigor in the first session of an ongoing group than they do in the *ad hoc* meeting.

Because less is at stake, the communication network, the roles, the norms, and other features of group process in the *ad hoc* meeting tend to be accepted uncritically and the use of stereotyping devices is common. Many presentations are received by *ad hoc* meetings. Selected persons often meet primarily to hear the presentation and take action on it, in a typical *ad hoc* meeting.

One of the most important tendencies in the *ad hoc* meeting is to accept leadership. Whether the person calling the meeting is a self-appointed moderator, or some organizational unit has assigned a person to lead the meeting, the members are likely to accept and appreciate guidance from that individual. The group needs quick help in getting underway. Members realize they have little time and tend to accept arbitrarily stipulated goals and procedures with little challenge.

Participants in *ad hoc* meetings tend to use formal organizational status or professional credentials as ways of assigning leadership and influence. Thus, if seven people in the meeting are all from the same company, the discovery that John Harris is production manager, the highest status of anyone at the session, will cause the others to look to him for guidance. If a group of citizens from various segments of the community gather together and discover one of the members is a famous lawyer, another a surgeon, and a third a public official, that information will help the others structure a hierarchy of influence and importance.

Once the discussion is underway, those members who do not hold positions of professional stature or who are not known by reputation tend to be quickly stereotyped on the basis of early contributions and behavior. Each individual strives to get some impression of every other and relies upon superficial cues. Thus, a person who does not speak for fifteen or twenty minutes may be stereotyped as quiet, shy, apathetic, or uninterested in the meeting and thus figuratively dismissed. Another, who speaks in a loud authoritative voice and expresses strong opinions and makes flat judgments, may be stereotyped as rigid or "bossy" or "pushy."

Thus, the members of an *ad hoc* meeting take short cuts to structure their group into a "pecking order" so they can get on with the business at hand. They are willing to risk substantial mistakes because of the shortage of time and because they often perceive the task as less important than the assignments characteristic of more permanent groups.

Members of *ad hoc* meetings also tend to accept a stereotyped picture of how a meeting ought to be run. Where the zero-history group that will meet for many sessions over several months will work out its own procedures for accomplishing its tasks, the *ad hoc* meeting must rely upon some other tactic since it simply does not have time to develop idiosyncratic modes of procedure. The culturally accepted picture of how a small-group meeting should be conducted includes the assigned role functions of moderator, leader, or chairman and secretary or recorder.

The moderator, leader, or chairman is expected to tend to the administrative details of setting up the meeting place. In addition, he also typically plans the agenda, sends out preliminary information, and schedules the meeting.

During the course of the session the assigned chairman is expected to "lead" the discussion. The chairman's duties are commonly understood to include the following:

A. Chairman's duties in regard to the task
   1. Start the meeting
   2. Act as "pilot" to keep group on course, remind members of the agenda, cut short unnecessary digressions
   3. Help group arrive at decisions (take votes when necessary)
   4. Provide transitions from topic to topic
   5. Summarize major portions of the discussion
   6. Control channels of communication to assure equal participation and that all sides get a fair hearing (encourage the quiet members, discourage the persons who talk too much)
   7. Follow up decisions and see that the results of the meeting are utilized
B. Chairman's duties in regard to social and human relations
   1. Introduce members to one another
   2. Help release initial social tensions and "break the ice" so people can relax and feel free to go to work
   3. Release later tensions generated by antagonisms and conflicts

The stereotype of a good participant for an *ad hoc* meeting is very general and does not provide for differentiation of role functions caused by a person's organizational status, community reputation, motive structure, or training and ability. The leadership role functions are consolidated in the "moderator's" duties. All other members are expected to conform to one standard role of *participant.*

The participant is expected to follow the moderator's lead and accept the directions that the chairman gives to the group. That is, when the chairman recognizes Member A to speak, the expectation is that Member B does not interrupt and take the floor. When the chairman cuts off a digression, the others in the role of participants will accept the judgment that the digression is unproductive and move on to the topic suggested by the moderator.

The stereotype of the participant involves the following duties:

A. Participant's duties in regard to the task
   1. Enter into the discussion with enthusiasm
   2. Have an open-minded objective attitude
   3. Keep contributions short and to the point

    4. Talk enough but not too much
    5. Speak clearly and listen carefully
B. Participant's duties in regard to social and human relations
    1. Respect the dignity of others
    2. Be well mannered
    3. Try to understand the other person's position
    4. Do not manipulate or exploit the other person

Of course, the picture of how a good *ad hoc* meeting should go varies considerably from the realities of even a short session. Participants do not all willingly follow the assigned moderator even when they know they should. They are, however, much more likely to do so in an *ad hoc* meeting than in a group that has the prospect of several meetings over a period of days or weeks. People who would in a more permanent group move strongly in the first meeting to test the assigned leader's abilities will not do so in the *ad hoc* meeting because such testing is time-consuming and tension-producing and the context does not justify that expenditure of time and energy. To be sure, the moderator or chairman will be evaluated by the others as to his effectiveness even if he is not challenged, but the tendency to accept his leadership is quite strong in the *ad hoc* meeting.

Even in a short meeting, role differentiation does take place. Status and reputation, as previously noted, produces some hierarchical ordering of roles. A few people do talk more than others despite the best efforts of the moderator. Some people are silent. Some members are friendly and humorous and likable. Others are well organized and insightful and contribute to the success of the group's work. Thus, the generalized stereotype of a meeting composed of one leader and undistinguishable followers soon evaporates under the pressures of the meeting.

The person preparing a presentation for a small task-oriented group formed for one session should understand the dynamics of the situation. The drive to hierarchical structure is widespread in our culture, and the superficial cues provided by organizational status, talking or not talking come to have much more influence in the *ad hoc* meeting than elsewhere. Thus, analyzing the audience for the presentation in terms of what organizational and community positions will be represented is important. If plant manager, shop foreman, lawyer, and university professor will be at the meeting, that information will be as helpful in analyzing the audience as the knowledge that Herman Albright, George Humboldt, Gregory Colfax, and Bill Douglas will attend. The speaker will also want to collect, if possible, such information as the fact that Humboldt, the shop foreman, is also a lay minister in a fundamentalist church and that lawyer Colfax is famous for defending civil rights and civil liberties causes.

MEETINGS OF SMALL TASK-ORIENTED GROUPS

Many presentations are made to small groups that have met one or more times before and that expect to meet one or more times in the future. Under circumstances of some permanence (even if the group expects to complete its work within four or five sessions and a period of several weeks) the inherent pressures to develop a sense of cohesion, to establish roles and order them into a hierarchy of ability, likability, and dominance, in short, to develop a unique group culture, are released. The pressures for group structure and allegiance are intensified if the members perceive their group as permanent and important. The more long term the group's prospects, the more important the group to the participants, the greater the initial tensions and the longer the testing period.

Small task-oriented groups are dynamic in that the communication networks and patterns, the interpersonal relations and transactions, and the operating procedures are always in process and ever changing. One of the most important dimensions of a group's life is the time factor. The first meeting of a new group is very similar to the *ad hoc* meeting, with the important exception that the willingness to accept structure is transitory. From the point of their first meeting forward the group begins to evolve its own social structure, a division of labor relating to the task, and a set of group norms. Once the group matures and the roles and common norms emerge, the group may stabilize for relatively long periods of time and the behavior of individuals and the performance of the group itself becomes quite predictable. However, even relatively stable groups go through cyclical developments with fluctuating levels of cohesion, with periods of crisis and complacency, and with readjustment of roles or changes in group norms. Fluctuations are usually caused by events in the external environment that put pressures upon the group. A different objective or a change in the job, a crisis such as a threat to the parent organization or to the group by some external group, or the addition of members or their removal will cause changes in the group's stability. Thus, the person making a presentation to a group must examine the time dimension to assess trends and changes.

Because the early meetings of all groups approximate the same evolutionary pattern, we will present a paradigm of the emergence of roles and norms in zero-history groups. Next, we will describe the functioning of mature groups under conditions of relative stability, and finally examine some typical instances of group instability and its effect on interaction and efficiency. The student of presentational speaking can apply the paradigm of group dynamics to a target audience and by checking some of the more obvious symptoms discover if the group is in a period of adolescent evolution toward maturity, in a mature and stable period, or in a period of upset and crisis. The response of a group in a stable and cohesive state is most predictable and the behavior of groups evolving or fluctuating least predictable. Nonetheless, if he understands groups in flux, a presentational speaker can plan more options for adaptation to varied responses.

Social tensions in continuing groups.   Group meetings are always social events with a significant proportion of communication about interpersonal matters. Every member comes to the first meeting with one major question, "How do I relate to these other people as a human being?" He wants that question answered as early as possible. Indeed, the question is so important that until it is answered for an individual that person is in a state of anxious suspense. The person is *tense.* The tension centers upon the responses of others and it is thus a *social tension.* (A person might be in a state of anxious suspense and excitement because his automobile stopped on a country road when the temperature was thirty degrees below zero, but the tension would not be social.)

The social tensions caused by our concern over the way others respond to us as people we call *primary tensions.* Every zero-history group represents a new challenge and a new opportunity to establish friendly or unfriendly, rewarding or unrewarding, interpersonal relationships. People in new groups, therefore, always feel a certain amount of primary tension. They are ill at ease. They do not know what to say or how to begin. The first part of the meeting is characterized by quietness and apparent apathy. People speak softly, sigh, and are polite. Although members may seem bored, they are really not. Every individual, however, gambles for high stakes when he plunges into the meeting and takes an active part. He may make a good showing and the others may be impressed with his ability. They may be irritated by him and decide that he is a show-off or stupid and uninformed. They may like and respect him or reject him.

If the early meetings do not release the primary tensions, the whole style of the group may be affected by the resulting uncomfortable pattern of communication. Social tensions are released through indications of pleasure such as smiles, chuckles, and laughs. It is important to the group that primary tensions be released as soon as possible and that every participant be made to feel accepted as a person. (The relief of primary tension is equally necessary but easier to achieve in the *ad hoc* meeting.)

When the members have relaxed enough to forget their concern with self, the group should go to work. Spending too much time on releasing primary tensions may be pleasant but will soon cause restlessness because busy people do want to get on with the job and resent spending unnecessary time joking, kidding, or gossiping. When the zero-history group begins to work upon its task, its deliberations are doubly complicated because it not only begins to process data and make decisions but it must also structure the group. The situation is analogous to one in which a group of people is presented with the necessary tools and materials and told to build a house. However, the builders have no blueprints and no notion as to who can do what. They are not allowed to discuss and plan how they will build the house but must begin the job. Someone takes the initiative and makes a suggestion as to how to begin. A few may follow his lead and start to drive stakes to lay out a foundation. Another person may suggest a different starting place as they get under way. They take turns digging, planning, arguing, pouring concrete, sawing lumber, and so on. During the process they discover a member with a flair for design and that person comes to take over the major planning, another who is good at blueprinting, several who are good at sawing and hammering, some who are good at finishing, painting and others who do less difficult but nonetheless necessary jobs like carrying lumber, digging foundations, mixing paint, and so on. When the house is completed, the group has not only built a house but has also come to know one another and to expect particular contributions from certain members. They did their assigned task and also accomplished another important job of structuring the group. Should the group be asked to build another house, it could move much more quickly and efficiently to the job because of the structuring that took place in the first experience.

The first meetings of a new group are understandably difficult and frustrating. In the process of deciding who will do what for the group, members often compete for particularly pleasant, rewarding, or high-prestige activities. They also may disagree about details of the job. When they disagree, seek conflicting personal objectives, or contend for conflicting positions within the group, they grow antagonistic and another kind of social tension is created. *Secondary tensions* are much more obviously interpersonal in nature and are louder than primary ones. People speak rapidly, interrupt one another, are impatient to have their say. They may get up and pace the room, gesture broadly, and raise their voices. When secondary tensions reach a certain level, the group finds it difficult to concentrate on its job. When that point is reached, the tensions must be released by humor, direct confrontation and the resolution of conflict, or by conciliation.

The process of role emergence. In the early evolutionary period of a group, one important structuring process is the emergence of roles for individuals. Each group has certain tasks that must be done if the group is to succeed. The various participants bring to the group their native ability and acquired skills and knowledge. During the first meetings members try one or another of the job-oriented roles and the group reinforces or punishes their attempts. Gradually, through punishment and reinforcement each member comes to expect to perform certain duties and to be rewarded for doing so. The others in the group expect this person to perform certain functions and when individual and group expectations coincide, the individual's role has emerged.

A person thus works out his role jointly with the group. A member does not *take* a role in the sense that we might say he took leadership but rather he tries out for a role and is awarded or denied it by the others. Two tendencies within the group dynamic play an important part in the awarding of roles. Members tend to reinforce behavior that they perceive to be most beneficial for the entire group and those task functions that a person performs most efficiently. When the two criteria conflict, the group tends to select a role for a person that is best for the entire group.

The general process by which groups make difficult role assignments is the same as the one they use to make difficult task decisions.[10] First, the members display their various abilities and are encouraged or discouraged in a mild way. In cyclical fashion these role tryouts proceed until conflicts come into the open and secondary tensions rise to intolerable levels. Groups then typically back off from role structuring to other matters only, of course, to return to them again. The more difficult decisions relate to the high-status roles. Typically, the last decisions to be made are those regarding important role functions in the task area which require great skill and training and the role of leader. Leadership emerges in the same pattern as a difficult task decision, by the method of residues. Members are eliminated as potential leaders until the group is left with the person it is most willing to accept. If two or more participants seem equally able, the process may take a long time, particularly if both contenders gain supporters during the shakedown cruise. The group may then divide into factions, with one or more neutrals holding the key to eventual group structuring. If the two or more people remaining after the process of elimination are unacceptable to a substantial minority, the high-status roles may never emerge. The group may always be plagued by instability, interpersonal conflict, and inefficiency.

When roles stabilize in a group, the environment becomes much more secure and comfortable. Groups normally experience a dramatic increase in cohesiveness when roles emerge and they can then concentrate a good deal more of their attention and energy on the job, as the

[10] For more detailed descriptions of the process of role emergence and of group decision-making, see Bormann, *op. cit.*

group building houses can operate more efficiently on the second house because of the role specialization that took place during the building of the first. (Of course, if roles did not emerge and the building crew split into factions with one group tearing down what the other built and vice versa, the second project might be a disaster.)

When the roles emerge, the group will tend to arrange them on a ladder from higher to lower importance to the over-all group objective. Thus, groups with a stable role structure tend to have informal but well-understood status relationships analogous to the formal status levels of permanent organizations. While groups with clear and stable roles tend to be cohesive and efficient, the attraction of the group is strongest for the members with high status and weakest for those with low status. Thus, the influentials within the group will tend to enjoy it and work hard for the good of the unit, while the low-status members will often be apathetic and dilatory in their efforts. The best groups are those in which the low-status members are provided rewards sufficient to commit them to the group.

The effect of changing personnel on stable groups. When members of a highly cohesive group with stable roles are removed, added, or replaced, the result is unsettling. All the roles undergo a reshuffling because new personnel do not assume the same duties as the old. If a new person is added to the group, the individual will bring his own skills and talents and a role will have to be found for him. The new member will take on some of the duties of the old members and thus cause a general reassessment. If a person is removed, that individual's tasks must now be performed by those remaining. If the absent member is a high-status or an influential person, the members who stand to gain by climbing upward will come into conflict and people who might have worked comfortably together in the presence of the influential member may not cooperate when he is absent.

In general, the effect of changing personnel is to repeat the dynamics of the original shakedown. The differences between the cyclical fluctuations of mature groups and the evolving of new structures in groups just getting organized are due to the influence of history. Quite often, a period of role instability and struggle surprises and frustrates the members, who have come to expect stability. People often do not understand what is going on and why it must go on. They respond by blaming the new members or they bemoan the loss of the old.

The fluctuations resulting from changing personnel are particularly difficult for groups characterized by absenteeism. The committee that must always meet with some members absent or the voluntary organization whose meetings are seldom attended by the same people is always handicapped by a lack of structure that may well be crippling in its effect.

The development of group norms. As a group develops a history, it also develops standard operating procedures that come to form "sets of expectations" for the members. The common expectations as to how the group will conduct its meetings, how the members will communicate (the communication networks and the style of encoding), how they will dress, how they will work, and so on, are called *group norms*. Groups develop norms largely through the process of suggestion. (Chapter 10 describes the process of suggestion in detail.) When a particular behavior is first displayed in a group, the way in which the function is performed exerts a positive suggestion and serves as a precedent for the next person. For example, a zero-history group in the opening minutes of its first meeting has few if any common precedents. It therefore tends to act according to the stereotype for the *ad hoc* meeting described above. But the stereotype's expectation of a meeting is very abstract and of little practical help. The group may decide that its members should introduce themselves. The first person may speak up in a strong voice with considerable confidence and go into detail about his background, experience, and interests. The second person will have a tendency to follow the model of the first and so on around the group. If the first person speaks softly and shyly, providing little more information than his name, the next will tend to do the same. The same mechanism will govern many of the interactions, transactions, and communications that take place. A dominant member may complain of being uncomfortable and remove his coat. Another may follow the lead, and soon all the men in the group are in shirt sleeves. One member may express an opinion early in the meeting in an informal and personal style. Others may follow, and soon the group has an expectation that the style of speaking in the group will be colloquial, slangy, and informal. The norms of a group constitute the group culture. They soon identify the insider and distinguish the members from the outsiders. They serve also as means to build *esprit de corps* and to make the social milieu familiar, predictable, and secure.

The group will develop norms relating to the task as well as to social interactions. The task norms or habits may include critical thinking or the uncritical acceptance of authoritative opinion, for example. The norms of a group function somewhat like the habits of an individual. The norms may be useful and productive to both member satisfaction and task efficiency or they may be destructive. Like habits, norms may be changed inadvertently or by conscious design. Groups may discuss their norms, discover their weaknesses, and by conscious effort change them.

Group pressures for conformity. One of the most important characteristics of group dynamics for the presentational speaker to understand is the power of nonverbal and verbal suggestion to induce conformity. The need to conform is greatest in cohesive units. A newcomer to a group meeting is under considerable pressure to act and talk in the same manner and style as the others in the group simply because everyone else follows a common mode of behavior. When the others all remove their coats, loosen their ties, and put their feet up on the table, the newcomer finds it difficult to keep his coat and tie on and sit erect with both feet on the floor. In important matters, members will put verbal pressure on a deviant, supplementing their nonverbal suggestion. They may kid, chide, plead, argue, and threaten if a member violates a group norm or fails to support an important group decision. The bandwagon phenomenon is prominent in the dynamics of a small group. If a few influentials lead the way and succeed in gaining majority acceptance, the pressure on the minority to conform is often extremely powerful and effective.

ANALYZING THE SMALL GROUP AS AN AUDIENCE FOR A PRESENTATION

John Jamison preparing his presentation for the Board of Control examined not only the individuals on the board but asked himself about the nature of the group and its structure. Jamison estimated the impact of the corporate organization upon the dynamics of the small group, noting that Perkins was president and had top organizational status. He analyzed the board as an ongoing task-oriented unit. He examined the dynamics of the group's evolution and decided that the board was in a period of role stability and had developed predictable decision-making norms. He knew that the decision-making process was dominated by three important influentials, Joe Perkins, Homer Lydgate, and Marshall Everding. Jamison then could assume that his audience would conform to the behavior of the three influentials. His next task was to study the three key influentials by making an intensive motive analysis of each.

In preparing for any presentational speech, analyses from the points of view of organizational context, small-group theory, and the dynamics of face-to-face communication will set the stage for sound motive analysis of individuals. As was the case with John Jamison's presentation, there are usually a few influentials who can be counted on to lead and reflect the motivations of an audience.

The speaker preparing for an *ad hoc* meeting can rely upon a quick and superficial analysis of the people to be present. He knows that organizational and community status and reputation will be major factors because the members of the meeting will be forced to make hasty judgments. These are the ingredients that must necessarily structure their perceptions of the meeting.

The real art of group audience analysis can be practiced with an ongoing group that has some history. The speaker can learn much about the development of the group from information about how long the group has been in operation. If the group has had only several meetings, the speaker should search for evidence that the process of role emergence is continuing. If several people are still in contention for leadership, they may approach the speaker before the presentation and indicate that an important difference of opinion exists in the group or that the speaker ought not pay too much attention to the other contender because the latter has proved troublesome and destructive in the past. If the group frequently changes its mind, sends out conflicting reports, if members talk about their difficulties with the group in social situations or at coffee breaks, the indications are that the group is in a period of role instability. If the group has clearly developed cliques that are antagonistic to one another, the speaker has further evidence of what happened during the early shakedown cruise. A person delivering a presentation to a group in an early period of role-testing and contention must expect that the question-and-answer period will prove a difficult one. Members may get off on procedural matters, may digress into fields far removed from the topic of the presentation, and the speaker's attempts to practice good human relations with one questioner may result in an attack from another.

Somewhat the same pattern of evidence coming from a group that has been in operation for several months or years will indicate a group undergoing a reshuffling of roles. The speaker would be well advised to search for a change in personnel, of circumstance, or in ability or interest on the part of a high-status member to account for the instability. The history of the group will continue to influence its dynamics, however, and people in influential roles will continue to be important. One ought, also, to search for those with less seniority who are trying for more influential roles and are likely to achieve them and adapt to these comers in much the same way that one would to the established influential members.

SUMMARY

In this chapter we considered the small task-oriented group meeting. The small group was defined as one consisting of three or more people, with an upper limit of twelve. The small-group meeting is among the most important forms of communication in any organization. Most important organizational decisions are made in committee meetings. The business meeting can also inform personnel directly about important matters in a situation where subordinates can communicate directly with superiors. The group meeting can build a feeling of commitment and involvement in the business or organization.

The small-group meeting is an extremely complicated communication unit and the common perception that it is relatively simple stems largely from the fact that many business and professional people have a vivid picture of what a meeting ought to be like that acts as a surrogate for reality. Group meetings are supposed to be brisk, efficient, and businesslike. The meeting is supposed to be well planned and the deliberations well organized. In reality, groups have short attention spans, tend to approach a new task globally and in a circular fashion rather than in a step-by-step linear path. They approach difficult decisions, and withdraw, approach again, and continue until the pressure of the situation forces a decision.

The two major kinds of meetings that provide audiences for presentational speeches include the *ad hoc* meeting and the session of an ongoing task-oriented small group. The *ad hoc* meeting is a communication event composed of a group of people drawn together for a purpose that is to be achieved in one meeting. The composition of the group is unique to the single situation. The session of an ongoing group is but one of a continuing series of communication events involving the same people. The fact that the ongoing group has both a history and a future influences the dynamics of the meeting and makes a considerable difference in the behavior of the audience listening to a presentation.

Because of its transitory nature, the *ad hoc* meeting accepts prescribed structures and uses stereotyping devices to provide procedures for doing its work. The ongoing group, on the other hand, develops a role structue including leadership, work procedures, and norms of behavior through a process of display, testing and validating within the context of its meetings.

In groups with some history and stable roles and norms, individuals will have risen to places of influence and leadership and their status will be legitimatized by group acceptance.

The speaker preparing a presentation for a small-group meeting should analyze the impact of related organizations upon the structuring of the group, distinguish between *ad hoc* meetings and sessions of continuing work groups, examine the dynamics of the group's evolution in the latter case, and evaluate the potential audience response by estimating their expected behavior as a group. The speaker who makes a careful analysis of the group is in a position to select certain key members of his audience for intensive motive analysis.

QUESTIONS FOR DISCUSSION AND REVIEW

1. What is meant by the concept of a *small group?*
2. In what way can an unrealistic picture of how a meeting ought to be run serve to make for unproductive conferences?

3. How do decisions emerge in a group discussion?
4. What are the distinguishing characteristics of a zero-history group? An *ad hoc* meeting? An *ad hoc* committee?
5. What are the typical expectations of duties for an assigned chairman or moderator of an *ad hoc* meeting?
6. What is meant by the concept of *primary tension?*
7. How do roles emerge in task-oriented groups?
8. What is the effect of changing personnel on groups with a stable role structure?
9. What are *group norms?*
10. What are some important things to keep in mind when analyzing the audience and the occasion for a presentation to be delivered at a small-group meeting?

REFERENCES AND SUGGESTED READINGS

BORMANN, ERNEST G. *Discussion and Group Methods: Theory and Practice.* New York: Harper & Row, 1969.

COLLINS, BARRY E., and HAROLD GUETZKOW. *A Social Psychology of Group Processes for Decision-Making.* New York: Wiley, 1964.

GALBRAITH, JOHN KENNETH. *The New Industrial State.* Boston: Houghton Mifflin, 1967.

GULLEY, HALBERT E. *Discussion, Conference, and Group Process.* 2nd ed. New York: Holt, Rinehart and Winston, 1968.

HARNACK, R. VICTOR, and THORREL B. FEST. *Group Discussion: Theory and Technique.* New York: Appleton-Century-Crofts, 1964.

CHAPTER FIVE

MOTIVE ANALYSIS: PREREQUISITE TO PRESENTATION

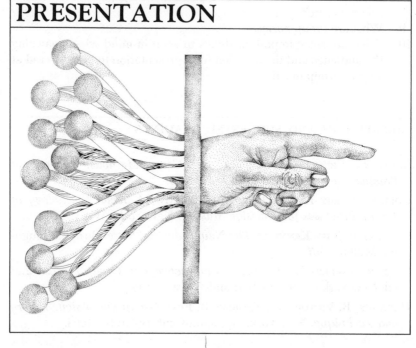

The advice concerning presentational speaking given in this book and all methods recommended depend upon the speaker making accurate estimates of the particular motivations in his audience. Only an analysis of motivation can establish the frame of reference within which main points and supporting materials are selected. Since an effective presentation is audience-centered, predispositions of the listeners are more important to the planning of the speech than any other factor. Hence, a speaker who wishes to influence others must have a systematic procedure for locating and estimating these behavior-determining tendencies in people.

MOTIVATION DEFINED

Unfortunately, the term *motivation* has been used with a wide range of meanings. Most of the generally accepted usages have little utility in interpersonal communication. From animal psychology come definitions like "A motive is a drive plus a learned mechanism to reduce the drive." Applying that genre of definition to human beings interacting in a modern organization is an exercise in futility. The dictionary definition, "What induces a person to act," is too broad to be helpful, since it includes all environmental influences and inherited abilities and limitations.

In current communication theory one misuse of this term has contributed to the often general and substantial confusion about motivation. Many authorities speak of one person "motivating" another person. The manager is led to think, "I can motivate Herb to get the job done." This usage assumes that an individual can transfer, or give, a motive to another. The point often overlooked is the fact that a motive is *within* the person who is activated by it. All of us respond to motives within us that have been conditioned and developed by our own experiences. A stimulus from the outside can arouse or "trigger" a motive that is in residence, but if that motive is not ready and waiting, no response occurs.

Several leaders in the development of theory of organizations have called attention to the above misuse of "motive" and "motivate" in striking fashion. Douglas McGregor says:

> Strictly speaking, the answer to the question managers so often ask of behavioral scientists— How do you motivate people?—is: You don't. Man is by nature motivated. . . . We do not motivate him, because he *is* motivated. When he is not, he is dead.[1]

Frederick Herzberg recounts recent attempts to apply the theory of motivation to management of human organizations and notes their superficiality and uselessness. Rewards and punishments proved ineffective because they failed to activate powerful enduring motivations. He satirizes the attempt to impose motivation from outside: "Let me rephrase the perennial question this way: How do you install a generator in the employee?"[2]

Obviously, you cannot install a generator. If one is there, you may be able to use it, if you know how to get it running!

Considering points made by McGregor and Herzberg, and many others, we would be unwise to use the verb *motivate* to designate the sending of messages to other individuals. A different term is needed. When a person attempts to communicate with another in an effort to control his belief and/or action, he becomes a persuader. We suggest that any unit of communication intended to influence the choice of

[1] Douglas McGregor, *The Professional Manager* (New York, 1967), pp. 10–11.

[2] Frederick Herzberg, "One More Time: How Do You Motivate Employees?" *Harvard Business Review*, 46 (1968), 56.

another person or persons be classified as "persuasion" and the habits, interests, needs, desires and goals that energize the responses of people be termed "motivation." The simple distinction can be made that motivation is *inside* the person being persuaded, while persuasion comes from *outside*.

Let us stipulate formal definitions for "motive" and "persuasion," to encourage more precise use of these terms and to increase understanding of what we are talking about. *A motive is an internal source of variable energy that causes a person to pursue selected options.* The motive, what we are interested in, energizes our response in a particular direction. Of possible outlets for this energy (choices or alternatives) we select one and pursue it. A motive is a "variable" source of energy, because, depending upon the intensity of our interest, we expend greater or lesser amounts of energy over shorter or longer periods of time following the chosen path. In the context of this definition, motive analysis is the process of identifying in an individual his energy-expending potential. Is he predisposed to follow (attracted to) a belief or course of action? To what degree is he likely to become involved in the pursuit? When we can answer these questions with some confidence, we have a foundation on which to build our presentation.

Viewing motivation in this perspective dramatizes the importance of pushing ahead rapidly in the empirical study of motivation in modern organizations. Herzberg's article cited above shows how little progress we have made in correlating motivation and behavior. Both happiness and productivity of human beings seem to require that people be provided constructive outlets for their motives. At present, we are inept in meeting the needs of others, in family, school, various organizations, and nations. The world's greatest untapped resource, relatively untouched because it is unexplored, may be human motivation.

Persuasion is the attempt to attach your recommendations to the other person's motives, thereby activating existing habits and interests. This is accomplished purposefully (excluding accidental influence, another category of behavior-shaping phenomena) and is implemented by interpersonal sending and receiving of messages, that is, by communication. A single definition emerges: *persuasion is communication intended to influence choice.*

What shall be the role of coercion (force or threat of force) in attempts to control the behavior of other human beings? The above definition excludes coercion from persuasion. As long as two or more viable options, possible beliefs or actions, are open to the receiver, he has the ability to choose, and successful persuasion may induce him to prefer one possibility to another. Coercion restricts choice. A person forced to do something finds alternatives other than the one he is coerced into accepting so punishing that they are no longer options.

The line between persuasion and coercion is a shaded area rather than a sharply defined boundary. Mild fear, for example, can be overcome, so choice remains. If the intensity of the fear increases, there comes a point where it dominates the fearful individual. We might call this his "terror threshold," and it varies from person to person. One person can live calmly with risk and danger that would paralyze another. A threat to fire one employee might be coercion because he will, literally, do anything to keep his job, while the same threat might be shrugged off by the man working beside him. For the latter employee, the possibility of being fired might be rather weak persuasion.

What we are suggesting is that one must consider the nature of the person receiving a message before its content can be classified as "persuasion" or "coercion," since a threat to one individual may not be at all threatening to another. Truly, individual differences make all the difference in the world, when fear arousal is a part of communication.

Admittedly, both persuasion and coercion are techniques of management. Also, although some people do not frighten easily, certain messages *can* produce a general fear response. Is terror a useful device in effective leadership? Rensis Likert provides evidence to help answer this question.

Likert[3] clusters "operating characteristics" under four systems of organization. Three he classes as exploitative authoritative, benevolent authoritative, and consultative. The fourth system he designates "participative."

Appeals to physical security, economic security, and desire for status motives are classified as characteristic of exploitative or benevolent authoritative systems, while appeals to ego, desire for new experience, and group-process motivations are classed as consultative and participative procedures.

Coercion, rewards, and punishments are associated with exploitative and benevolent authoritative systems, while rewards based on compensation developed through group participation, involvement, and participation in goal setting are classified as consultative and participative activities.

Consistently, management systems including predominantly consultative and participative elements outproduce and are preferred to exploitative and benevolent authoritative systems. Can a business organization modify its persuasion-coercion emphasis? It would seem so. Certain companies have been changed from exploitative to consultative and participative over a period of two to four years, as noted by Likert. The shift from coercion to persuasion was accompanied by increases in productivity and morale.

[3] Rensis Likert, *The Human Organization* (New York, 1967), chap. 3.

EMOTIONS AND MOTIVES

As a term in current use in communication theory, *emotion* is as misused and misunderstood as "motive." Its meaning has been blurred by expansion to include all human responses other than critical thought. The ultimate absurdity that contributes to destruction of the utility of this necessary word is to confuse it with "motive." Let us see why "motive" and "emotion" should not be used interchangeably.

From the range of definitions assigned to "emotion" we will stipulate one that is suited to the study of communication. *Emotion is a generally upset condition sufficient to cause shock, diffusion, and transference.*

We reserve the term *emotion* for a definite psychophysiological arousal that many psychologists label "the emotional condition," identified by three symptoms, shock, diffusion, and transference. We judge it unwise to speak of a response as "emotional" unless the respondee is disturbed significantly in this manner. We refer to lesser affective states that exist without these symptoms as "feelings."

Our stipulated definition enables us to distinguish "emotion" from "motive." As an internal source of energy that is directional, a motive propels an individual toward a selected option. The emotional condition is nondirectional. Motives operate with or without a concurrent emotional condition. When a person is emotional, his motives operate differently than when he is calm, but they are the same motives. Generally, an emotional condition increases the energy output associated with the functioning of a given motive.

The effects of emotion upon behavior are clarified by an understanding of shock, diffusion, and transference. An emotional person is in a state of shock, to some degree. This does not mean that he is unconscious, in a cataleptic rigidity. Shock is loss of critical faculties, and if sufficiently extreme, the individual would indeed lose consciousness. But in the usual case shock consists of lessened ability to think clearly and solve problems.

Diffusion is a physical phenomenon, consisting of a tendency toward excessive, total bodily movement and loss of ability to make small, precise, isolated adjustments of parts of the body. The pacing and arm waving associated with anger illustrate diffusion.

Transference is a "spilling over," the tendency to release emotional energy in situations and toward people unrelated to the emotional condition. Angry people often drive automobiles recklessly, "taking it out on the machine." After a frustrating morning on an unyielding problem, an advertising account executive said, "I'm going home for lunch. If my wife doesn't have it ready, I'll give her hell. If she does, I won't eat!"

Visualize how a severe emotional condition can affect the performance of a key member of an organization. He is unable to think clearly (shock), so his normal good judgment cannot be relied upon. His manual dexterity is lost (diffusion) and he treats everyone as though that person caused the emotion (transference). Obviously, emotion among members of an organization, if it is at all prolonged and general, lowers productivity. Other things being equal, the organization that operates with less emotion is more efficient. Good management strives to eliminate causes of unnecessary emotion.

A heightened or depressed "tone" of the human organism is possible without emotion. Enthusiasm, or euphoria experienced on a beautiful spring morning, or the gloom associated with illness or a hangover, are states that affect the ways our motives operate. Because these "tone" variations do not show the symptoms of shock, diffusion, and transference, they are not emotions. They can be appropriately termed "feelings." Positive feelings like loyalty and warm regard for one's associates can enhance performance, since the destructive influence of shock, diffusion, and transference are not experienced.

Usually, one can safely arouse feelings that facilitate a desired response in persuasion, up to a point. There is always a danger that a feeling, encouraged and reinforced, may become sufficiently intense to precipitate an emotional condition. Then shock, diffusion, and transference complicate the picture. The football coach, in his pregame presentation, tries to strike a delicate balance. He wants to generate eagerness, anticipation, confidence, and enthusiasm. But if in so doing he creates anger or fear emotion, the performance of his team will be adversely affected. An angry quarterback will not be able to call the best plays (shock), will not throw the ball well (diffusion), and will probably transfer his anger to officials and teammates. Arousing emotion as a technique of persuasion is dangerous business. The side effects often outweigh the benefits.

A SYSTEM FOR MOTIVE ANALYSIS

Motive analysis has been needlessly elaborated and vastly confused by psychologists. All of us analyze the motives of other people every day at a more or less superficial level. All planning of communication necessitates predicting how people will respond. Whenever we predict the behavior of a person from information about his habits, desires, needs, interests, and goals, we are analyzing motives. The motive construct we hypothesize is usually part of a particular context, and we estimate the probable interaction of our motive construct with some proposed stimulus. When a husband induces his wife to accompany him to a professional convention by mentioning opportunities to shop rather than a chance to learn about marketing widgets in Outer Patagonia, he is utilizing motive analysis.

One's abilities to analyze the motives of others can be increased by observation and study. A do-it-yourself approach consists of making two lists, one of ways in which people are predictably alike, and the other of response patterns in which human beings tend, reliably, to differ. The lists should be cumulative, kept in written form, over months and years. Items on the lists come from introspection, from writing brief analytical descriptions of interesting bits of observed behavior, and reading.

Printed materials on "what makes people tick" abound. The self-taught student of motivation will read every article available to him that purports to help readers better understand people in popular magazines and scholarly journals. Proceeding intuitively, the student selects behaviors that seem to be capable of being generalized and adds them to list 1 or list 2. As the lists grow, they can be kept manageable by creating categories to group similar items. The classification system can be taken from some authority or it can be devised by the student. The important criterion is that the categories relate as closely as possible to the kind of communication problems confronted by the student.

The list-building project develops greater understanding of certain universals of motivation. In particular, the different *varieties* of motives common to all people will appear in our lists. Certain to be noted repeatedly are three major and distinct kinds of human motivation: habits, deficit motivations, and other-than-self centered motives.[4] We now explain and exemplify these basic motivational categories.

HABITS AS MOTIVES

The generalization "man is creature of habit" will come as no surprise to our reader. Human inertia, resistance to change, is one of the most impressive and predictable characteristics of people. Individually, habit operates to keep us doing what we are doing the way we have been doing it. Collectively, it protects us from impulsive improvements (or unwise "bright ideas") in our communities and leads to the maxim respected by sociologists and politicians: "Social change comes slowly." Consider the effort to reduce tooth decay through fluo-

---

[4] For a more complete treatment of motivation, see Ernest G. Bormann, William S. Howell, Ralph G. Nichols, and George L. Shapiro, *Interpersonal Communication in the Modern Organization* (Englewood Cliffs, N.J., 1969), chaps. 14–16.

ridation of municipal water supplies in the 1950s and 1960s. Long after the health and economic questions had been answered satisfactorily thousands of critics were still fighting the battle to gain the popular support necessary to begin fluoridation.

All people are habit-bound, but the *degree* to which habit controls their decisions day in and day out varies widely. It is realistic to envision your associates as scattered along a continuum labeled "addiction to routine." At one end of this continuum we find a cluster of the more rigid members of the group, those who somehow learned to enjoy redundancy most. These people receive "psychic income," experience deep satisfaction, from living each day the way they lived the day before. The man who is typically rigid in this sense likes to go to bed and get up at uniform times. He likes to have the same breakfast every day. He arrives at work the same time each morning, and his day is ordered, with an unvarying sequence of events. He can be a perfectionist, because he practices everything over and over. So his satisfaction in routine can come from doing his job well and from the security of knowing what tomorrow will bring. But because he has a vested interest in perpetuating the status quo, he is more disturbed by change or the possibility of change than are less rigid people.

At the other end of our "addiction to routine" continuum are those who, relatively, find novelty rewarding. While they are fundamentally committed to the mores and folkways of their culture, they attach importance to variety in the little details of living. They enjoy varying the workday. Their sleeping and eating patterns tend to be irregular. They buy new products on impulse. Initially, almost any change is attractive to them. Later, their judgment leads them to reject most proposed changes, revealing their deep-laid habits of delayed judgment and critical thought.

One important step in motive analysis is to assign the person being analyzed a position on the "addiction to routine" continuum. If he is near the rigid end, his responses to a recommendation for change will be vigorously negative, at least at first. Later, his judgment may force him to overcome his initial reaction. An individual near the flexible end of the scale will tend to like the recommendation of change, and the more bizarre it is, the better he will like it—at first hearing. As with the rigid person, later judgment will often revise the initial acceptance or rejection.

Since presentational speaking is usually innovative, the ability to accurately predict the initial reaction to proposed change becomes highly important. If key members of the audience are rigid, the speaker will understand that he must design his presentation to provide relevant information and time for them to revise their initial negative response. To reduce the impact of their automatic rejection response, his language must be selected to be perceived as routine, to cause the proposal to seem to be a minor change from the status quo. Elements of continuity from the past and present should be stressed.

To adapt to the flexible receivers, the persuader can be dramatic to heighten the novelty of his proposal. His language can maximize change, and he can picture the circumstances resulting from his proposal as "new" and "different." Impulsive listeners will respond favorably, but here again the thoughtful speaker will realize that this first reaction may well be modified by judgment. So he never accepts the initial acceptance of a flexible person as final. He continues to supply information and develop his proposal until he is sure that reexamination of the positive impulse decision will not change it.

Perhaps we are belaboring the obvious, but it seems to us that so many causes have been lost because they have been presented to rigid people as exciting and dramatic changes, that we must warn against it. Less catastrophic but equally regrettable is the failure to stress novelty when presenting a recommendation to flexible men. Any presentation should incorporate adaptaton to the "addiction to routine" characteristics of its audience.

Now we turn to a scaling of habits relevant to communication in terms of their complexity. If the reader will forgive our "habit" of thinking in continua, we suggest another continuum. A habit is a unit of behavior, which, once started, tends to complete itself. One movement, or thought, triggers the next until the familiar cycle has run its course. Like the record player, started by a push of the "on" button, which plays a stack of records and turns itself off, the human habit needs no conscious assistance once it is under way. Most people understand this automatic, programmed nature of habits, but few appreciate how complex habits can be. We tend to think of habits as simple and mechanical, examples being lighting a cigarette or starting an automobile engine. But mental habits are just as real as physical habits. Due to the almost infinite number of associations possible in the human brain, mental habits are often elaborate and extensive.

Our continuum of habit complexity ranges from a minute movement like wrinkling our nose or lifting an eyebrow while concentrating upon a knotty problem to complicated physical patterns like putting a golf ball, hitting a tennis service, or driving a car to mental habits like suspending judgment or jumping to conclusions. An entire problem-solving routine can become habitual. Many executives have acquired the Dewey sequence of problem-solving as a habit. Automatically, they tick off the steps of (1) defining, (2) limiting, (3) exploring, (4) listing possible solutions, and (5) selecting the best solution. Considerably more complicated is the Kepner-Tregoe method of dealing with managerial problems in organizations.[5] Study and drill over long

5 Charles Kepner and Benjamin Tregoe, *The Rational Manager* (New York, 1965), pp. 54-55.

periods of time have implemented the Kepner-Tregoe procedure as a habit in managers who applied themselves assiduously to it.

Much behavior can be predicted if you know how a person habitually thinks. Does the man to whom you propose change automatically ask (silently), "What's in it for me?" or perhaps, "Will this help us do a better job?" or, "Will it save money?" These are three typical responses associated with particular people in all kinds of organizations. Originally, the motives we will discuss later under "deficit" and "other-than-self centered" categories contributed to the formation of these response tendencies. But after enough repetitions habits were formed. Responses were selected, reinforced, and became as predictable as a knee jerk reflex.

Nowhere is the "creature of habit" description more applicable than to man's thought processes. All of us settle comfortably into our mental ruts, conforming happily to comfortable, familiar stereotypes. We read the magazines and books of the types we know best, we lead social lives in imitation of those around us, we work the way we have seen others work.

A maxim current in teacher-training colleges is revealing: "The beginning teacher teaches not the way he was taught to teach, but the way he was taught." Creativity, breaking out of usual thought patterns, is *not* our norm. Training people to be more creative, in school and in industry, has made but slight progress toward freeing men's minds from the shackles of habit. Perhaps we can devise ways of training people in the habit of being nonhabitual (i.e., creative) when they are stimulated by a problem!

DEFICIT MOTIVES

A second large cluster of motivations common to all people is appropriately labeled "deficit." These sources of energy are directed toward an objective that we might describe colloquially as "beefing up the ego." Deficit motives act to protect their owner from harm, present and future. In this sense they operate defensively, always reacting to actual or possible attack. Abraham Maslow suggests that the defensive character of this motivation, always acting to hold or restore something, is a negative element. Instead of advancing to new goals, the motive attempts to prevent regression or to regain what has been lost.[6] Hence, we label such motivation "deficit." We would add that another characteristic of deficit motivation is its self-centered nature. Benefits from successful operation of a deficit motive are always predominantly selfish and personal. Understandably, anxiety is associated with deficit

[6] A. H. Maslow, *Motivation and Personality* (New York, 1954), p. 105.

motivation more than with habit or with other-than-self centered motives.

Maslow postulated a "hierarchy of basic needs,"[7] which has become a generally accepted and essential part of many theories of motivation. We will modify his original categories freely, but retain the helpful notion that basic needs are sequential, that is, form a hierarchy.

Figure 5.1 represents the four deficit motives we consider to be

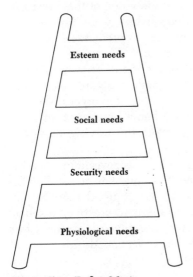

Esteem needs

Social needs

Security needs

Physiological needs

Figure 5.1   Deficit Motives

universal and important arranged in a "ladder" that suggests their hierarchical relationship.

A person "climbs the ladder" in the sense that the lower needs must be substantially satisfied before higher needs become important to him. Attaining maturity is, to some extent, a matter of moving up the ladder. As an individual develops mechanisms (habits) that adequately and automatically satisfy his deficit motives, he becomes free to respond to other, less self-centered motives.

Physiological needs are those upon which the health and well-being of the body depend. When a person is physically in good shape, well fed and well cared for, his physiological needs seem unimportant. Then "security" becomes a matter of concern.

We can define "security" as the ability to look ahead without anxiety. If you can contemplate tomorrow, next week, next month, and next year without worry, you are secure. In a culture where the hus-

---

[7] *Ibid.*, p. 97.

band supports his family, this peering into the future is done on behalf of the members of his family as well. When circumstances are such that an individual has relatively little reason to worry about his source of support or his ability to provide for those dependent upon him, security becomes inactive as a motive.

Man is a social animal. When his security is no longer a matter of concern, he is motivated toward building and improving his human relationships. All of us need people to relate to, fairly intimately, and some of us need many more than others do. A person who has recently moved into a new community will find it important to locate people with whom he can communicate freely and enjoyably. When he is happy with his associates, his social needs are met and his quest for human contact becomes unimportant. Again, a satisfied need no longer motivates behavior.

A person with physiological, security, and social needs well in hand (which is another way of saying that he has delegated them to his habit systems) typically finds himself preoccupied with the fourth deficit motive, his need for esteem. Esteem as a motive is concern over one's self and public images. The self-esteem component is satisfied when a person meets his own standards of performance, socially and on the job. Public-esteem needs are met when one receives evidence that he is well regarded by his peers, his family, his rivals, his subordinates, and his superiors.

When an individual is able to inventory his image and finds (1) he is meeting his own standards quite well and (2) the evidence indicates that his associates regard him highly, he typically quits worrying about esteem, and that motive, like the earlier deficit needs, ceases to be a directive force in his daily life.

We have sketched in the movement up the ladder of a well-adjusted person. Few of us can claim that status. Most of us have difficulty clambering over one or more of the deficit rungs. For example, *security* is a "hang up" for many people. If you feel insecure when all around you feel secure, if risk is minimal for them and frightening for you, then a nonrational concern for security has become, for you, a dominant motivation. You then worry about security more than the circumstances warrant, a pathological behavior. It takes time and energy to be insecure. This time and energy must be subtracted from some more worthy endeavor. Basically, this lowering of productivity is the price paid for emphasizing, nonrationally, any of the deficit motives.

For reasons that are complicated and little understood, certain people find it similarly difficult or impossible to satisfy one of the remaining three deficit needs and relegate it to habit. We have all known persons who had an insatiable desire for praise and notoriety, others who were constantly concerned because their relationships with people were unsatisfactory, and less frequently, individuals whose unjustified concern over their health prevented their normal functioning in society. These unfortunate human beings are penalized by the dominance of a deficit motivation, a personality need for unrealistic amounts of esteem, social success, or attention to their bodies. Until an adjustment occurs that returns the "out of kilter" motive to a normal perspective, such persons can function only partially at work, in recreation, and at home.

To the man with a dominant deficit need, other reasons and interests seem unimportant. The insightful persuader never fails to trigger the dominant motive. To show an esteem-starved person that what you recommend will cause him to be respected by his associates will in all probability release a flood of energy directed to the suggested belief or course of action. Similarly, promises of security appeal to the person lacking security, and the prospect of being sought out as a friend appeals to the person who needs friendship. The hypochondriac responds to the drug advertisement that promises to restore his long-lost feeling of physical well-being. Truly, a persistent, dominant deficit motive is close to the center of human motivation. Any motive analysis that fails to identify such a powerful source of energy is deficient, indeed!

The high price one pays to support a dominant deficit motive should concern us. While it is a key to successful persuasion and thus facilitates social control, the individual with the enlarged motive would be better off without it. Correcting the pathology is no easy task. Possibly, the distortion of reality is sufficient to justify securing psychiatric help. Usually, understanding counsel of associates is worth a try. The person with a chronic thirst for praise, for example, is typically unaware of his condition. If he can be led through an analysis of his own motivation and thereby develop insight into his own behavior, the excessive dominance of the esteem motive will be reduced. Talking openly about feelings and reasons for beliefs and actions is good for most of us. Externalizing any problem in this fashion makes it easier to live with. Confronting facts about ourselves is often difficult but always beneficial.

OTHER-THAN-SELF CENTERED MOTIVES

Peter Drucker in his thought-provoking book, *The Effective Executive*, cites "commitment to contribution" as characteristic of the successful high-level manager. By "contribution" he means the job to be done, the services to be rendered to the public *outside* the executive's organization. The nature of the motivation promoting dedication to "contribution" is made quite clear in Drucker's explanation.

The focus on contribution turns the executive's attention away from his own specialty, his own narrow skills, his own department, and toward the performance of the whole. It turns his attention to the outside, the only place where there are results. He is likely to have to think through what relationships his skills, his specialty, his function, or his department have to the entire organization and *its* purpose. He therefore will also come to think in terms of the customer, the client, or the patient, who is the ultimate reason for whatever the organization produces, whether it be economic goods, governmental policies, or health services. As a result what he does and how he does it will be materially different.[8]

Commitment to contribution as a motivation differs sharply from deficit motivation. Where a deficit is self-centered, causing a person to focus on benefits to himself, contribution is other-than-self centered. Concern with contribution is interest in consequences affecting other people. It evelutes one's behavior in terms of benefits to others. People strongly motivated by commitment to contribution seldom consider consequences to themselves in making decisions. Their deficit needs are adequately met by habitual routines and they are free to preoccupy themselves with results.

Commitment to contribution is one of a cluster of other-than-self centered motives that only recently have been recognized as important determinants of human behavior. Prior to the discovery that strong motives could be turned outward, away from the self, human motivation was often assumed to be totally selfish, turned inward. For many years we tried to explain the beliefs and actions of people through their deficit motivations alone. This led to grotesque distortions, such as accounting for the helping relationship by assuming that the sole reason a person aided someone in distress was to make himself feel good.

Much credit for persuading people in the world of business to believe in other-than-self centered motives must be given to Douglas McGregor, who in 1960 postulated his Theory X and Theory Y as alternative explanations of human nature and human behavior at work.[9] Theory X he presented as a set of beliefs about people currently held in organizations: that people dislike work, that they must be coerced and threatened to get them to work, and that they prefer to be directed, dislike responsibility, and value security above all else. McGregor's Theory Y was a contrasting set of beliefs: that work is as natural as play, that men exercise self-direction and self-control in pursuing work objectives, that people under proper conditions seek responsibility.

[8] Peter F. Drucker, *The Effective Executive* (New York, 1967), p. 53.

[9] Douglas McGregor, *The Human Side of Enterprise* (New York, 1960), chaps. 3 and 4.

Theory X restricts man to deficit needs. Theory Y assumes he is directed also by other-than-self centered motivations. Theory Y beliefs have been built into organizations with favorable results, an example being extensive experiment with varied forms of participative management. Over the decade beginning in 1960, policies and practices of management were modified significantly in an effort to apply the assumptions of Theory Y.

We can identify two kinds of other-than-self centered motivation. One is preoccupation with people and the other is preoccupation with processes.

As an example of a preoccupation with people that acquired the strength of a motive, we will mention the sales manager of a corporation that manufactured electronic devices. He retired relatively early with completely adequate financial resources, but chose to resume work because of the satisfaction he received from helping young men improve as industrial salesmen. He was a skilled supervisor who was intensely interested in every employee he managed. The young salesmen sensed his interest and quickly became excited about their work for its own sake, because their supervisor enjoyed helping them do it better. Human relationships were informal and open. There was much fun on the job, and many work days were prolonged voluntarily because the employees became involved in the group effort. And the supervisor found his work more stimulating than any play activities he attempted during the period of his retirement.

Preoccupation with process as a motivation often occurs in research or product-development activities A design engineer became intrigued with the problem of "fixing" a communications satellite in one position above a selected point on the surface of the earth. He and his associates experimented with star-sensing circuits. As they made headway toward their objective, excitement increased. Often they preferred returning to the laboratory in the evening to movies or socializing. Just as the creative artist gets "caught up" in the music he is composing, the picture he is painting, or the novel he is writing, the design engineer found himself motivated more strongly by his task than by any other need. His effortless expenditure of energy exemplifies the results that follow preoccupation with improving the "state of the art" as an end in itself.

At this point, we warn the reader not to confuse other-than-self centered motivation with "doing good" or altruism. Many people vigorously propelled by other-than-self centered motives are definitely not "do-gooders." The bank robber who works for years to plan the perfect holdup, the protesting university student who dedicates all his time and intelligence to plotting ways to bring his university to a halt, the housewife who schemes with her best friend's husband to arrange an adulterous affair that will not be detected, all these may well be energized by other-than-self centered motivation. The point is that other-than-self centered motives may be wholesome, neutral, or unwholesome for the people involved. What makes them other-than-self centered is the location of the focal point of interest in people or processes outside the self.

SUMMARY

Let us return to John Jamison and his presentation, discussed in some detail in Chapter 1. John designed his speech to trigger dominant motives in three men. Were these important motives habit, deficit, or other-than-self centered? We will look at each in turn.

President Joe Perkins had as his central concern the costs of introducing a new cereal, particularly the "outgo" from the time it is marketed until it begins to show a profit. This is a process orientation and would seem to be other-than-self centered. However, Lydgate, head of marketing, was interested mainly in possibilities of the new cereal for novel advertising. Viewing a new product from the dimensions of advertising is a part of the process of supplying cereals to the public, and would appear to be other-than-self centered. Marshall Everding's desire for a complete product line is also, on the surface, an "improve the state of the art" motivation, definitely other-than-self centered.

The John Jamison presentation *may* have appealed to only other-than-self centered motives in his auditors. We say "may" because, as stated, the three dominant interests probably involved other motivations. Habit seems certainly to be a part of the motivational setting. Each of the three men had produced the same reactions to new proposals repeatedly in the past. Evidently, previous responses had rewarded and reinforced expression of these interests. The ingredients of habit formation were present. If the predicted responses are habitual, as they must be to some degree, the habit portion of the response mechanism is secondary, since initially the interests were likely to have been other-than-self centered. Later, their repetition became habitual, but the origin of each is found in the preoccupation of its owner, centered outside himself.

Except—there remains a possibility that the fundamental motive in one or more of these men was deficit. Perhaps social esteem or security needs could be met by any of them vigorously applying his particular criterion. This is unlikely, because the interests as asserted seem remote from personal consequences, and because these men were established and successful, so probably had little remaining deficit behavior. But the possibility remains. Jamison would have been wise to examine the likelihood that any of the three might be serving a deficit personality need. If such should be the case, a slight modification of the presentation could connect an appeal directly to the dominant deficit motive.

QUESTIONS FOR DISCUSSION AND REVIEW

1. What is the relationship of motivation to the process of persuasion?
2. What is included in the concept *motivation?*
3. How are "emotion" and "motivation" different, and what is their interaction?
4. What is an example to show how a habit can function as a motive?
5. How can you set about estimating the "flexibility" of another person?
6. Why are the four deficit motives said to be "sequential"?
7. What are the differences among security, social, and esteem needs?
8. What are the implications to the persuader of the maxim, "A satisfied need does not motivate behavior"?
9. What are the opportunities in your profession to develop other-than-self centered motivations?
10. How does McGregor's "Theory X and Theory Y" relate to the concept of other-than-self centered motives?

REFERENCES AND SUGGESTED READINGS

Brembeck, Winston, and William S. Howell. *Persuasion.* Englewood Cliffs, N.J.: Prentice-Hall, 1952.

Clevenger, Theodore, Jr. *Audience Analysis.* Indianapolis: Bobbs-Merrill, 1966.

Cronkhite, Gary. *Persuasion: Speech and Behavioral Change.* Indianapolis: Bobbs-Merrill, 1966.

Keltner, John W. *Interpersonal Speech-Communication: Elements and Structures.* Belmont, Calif.: Wadsworth, 1970.

Minnick, Wayne C. *The Art of Persuasion.* 2nd ed. Boston: Houghton Mifflin, 1968.

Oliver, Robert T. *The Psychology of Persuasive Speech.* 2nd ed. New York: Longmans, 1957.

Scheidel, Thomas M. *Persuasive Speaking.* Chicago: Scott, Foresman, 1967.

PART II

TECHNIQUES OF PRESENTATIONAL SPEAKING

With an understanding of basic concepts and theories involved in presentations, the reader is ready to advance to specific techniques. In Part II, techniques are treated in roughly the order in which the maker of the presentation should confront them in his planning. His first decision is to select his strategies of organization and within that frame-work materials are arranged.

Forms of support, statistical and nonstatistical, are treated in detail. Both reasoning and suggestion are explored and compared as means of presentation. Audio-visual aids of all sorts are examined as they clarify and support key items of presentation. Finally, the role of the listener as an active participant is investigated and ways in which he may respond constructively and helpfully are explained and exemplified.

CHAPTER SIX

ORGANIZING THE PRESENTATION

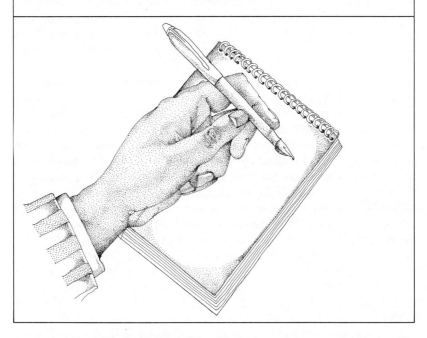

An interesting phenomenon of speech communication appears when we analyze the talk of managers, executives, and leaders in professional organizations. Striking differences between the speaking of successful and unsuccessful leaders become obvious. The less successful persons lack fluency and directness in their talking, fail to sense the responses of their listeners (they do not use feedback), and most striking of all, they do not enjoy business conferences, meetings, and making presentations. In fact, unsuccessful managers typically fear speaking to anyone other than a few close associates, and consequently, they avoid making presentations whenever possible. As a result, they often delegate to others the job of giving presentations, to the detriment of themselves and their divisions.

Surprisingly, what these unsuccessful communicators say is often very much to the point. Usually, they are well-trained and intelligent people, as their having achieved management positions indicates. But they have failed to take advantage of the spoken word as a tool for getting the day's work done. Consequently, they phrase their thoughts so ineptly that they are seldom understood, they do not adjust to particular situations and listeners, and they "step on the toes" of others by saying things in a tactless fashion. Their good ideas and valuable information go unused.

The successful leader in business or the professions has none of the above speech problems. He is fluent, often eloquent. He enjoys talking and does his work via the spoken word as much as possible, using the telephone often. He is sensitive to the responses of people around him (uses continuous feedback), adjusting what he says and how he says it from moment to moment. The people he talks to are uniformly impressed.

The fluent and outgoing person who aspires to be or who is a successful leader may assume that he has no need to learn more about the making of presentations or any other speech-communication skill. We hasten to dispel any such illusion. Are the good speakers who direct our organizations well-rounded experts in the use of the spoken word, or do we find substantial deficiency in their speech communication? Our experience in teaching managers of many different organizations the basic speech-communication and presentational-speaking skills leads us to answer that even superficially fluent managers are not uniformly talented in all aspects of speaking. Often, successful managers excel in fluency, use of feedback, vocabulary, and delivery. However, as communicators they are inefficient. They expend too many words per idea. They talk while they are thinking of something to say next. They lack the ability to arrange items in a message so that each successive idea follows the preceding one naturally and inevitably. If we were to select the one most important defect in the presentational speaking of even the most fluent and successful managers, including executive officers of large corporations, it would be lack of sound organization. What the successful leaders need most to improve their speech communication is the understanding of the principles of organization and the ability to implement them in construction and transmission of messages.

A person's inability to organize ideas poses difficulties in the brief and fragmentary messages that occur in daily routines of working with people. Rambling, disjointed, and repetitive comment in a conference, meeting, or on the telephone is bad enough, but bad organization in a presentation is disastrous. The presentation must be a unit, with the parts tightly articulated in harmony with an obvious organizing principle. To "lose" a listener because his good judgment tells him that two items which the speaker asserts are related are, indeed, not related, is often to lose the final decision.

The basic reason why even good leaders who have considerable native speaking ability organize their spoken messages so badly is that they have no knowledge of the process of structuring ideas for oral presentation and are not acquainted with organizational patterns best suited to their needs.

THE EARMARKS OF SOUND ORGANIZATION

Many of us have only a vague notion about what constitutes organized material. If a message can be outlined or is presented in outline form, we often judge that it is well organized. (Indeed, many business and professional people make a habit of developing messages in outline form. Somehow, they seem to assume mistakenly that a series of assertations, each properly numbered and indented, will carry more important information more quickly and clearly than an integrated series of clear topic sentences with explication and supporting information.) Actually, all that outlining indicates is that someone has listed and numbered some points, provided a list of alphabetized subpoints, and, perhaps, a further listing and numbering of sub-subheads. The process of systematically skeletonizing a series of sentences or phrases does not insure that a given sub-subhead fits logically as a supporting point for a subhead and that the subhead in turn fits logically under the main head. Nor does such outlining require that the sequence of ideas presented in the outline be the best for a particular topic, occasion, message source, or group of listeners. Sound organization, on the other hand, is characterized by unity, coherence, relevance, conciseness, and comprehensiveness.

Unity. A well-organized message has unity. One can evaluate the unity of presentation by first searching for and finding a central theme to which each element logically relates. Usually, the central theme is expressed or implied in terms of one clear statement. Frequently, the central statement is expressed explicitly in the message and highlighted by the speaker in a way that makes it obvious. All major subdivisions of the unified message are related to the central theme and often to some of the other subdivisions. We can think of phrases and sentences showing the relationships among the various parts of a message and their connection to the central theme as "big-picture" comments. The speaker cannot assume that each listener will provide the structuring necessary to fit the individual pieces of the presentation into a coherent pattern. Big-picture comments accomplish this by including material like the following: "In terms of our ultimate decision to develop this product the immediate and long-term cost implications are, to my mind, the most important. Given our current capitalization crisis and the pressure of competitors on some of our standard products, I believe cost considerations are crucial, particularly the short-range costs. So let's look at the immediate costs of product development."

Coherence. A well organized presentation is coherent. Coherence, in this sense of the term, refers to how the various parts of the message cluster together. Each part of a coherent presentation relates to every other part in a way that reveals some global design. The practical demands of structure are generally met by having each element closely related to the immediately adjacent element. Thus, when building a structure of bricks, each brick is cemented to its neighbors. The ultimate design of the building is clear only after the completion of all of the connections and when one can step back and see the finished structure. Similarly, each element of the presentation should be related to the preceding and succeeding parts to establish a coherent message. When communication units are small, the fact that one utterance succeeds another in time may be sufficient to indicate the relation of one to another. When the elements are somewhat longer, inflections or gestures or pauses may indicate the connections between parts of the discourse, but when the elements get still larger the speaker ought to provide verbal connecting links. Linking statements are designed to make apparent the coherence among various elements of the message. We will henceforth refer to such material as transitions.

Relevance. A well-organized message contains only those ideas and information that are clearly and directly related to the central theme of the presentation. If the speaker feels that a seemingly unrelated element is important and relevant, he should explain his line of reasoning to the audience. One of the most common problems of the individual who organizes poorly is that he includes material that comes to mind whether it is related to the topic under consideration or not. When a person prepares a speech, his mental processes are stimulated by many different impressions. Many of us "free associate" ideas. One notion gives way to another, one mental image triggers other images, one anecdote, experience, or thought leads to another, quite often through idiosyncratic and illogical processes. We include these irrelevant materials because, at the moment, they interest us, but there is no reason to assume that such materials will seem logical, interesting, or useful to others.

Conciseness. A well-organized presentation is concise in the sense that it is not repetitious. Each topic is dealt with in comprehensive fashion and then not dealt with again except for emphasis, as in summaries, transitions, or conclusions. A very common organizational fault is to deal with a topic, drop it, take up a second idea, perhaps a third, and then return to the first. The beginner is learning to be concise when he can cut his message into parts and paste it together again so that all of the statements about a given topic are clustered together.

Comprehensiveness. A well-organized message is comprehensive in that it deals with all of the important topics relating to the central theme. Of course, the comprehensiveness of speech communication is a function of the audience and the occasion. The comprehensiveness of John Jamison's presentation was restricted to what was possible with an audience composed of the Board of Control and the time limitation of twenty minutes. Comprehensiveness implies that the presentation is limited to territory that can be covered in the time allotted, given the understanding and interests of the audience. The Board of Control had a high level of interest in and knowledge about the topic; thus, John could cover more territory than he could if he were making a presentation to people unfamiliar with the business.

MESSAGE PREPARATION

Presentations that are unified, coherent, relevant, concise, and comprehensive result from a two-stage process of message preparation. Many less formal speech communications within the organizational setting require less time to make ready than the presentation (and sometimes the exigencies of the situation make preparation next to impossible); nonetheless the ideal of complete two-stage processing of oral messages is a good one for all interpersonal communication as well as for presentational speaking.

The analysis stage. Once a person has received an assignment to deliver a presentation, he should assemble all of the information he thinks important and begin to study it. Some of his thinking ought to be systematic and disciplined and some ought to be more freewheeling and creative. The beginning ought to be systematic. Collecting and reading the basic information relating to the topic sets the stage for a process we term "mulling over." The function of the mulling over is to make an analysis of the topic.

The process of analysis consists of close study of the materials to find important points, basic questions, and core issues. When a person begins the study of a topic, many pieces of information may seem equally important, and even those ideas that appear significant may not relate clearly to other significant ideas. John Jamison may have a feeling that information about the crossover point for the new product is of vital importance, but early in his preparation he may not know precisely how and when he will use it.

Once a person has discovered the core issues in a body of material, the process of analysis continues on to reveal the central focus and, ultimately, the way each of the basic parts relates to the central theme and to one another. When the process reaches its conclusion, the end product is a logical brief that lays out the basic points in tightly ordered and reasoned fashion as they support the main topic.

When one makes an analysis of a complicated subject, the parts seldom fall easily and neatly into place. After the systematic collection of data and careful study, a person should make an attempt at arranging and structuring the main points. The typical first result of such arrangement will be the kind of outline we referred to above; that is, an unsatisfactory listing of points of differing levels of abstractness in an order that could be shuffled without disturbing any logical progression. When a person reaches a dead end, the time has come for more freewheeling "mulling around." At this point, creativity is to be encouraged.

Usually if time permits, and presentations often are carefully prepared so there is some time for preparation, the speaker is well advised to put the topic out of mind for a bit when he reaches the end of fruitful disciplined planning. Typically, the topic of the presentation will come to mind at those times when his attention is not directly engaged. When a person is driving a car, walking, doing routine chores like mowing a lawn or cleaning a house, or shortly before dropping asleep at night, he often finds thoughts about important matters tumbling through the consciousness. The images are sometimes free associative and fragmentary and, on occasion, ridiculous, but many times during these periods of purposive daydreaming an important organizing principle will come to mind or a particularly apt illustration or anecdote to be used in the presentation will surface.

Many busy and productive people keep a notebook or note cards to jot down ideas that occur to them during such periods. Quite often they have these handy by their bedside, for example, if they are likely to get an idea before going to sleep. The best presentations often result from a particularly happy insight arrived at during one of the freewheeling mulling around periods that reveals a basic pattern or structure for the whole topic of the presentation.

Some psychologists refer to an insight of the latter sort as an "ah ha" experience because a light suddenly turns on and illuminates the entire problem. When one has an authentic "ah ha" experience, the feeling that accompanies it is one of excitement and pleasurable anticipation. A person wants to try out the idea and see if it will work and if it is, indeed, as elegant and gratifying as it seems. The testing or verification of the insight again requires systematic disciplined thought.

After a person finishes a careful verification of the ideas developed during the creative phase of analysis, the result will be an outline of the topic, but this time the outline will consist of subpoints of the same level of abstraction, each with carefully defined limits that do not overlap, selected in such a way that taken together they exhaust the topic. The subpoints will be arranged in a logical progression so that moving them about arbitrarily would do violence to the chain of reasoning which they represent, and all of them relate to the major theme. With the final verification this first stage of the preparation comes to a close.

The audience-adaptation stage.   After a sound analysis of the topic the speaker has a thorough understanding of his material. The job of preparation for a presentation is not yet finished, however, because the good speaker does not simply present every audience with the analysis that he found convincing, for what is necessary to convince him may be different than what is necessary to convince his listeners. The untrained person often wants to include everything that led to his understanding of the question and finds time limitations frustrating. Certainly, if a person wants to present the complete analysis that results from months of study and labor by a division of his organization, thirty minutes or an hour is too short, but usually, the occasion does not require the complete analysis. The presentation is set up to give key people only that part of the analysis that they require to do the job. On the other hand, a speaker may be so sophisticated in his job that even fragmentary items in the analysis are more meaningful to him, but for his listeners they must be spelled out, amplified, and made operational.

Presentational speaking is a subfield of the ancient art of rhetoric whose essence is to take information already in mind and artistically fashion it for a specific audience and occasion. For our concerns, therefore, the second phase of message preparation is crucial. In the second phase the speaker with a thorough understanding of his topic begins to analyze his audience to discover the best way to present all or part of his ideas to them.

Again the preparation in the second phase should be disciplined and systematic at times and at others should be more freewheeling. For the systematic analysis a person can begin with the topics considered in Part I of this book. What is the formal organizational context for the presentation? What is the message source's formal status, authority, and responsibility? What is the receiver's formal position? What does he know of the actual power and esteem of his listeners? What about their individual idiosyncrasies, interests, attitudes, drives, and preoccupations? Jamison had already gone through the first stage and he knew what he wanted to say, he thoroughly understood his case, but what he needed was help with the second stage of preparation when he adapted and organized his material for the twenty minutes he had with the board.

THE PROCESS OF ORGANIZING MATERIALS FOR A SPECIFIC AUDIENCE

The last steps in preparing a presentation may be thought of as the nuts-and-bolts organization of the message. These latter steps consist of selecting, arranging, and proportioning the material for the presentation and of bolting the parts together with transitions.

Selecting material. The first stage in organizing details of a presentation for a specific audience is to select from all of the information that could be included that which will be used in the speech. When the time limits are short, the selection of material is crucial. The point is illustrated by the old witticism about how half of what we do in our sales presentations is a waste of time and we ought to cut it out except we do not know which half. When someone must make a presentation in twenty minutes, as John Jamison did, then he must forego the luxury of including 50 percent garbage in his message.

Identifying the most important material for each of the key people in the audience is an extremely practical way to select items for the presentation. Speech consultant Paul Osterhus recommended to John that he analyze the motivation of the people who would hear the presentation to discover their priorities of interests and that he use that criterion as the basis for the selection of material.

Another aid in selecting material is stating the central thesis in the form of a single, simple sentence. The technical name for this focal point of the presentation is the *proposition.* The proposition is the essence of the speaker's proposal in that it tells precisely what he wants the audience to believe or do as a result of his talk.

One should always strive to get the kernel of the talk into one sentence. If the central statement becomes a paragraph, the speaker will know that his thinking and preparation are not yet adequate to the task. A paragraph provides a very fuzzy focus for a speech. The presentation which drives home a proposition phrased clearly in one sentence is effectively unified.

When we say that the proposition should be phrased as a simple sentence, we are not referring to the content, which may be complicated, but to the grammatical form. A simple sentence has one subject and one predicate and therefore serves to present but one idea. A compound sentence, on the other hand, consists of two or more separate ideas and puts a great burden on the speaker, for he must try to balance these points equally throughout his speech. For example, Jamison might phrase his central proposition as a simple sentence as follows: "We should immediately authorize the expenditure of $740,000 to discover the sales potential of product X." A compound sentence such as the following would not do. "We should recognize the need to diversify in the direction of new product X, and the expenditure of $740,000 in market surveys is justified."

In addition to being a simple sentence, a good proposition ought to be concrete and specific. John might have used as his central proposition the simple sentence, "I want to tell you the latest developments in regards to product X." The latter proposition suffers from vagueness. The phrase "latest developments" would allow almost anything about product X to work its way into the speech.

The concrete and specific proposition that contains a single, clearly expressed idea serves well as a second yardstick to use in selecting material. Every item that John Jamison uses should not only pass the test of audience need but should also be clearly and significantly relevant to his central proposition, "We should immediately authorize the expenditure of $740,000 to discover the sales potential of product X." Consequently, he would not include an interesting anecdote about how a major developmental breakthrough in regard to product X was made by accident, no matter how entertaining and interesting the story.

Arrangement. The second step in planning the organization of a presentation is to arrange the material selected in suitable order. The presentation takes place in a time-space continuum and therefore some material must come first, some second, and so on. We feel that the major decision in the last stage of message preparation is the choice of an over-all pattern. We have discovered a repertoire of three basic, tested patterns of arrangement in our study of presentational speaking in business and the professions. Everyone can readily master the three basic patterns, and the great majority, over 90 percent, of presentations will fall into one of them successfully. Indeed, because understanding the necessity for and the use of a basic organizational pattern is one of the most important skills for all leaders in business and the professions, we devote the latter part of the chapter to step-by-step directions on the use of the three basic patterns in presentational speaking.

Proportioning. The final step is for the speaker to estimate the relative importance of the various elements of the message for the audience, purpose, and occasion. The amount and kind of supporting material used depends upon the speaker's judgment concerning the importance of the various divisions of his present action. Proportioning requires a mature weighing of varied possibilities. A sound analysis of the topic in the first stage of preparation is crucial to wise proportioning of materials, but in the final analysis no mechanical aids to proportioning are available. A good proposition is one-half of the battle in selecting material, a good basic pattern of arrangement often comes from the recommended patterns, but judgments about proportioning of time and effort in the presentation outline come from experience and wisdom.

Transitions. Carefully selected, arranged, and proportioned materials must be tied together by transition material. The sequence of properly selected elements of a speech may be worthy of praise, but many listeners will miss some important relationships unless appropriate transitions highlight and reinforce vital connections. Further, transitions add *movement* to a speech. Properly used, they contribute variety, interest, and a sense of steady progress toward a predetermined goal.

Transitions may be nonverbal as well as verbal. A speaker can indicate the relationship between elements of his speech by a variety of gestures and vocal inflections. He can pause and resume speaking at a contrasting tempo to let his audience know he is progressing to another point. He can use gesture or bodily movement to the same end. A long pause and a movement of several steps suggest a substantial change in his topic, while a hand gesture or a tipping of the head suggest a minor shift. Moving to a climax of intensity in delivery through a sequence of several items tells the audience that the elements are related and that they build upon each other with cumulative effect. Stepping forward while talking about a series of points shows that they are related, and a favorable relationship is further suggested by nodding one's head at the end of each point. Shaking the head and movement to the side contrast elements in the sequence and hint at their incompatibility.

Voice transitions are made by shifting to a different vocal pattern, which can involve definite changes in pitch, tempo, voice quality, volume, and manner of speaking. Quite often, when a division of the presentation has been delivered in a way that builds to a climax, vocal transition is indicated by a change to a less tense and more conversational manner of speaking. Voice transitions are often more effective when supported by facial expressions and other gestures. Because possibilities for nonverbal transitions are unlimited, we will leave the reader to begin where our list of examples stops. He can devise his own repertoire of other-than-words transitions, combining voice and bodily action in ways that help his audience read maximum appropriate meaning into his spoken messages.

Verbal connectives may consist of words, phrases, and sentences. The simplest verbal transition is a one-word indicator that the speaker is moving on to another idea. Perhaps the two most frequently used one-word transitions are "next" and "also." We do not recommend one-word transitions as a general rule. At the point where an inexperienced speaker might say "next" or "also" or even "another thing," the skillful presentational speaker will provide a phrase or sentence that relates one idea to another.

Transitions relate ideas by forecasting the next point, by summarizing the point that is being concluded, or by summarizing one point and forecasting the next. The simplest form of the transition to forecast is the use of enumerations such as "First, let us examine present market conditions. . . . Second, I would like to turn to future trends. . . . Third, what should our investment policy be?" Using enumerations to forecast the next division of a presentation provides efficient transitions, but we suggest that the reader *omit* the "ly" that is often added to each number to form "firstly," "secondly," and "thirdly."

Transitions that forecast the next point to be made often indicate typical parts of a presentation and in form they are rather well-standardized as, for example, "Let us look at the causes of our difficulty" and "We cannot ignore the need to win popular support."

Summaries serve to bring divisions of the presentation to a conclusion and indicate that a new point follows logically. Statements such as "Thus, we see that present market conditions are conducive to the introduction of the new product" serve as excellent transitions.

On occasion, when tying together major sections of a presentation, the speaker may wish to both summarize the previous point and forecast the next as, for example, "Clearly, present market conditions are conducive to the introduction of the new product. But what of future trends? Can we expect conditions to remain favorable five years from now?"

In addition to summarizing and forecasting, the transition material may aid in presenting the audience with the speaker's estimate of the relative importance of various ideas. For example, proportioning of material is facilitated by transitional comments like the following: "Third, and something we often forget . . ."; "Most important of all . . ."; and "Of less significance but nonetheless we must not overlook. . . ."

Transitions can also show contrast and dissonance and thus create interest and attention by pointing up paradoxes or contradictions like the following: "To look at the situation differently . . ."; "In sharp contrast, many people believe . . ."; and "We must recognize there is another side to the story. . . ."

Questions are among the most flexible and useful techniques to provide transitions. They stimulate the audience to provide an answer and thus add interest and lead the thought processes forward. Many excellent presentational speakers join nearly all parts of their messages with questions that lead their audience's thinking neatly into the next channel. To illustrate how transition questions can contribute to a sense of organization and progress in a presentation, we list below ten questions without the content of a message. The reader should have little difficulty building a well-organized oral report or presentation around this sequence of transition questions:

1. What is the problem?
2. Why should we be concerned?
3. What is the significance of all this?
4. What is the other side of the story?
5. What are the possibilities for us, here and now?
6. Which is the best possibility?
7. Does the proposal have any serious disadvantages?
8. How much will it cost?
9. How soon can it be implemented?
10. What can we anticipate by way of results?

PATTERNS OF ORGANIZATION FOR
PRESENTATIONAL SPEAKING

Every good presentation should have a beginning, a middle, and an end. Rhetoricians often refer to these parts of the speech as the introduction, body, and conclusions.

While it is a good idea to prepare your audience for your message, deliver it, and finally, make a statement or two to "wrap it up," the three-part pattern offers little help in selection and arrangement of the precise points, illustrations, sequences of items, and transitions in the part of the speech that carries the load, the body. Actually, the main benefit from remembering the three-part division is that it reminds us that a speech is not a written report, and that fact makes a difference in preparation. For example, when one delivers an extended message to an audience, he should catch the attention and arouse the interest of his listeners before he begins the body of his discourse. The writer of an essay on the same subject may well assume that the reader is attentive and take up his main theme more quickly. Listeners also demand a feeling of completeness at the conclusion of prepared remarks that differs from the demands made by a reader of a written report.

Patterns that provide a useful principle of organization serve as a guide to arranging items of content in a consistent manner, suited to topic, audience, and occasion. The range of possibilities is great, embracing logical and nonlogical rationales derived from our knowledge of the ways in which the mind of man functions. A representative listing of various time-honored patterns of organization drawn from popular texts in public speaking reveals the diversity of approaches and some of the minor variations that have proved popular over the years.

1. Time order (historical or, when giving directions, what is to be done first, what second, etc.)
2. Space order (geographical, left or right, upper or lower, etc.)
3. Classification (points fit into a classification scheme, such as engineering, machining, assembly, etc.)
4. Cause and effect (first outline causes, then discuss effects, useful in predicting future events)
5. Effect to cause (first discuss effects, then suggest possible causes, useful in analyzing present problem)
6. Comparison and contrast (begin with how several things are alike, then discuss their differences)

7. Method of residues (list representative solutions, then object to and eliminate all but the last)
8. Climax order (list points in order of increasing importance)
9. Anticlimax (list points in order of decreasing importance)
10. Simple to complex (begin with simpler elements that audience understands, introduce more complex points gradually)
11. Problem-solution (begin by analysis of problem, then suggest solution)
12. Proposition-support (state your case, then provide evidence)
13. Support-proposition (provide evidence, then draw the proposition as conclusion or allow audience to infer the proposition)

The reader will get the general idea of the above organizing strategies without a detailed elaboration of each. The point we would make is that the speaker can benefit from reflecting upon his speech content and purpose to see if any of the possible ways of arranging events would prove helpful on a particular occasion or in a particular environment. Any standard pattern can be used totally or partially. Any pattern can structure a total presentation or be used to develop one portion of it. Organization becomes challenging because dozens of combinations are possible in even a brief presentation.

Let's return again to John Jamison's presentation. What was his organizing principle? John used what he thought of as a five-part strategy. First, he described the new cereal he was proposing, giving the facts essential to understanding of his later points. Three sections followed. One dealt with costs of production aimed at Joe Perkins; another focused on the advertising potential of the new product, and was tailored to Homer Lydgate; and the third fitted the new cereal neatly into the company's product line for the particular benefit of Marshall Everding. The fifth and final phase consisted of making any summary statements that seemed to be absolutely necessary, and receiving questions from board members.

By this procedure Jamison developed an organization that was adjusted to the five elements of presentational speaking: the central tasks of presenting recommendation and self, and the situational adaptations to standard human obstacles, particular circumstances, and the motives of individuals. Whenever a speaker applies or designs a pattern of organization, his ever-present problem is to ascertain that full justice is done to all five elements.

Why follow an arbitrarily selected pattern in presentational speaking? To achieve certain objectives that are difficult to accomplish without a pattern. The speaker who chooses an appropriate pattern and follows it wisely reaps these benefits.

1. Speech materials that will have maximum impact upon this particular audience will be more readily selected.
2. The pattern helps him arrange the content of his speech for greater possible clarity.
3. A properly applied pattern produces a speech that *moves,* one with a sense of steady, almost inevitable progress from point to point.
4. Unproductive repetition is prevented.
5. The optimum utilization of time is insured.
6. Unity, coherence, and proper emphasis in audience perception of the speech is increased.
7. The speaker will be able to conclude on time, in a manner that sounds finished and complete.

We now turn to our recommended patterns, the three designs for speeches that help to answer the question, "How can I arrange my materials to best achieve their potential effectiveness?"

THREE BASIC PATTERNS FOR PRESENTATIONS

The scientific problem-solving pattern. The scientific problem-solving pattern is particularly useful in two situations: (1) when the problem is complicated and hostility is anticipated, and (2) when the problem is complicated and the audience is relatively unfamiliar with the facts involved. The great strength of the inductive scientific approach is that it provides an easy-to-follow order in a topic which might well be baffling and chaotic. The bases for the inductive pattern are the sequential steps in problem-solving, introduced by the philosopher-educator John Dewey at the beginning of the twentieth century.[1] Dewey observed how the trained mind attacked a problem in the scientific laboratory. He noted the way an individual begins reflective thinking with a felt difficulty—an irritation or disturbance that sets the person to puzzling or acting to relieve the tension. He discussed the way a person casts about and tries to discover the reason for the felt difficulty. As the vague feeling of perplexity comes under rational analysis, the causes of the problem become clearer and the mind leaps forward to suggest possible solutions. Trial-and-error problem-solving is characterized by trying each solution as it pops into the mind. Reflective thinking, on the other hand, postpones the implementation of a solution until the representative answers have been weighed pro

[1] John Dewey, *How We Think* (Boston, 1910).

and con. Only after methodical reflection does the person select the best of the solutions to try.

Dewey's analysis provides the basis for a step-by-step consideration of a problem beginning with an introduction, definition of the problem, exploration of the problem, listing and examinations of representative solutions, and the selection of the best solution.

A presentation structured in the way Dewey found that a critical thinker solves a problem is an effective way to communicate. The person making a presentation can use the scientific inductive pattern to exploit another tendency of human decision-making processes. People tend to eliminate undesirable solutions first and allow the best answer to emerge as the only remaining option. If the speaker prepares his list of representative solutions with his recommendation last, he can then systematically consider and reject all the other courses of action, allowing his proposal to emerge as obviously the most desirable. This latter version of the scientific pattern is called the "method of residues." It is a very powerful way to persuade, since it follows natural tendencies of decision-making psychology.[2]

The pattern established by Dewey's analysis of reflective thinking leads listeners to be objective and thoughtful and disarms them of some of their prejudices as they are led along what appears to be a completely reasonable sequence. Hostility is difficult to maintain in the face of a completely open investigation of a problem, through the inductive procedure. The speaker says, now let us define the problem so we all agree on just what it is and what it is not. Then he says, let us explore the problem we have defined to discover what caused it, what its effects are, and what criteria must be met by any satisfactory solution. After exploration, he says, let us list all the possible solutions we can think of and compare them. The openness of the pattern leads even persons with prejudice to follow along thoughtfully, examining facts and interpreting them in each step. If the speaker is comprehensive and thorough, and if he reasons soundly, it will be difficult for competent thinkers in his audience to avoid joining him in the final selection of a "best" solution.

In the second circumstance, when the audience is less than informed on facts of the case, the inductive development of the topic furnishes a natural framework to convey essential information. In short, the inductive approach is an excellent teaching device as well as

[2] Recent work in the small-group-communication seminar at the University of Minnesota indicates that group problem-solving proceeds by the method of residues. See particularly, B. Aubrey Fisher, "Decision Emergence: Phases in Decision Making," *Speech Monographs*, 37 (1970), 53–66.

an effective means of persuasion. In defining and exploring the problem elementary facts can be tactfully mentioned by prefacing them with "As you know . . ." or "You will recall . . ." and so on. And when he comes to listing solutions, the speaker can say, "Although many of these solutions are familiar to you, we will include them, because we must be able to compare all reasonable possibilities."

One caution to speakers using the inductive pattern: because its posture is one of objective problem-solving, that is, applying the scientific method to human affairs, any emotive or "loaded" language is out of place. The ideal manner of speaking to implement the inductive approach is "report language," the matter-of-fact, direct, and "unloaded" use of words that minimizes emotional response. Even a single prejudicial term may seem so out-of-place and improper that it could imperil the outcome of the presentation.

Here is an example of a speech plan using the scientific problem-solving pattern of organization. The outline is a hypothetical one developed by Eric Bolton, son of the founder of Ira S. Bolton Publishing Company, for a presentation to top management recommending that Bolton Publishers expand in the direction of a nationwide service of custom-printed texts (texts for large beginning courses written by the local professors who teach the courses). Since Eric Bolton anticipated considerable resistance among top management for his proposal, he developed it along the lines indicated in the following outline, here in the form of his speaking notes.

CUSTOM-PRINTED TEXTS AT BOLTON HOUSE

1.0 New Directions for Expansion. Impartial examination of custom-printing. All facts, pros & cons. Wisest decision vital

2.0 Our problem "What shall we do about custom-printing textbooks?"
    2.1. How fit expans. plans?
    2.2. Relate to profits

3.0 Status quo—custom-printing texts for professors
    3.1. The record (5 o'head charts & graphs)
    3.2. Present projects (chart on easel)
    3.3. New business (blackboard)

4.0 Solutions
    4.1. Drop custom-printing
    4.2. Phase out custom-printing
    4.3. Push in Midwest
    4.4. Go national

5.0 Past record, present profits, future prospects justify national promotion of custom-printing.

State the case and prove it.   One of the earliest and most famous books on preparing material for oral presentation that has survived from antiquity is attributed to the famous Greek philosopher Aristotle. In that work, the *Rhetoric,* Aristotle suggested that the speaker met the minimal organization requirement when he stated his case and proved it. The pattern is a straightforward development of a central thesis by supporting elements each of which begins with a topic sentence (a contention) followed by supporting material. Typically, the pattern would consist of

1. Introduction
2. Proposition (thesis)
3. Contention 1, plus support
4. Contention 2, plus support (etc.)
5. Summary and reiteration of the proposition

An oversimplified version of the state-your-case-and-prove-it pattern is "Tell them what you're going to tell them, tell them, and then tell them what you told them."

In a sense, stating your case and then proving it reverses the scientific problem-solving pattern. Where the latter looks at the facts of the case and draws a general conclusion, the former starts with the general conclusion and attempts to prove that it is justified. Eric Bolton using the inductive method led up to his conclusion, which was not revealed until almost the end of his speech. The speaker using the pattern that moves from the general to the specific begins with his recommendation and devotes his speech to proving and reinforcing it.

The particular utility of the second pattern is found in handling familiar, much argued topics of controversy. When a person addresses himself to a well-worn issue that his audience has heard discussed many times, there is little reason for him to explore it comprehensively and gradually develop it. Usually, he is well advised to state his position, and support it as clearly and systematically as possible. This the second pattern is designed to accomplish.

The introduction of a presentation based upon the state-your-case-and-prove-it pattern is nearly always an explanation of why it is necessary and appropriate to reopen discussion of an unresolved problem on this occasion. Probably recent events, or new knowledge, have modified a previously stable situation, and the old controversy needs to be reexamined in a new light. If successful, the introduction will leave the audience eager to learn the effects of the new situation on the old problem.

The central thesis is usually stated immediately after the brief introduction. If the central thesis is stated clearly and highlighted by the speaker's manner of delivery, the audience will remember it as the main idea of the speech and test every argument and bit of evidence to see if these do, indeed, support the proposition.

Contentions with proof for each follow the proposition. The speaker indicates that the contentions logically support the proposition by means of clear "big-picture" comments and transitions. The speech ends with a summary that is not simply a mechanical repetition of the contentions but which is an effective reminder of the highlights of the evidence and reasoning taken from the several contentions. Reiteration of the proposition terminates the speech, encouraging the audience to reflect once more on the adequacy of the proof that was presented. If the proof is conclusive, the reasonable auditor finds it difficult to resist the recommendation.

A variation of state-your-case-and-prove-it has developed from the experiences of many speakers who were forced to make a presentation when preparation time was minimal. It can be used even on those occasions when, without warning, someone tells you he is expecting you to "say a few words" within the next ten or twenty minutes! We call this variation of stating your case and proving it the "Impromptu 1" pattern, because it serves the cause of impromptu speaking—speaking with little specific preparation—so well.

IMPROMPTU 1
1. *Begin* with an illustration.
2. Overview (number points).
3. Follow through (cover each point in turn).
4. Recap, with a *twist*.

The impromptu variation begins, *without explanation*, with an example. The speaker simply supplies an illustration, preferably one with human interest and visual imagery, that is intimately involved with the topic and the audience. He does not say, "I am going to talk about . . ." or set the stage for his example in any way. He just begins and tells it, and the resulting response is twofold: high interest, and curiosity as to what the purpose of the illustration may be.

The second step is the overview (state what you will talk about), consisting of listing and numbering the points to be covered by the presentation. For example, the speaker says, "Today I'm going to make three points, first . . . second . . . and third . . ." The points should be crisp and concise in their wording. The third step is to carry out the speaker's commitment to develop the points in the order he promised.

When the numbered points have been covered, the speaker rounds out and ends his speech with the fourth part of the pattern, which is a recap, with a "twist." A recap is an extremely short reminder of each point talked about, in different language. The "twist" is a surprise ending that makes the speech sound finished by referring back to the opening example with a tie-in that shows the relevance of the introduction and unifies the speech.

The impression produced by (1) an opening example that is central to the presentation, (2) a crisp, numbered overview that is meticulously carried out, and (3) a "twist" ending that sensibly relates the conclusion to the beginning is that the speech is thoughtfully planned and well organized. Audiences tend to believe that if a speaker can remember how he began at the end of the speech, he must have prepared it very carefully indeed!

In actuality, Impromptu 1 turned out to be useful in other than impromptu situations, and it met the needs of varied presentations so well that the anticipated modifications of the pattern, 2, 3, and so on, were not developed. The authors are somewhat concerned because this pattern is so easy to learn and use, and it produces a speech that is so obviously well organized, that many neophyte speakers are inclined to use no other arrangement. Hence, we caution the reader to avoid relying totally on Impromptu 1. You will find it useful but no universal panacea. On many occasions another pattern would be more successful.

However, since the "impromptu" variation of the state-the-case-and-prove-it pattern can be utilized not only in thoroughly prepared presentations but in off-the-cuff comments, oral reports, and other occasions when people in business and the professions must speak with limited preparation, we will examine its application by means of a case study.

The case of Bob Gibson and employee participation.   Bob Gibson is one of a dozen members of an "idea group" in his plant, Basic Electronics Parts, Inc. Each Friday they meet in a private room at Coco's, a pleasant restaurant nearby, for lunch and a talk by one of the members, who contributes an idea for the group's consideration. Bob is taking his turn at "utilitarian creativity" next Friday. He begins his planning on Sunday afternoon.

Bob's idea is nontechnical, a proposal to improve morale and increase productivity in the plant through involving all the workers in decision-making. He intends to recommend a program in which production and other employees will elect representatives who will meet with all regularly constituted management and engineering committees and have a voice in their deliberations. The labor union to which all the workers belong will be asked to handle details of participation, getting representatives elected and instructed, reporting back to their membership, and so on. The major obstacle to overcome in selling his recommendation to the "idea group" are (1) nothing like it has been tried in Basic Electronics Parts, Inc., and (2) a majority of the group is anti-union and unethusiastic about participative management.

Without worrying about how to begin or end his speech, Bob concentrates upon his audience and searches for ideas that would gently persuade them to react favorably to his proposal. The first point should be practical, noncontroversial and clear, moving them in the desired direction. He words it tentatively, "We'll get some good ideas we otherwise would not know about." Because there has been great dissatisfaction in recent months over poor inplant communication, he decides to make that the second point: "Communication, upward and downward, will be improved." Because he must be explicit about participative management, the controversial area of his topic, he decides to place that in third position and word it so that the present audience is involved: "Teamwork will become more important throughout the plant, and to all of us."

With themes of his talk in order, Bob now needs an *opener*, the illustration central to his proposal, which will catch interest without revealing too much. Ideally, he wants a familiar and critical happening important to the audience, something that makes a difference *to them*. He decides to relate an incident that involved three of the twelve, and which several of the others have heard about, incompletely and probably inaccurately. The incident concerned a production bottleneck in manufacturing electrolytic condensers. The best engineering brains in the company had tried to cure the foil-winding machine of persistent malfunction, to no avail. After several weeks of costly breakdowns, a production worker approached the engineer who was at the moment contemplating the stubborn machine and said timidly, "Sir, may I make a suggestion? Why don't you try nickel-plating that little roller?" Perhaps because all other ideas had given out, the roller was plated, and the malfunctions ceased. Bob visualizes how he can tell the story with drama and touches of humor.

With a transition to his already selected three points, he will have the major structure of his talk outlined. As we noted earlier, questions make good transitions. Bob decides that, after narrating the example, he will ask rhetorically, "How can we get these simple ingenious suggestions earlier?" and answer it, "By adopting a program of active employee participation." Then another question, "What could we expect to accomplish by such a program?" would lead to the *overview*, the listing of his three points, with the development of each, in turn, to follow.

Before devising his ending, the "recap with a twist," Bob decides to arrange supporting materials for the three main points. With a rough time allotment as a guide, he decides to treat the first point of "getting good ideas" briefly, since his "opener," the engineering example, supports it indirectly. The second point on improved communication he plans to build around two visual aids, one chart representing present inplant channels of communication and the other, channels under the proposed system. He selects two successful employee-participation systems for reference as he talks about applying his recommended system at Basic Electronics Parts. The final point, improved teamwork, he decides to develop hypothetically, sketching in three possible situations where the new arrangement would simplify needed cooperation among employees and units of management that find it difficult to coordinate their efforts under the present system. Although the cases are imaginary, he plans to develop them in realistic detail, with a judicious amount of dramatic color.

With his support sketched in, Bob sees a natural "recap with a twist" to make his presentation sound finished. After reminding his listeners of the three benefits he has been talking about, he can say, "What would have happened under the proposed system when that foil-winding machine acted up?" Then he can show precisely how the employee with an idea would have been encouraged to communicate it immediately, through his representative. In all probability, the difficult period of several weeks would have been reduced to two or three days.

From Monday through Thursday Bob uses his available time for mulling over the details and "fleshing out" his talk. He prepares his visuals and rehearses the delivery. Rehearsal is kept extemporaneous, with no memorizing but plenty of practice, saying things until they are comfortable and efficient. He keeps in mind the sequence of ideas, not words, and discovers that with each rehearsal his fluency increases and the apt description or the added touch of humor appears again and again while the less useful phrase is forgotten. By Friday, Bob's notes are ready. They are properly brief and neatly typed on 4 × 6 cards as follows:

EMPLOYEE PARTICIPATION FOR BASIC ELECTRONIC PARTS, INC.
1.0   Foil-winding malfunction incident
       How get questions earlier? Program-emp. partic.
       What accomplish? Overview 2.1, 2.2, 2.3
2.0   Advantages
       2.1. Get good ideas
             Jones and Smiley examples
       2.2. Up and down communication
             Charts 1 & 2
       2.3. Better teamwork. Hypothetical:
             2.31 New transistor changing existing circuits
             2.32 Closing out a production line
             2.33 Doubling capacity to produce high pass filters
3.0   Recap 2.1, 2.2, 2.3. Suppose new system in foil-winding malfunction. Show steps.

Psychological-progression pattern.   One of the most used and useful patterns of speech organization is the psychological-progression pattern, the third and final basic arrangement for presentation. It brings together logical and nonlogical modes of thinking and feeling to evolve a solid persuasive presentation. The psychological-progression pattern was first discovered by evangelical preachers in the early part of the nineteenth century. In more recent times Woolbert and Weaver applied the findings of contemporary psychology to the problems of public speaking and grouped all purposes of speaking into five categories: (1) attentiveness, (2) understanding, (3) deciding, (4) acting publicly, and (5) yielding fully.[3] Monroe adapted these ideas to public speaking in an attractive pattern that he called a "motivated sequence" and his arrangement has served as a basic plan for a public speaker in a series of popular textbooks.[4]

The psychological-progression pattern is an adaptation of the historically effective structure to the particular needs of the presentational speaker. It consists of five steps: (1) arouse, (2) dissatisfy, (3) gratify, (4) picture, and (5) move.

An attractive feature of the psychological-progression pattern is the ease with which it can be remembered. Five key words, each indicating clearly the purpose of that part of the speech, arranged in an order that follows so naturally that the steps are not ordinarily interchanged, result in the person, having once become acquainted with the sequence, finding it difficult to forget. Many people who give frequent speeches use the five divisions as a means to adapt to different audiences. In an automobile or on a plane they can rearrange familiar speech materials by asking themselves questions about the specific audience they will next confront. How will I *arouse* the audience's interest? How can I *dissatisfy* them by showing them the mess we are in? How can I show them that my recommendation will *gratify* the need? How can I get these people to *picture* the concrete results when my recommendation is implemented? How can I *move* them to act appropriately and expeditiously on my proposal?

Another virtue of the psychological-progression pattern is that a person can eliminate some of the early steps to fit the needs of an audience that is already interested in the topic or that is already aware of the mess that it is facing. Such an audience will be ready and waiting to hear the speaker's gratifying proposal. When planning a presentation using the psychological-progression pattern, a person should estimate the audience's willingness to bypass the first couple of

[3] Charles H. Woolbert and Andrew T. Weaver, *Better Speech* (New York, 1922), p. 252.

[4] Alan H. Monroe, *Principles and Types of Speech*, 6th ed. (Chicago, Ill., 1964).

steps, for it may become impatient if he insists upon discussing them when the audience is already in agreement.

By now the reader has probably noted that the pattern is nicely adapted to the central task of most presentations, to innovate and bring about change. The psychological progression is basically a problem-solution format most useful for persuasive purposes and less widely used by people seeking to inform or to entertain.

THE USE OF NOTES

In the case studies that illustrate the patterns of organization we have included notes used by the speakers during the presentations. This may have given the reader the impression that notes are a necessity and that all speakers should use them. Of course, this is not the case. We can generalize that all speakers tend to use more notes than they need, and to stare at their notes instead of maintaining contact with their audience. People who are completely familiar with their subject need no notes. To some degree, notes break the contact a speaker has with his listeners. To use them when they are not needed is to place oneself under an unnecessary handicap.

On some occasions notes may be necessary. When the speaker wishes to be absolutely accurate about statistical information, direct quotations from authorities, or about factual detail, he may need to have the information before him. Some individuals feel much more confident and thus improve their delivery when they can have a brief outline of their presentation available should they need it.

The speaker who is using notes should not try to hide that fact from the audience. The listener who discovers that a speaker is trying to hide his notes often becomes diverted from the ideas in the presentation in his eagerness to catch the speaker's furtive references to his cards. The best procedure is to use notes openly and only when absolutely necessary. A speaker ought to guard against the tendency to glance at his notes whenever he loses his poise. Looking down to keep from looking at the audience can become a bad habit.

A speaker should also be careful not to twist, bend, or rumple his notes in a random aimless way, for audiences are often distracted by such movements.

The person who wishes to speak without notes does not memorize the details of the presentation but concentrates on getting the major points of the outline in mind. If the speaker remembers the three main points, he can then turn to the first point and memorize the two sub-points under it, and so on. By getting the organizational pattern firmly in mind, the person making a presentation can largely do away with manuscript or detailed notes and free himself for speaking directly to the listeners.

We should mention something about notes that many of our readers have figured out for themselves. Properly prepared visual aids may make notes unnecessary. Also, when an overhead projector is used, notes can be written on the cardboard mounting of a transparency.

SUMMARY

A well-organized presentation is unified, coherent, relevant, concise, and comprehensive. Clear organization results from a two-stage process of preparation, beginning with an analysis of the topic and concluding with a careful adaptation to the specific audience.

The process of organizing a presentation consists of selecting, arranging, and proportioning materials. The understanding of the audience and a clear proposition aid in the selection of material. To arrange selected content to maximize its impact certain basic and time-tested patterns of organization are available to help in structuring presentational speaking. Proportioning of material requires judgments about the important points relating to the topic as well as an understanding of the background, information, interests, and motivations of the auditors.

The three basic patterns recommended particularly for presentational speaking are the state-your-case-and-prove-it pattern, the scientific problem-solving pattern, and the pattern of psychological progression. A substantial majority of presentations, perhaps 90 percent, will benefit from being fitted into one of these three arrangements.

QUESTIONS FOR DISCUSSION AND REVIEW

1. What are the major characteristics of a well-organized presentation?
2. What is the relationship between creativity and topic analysis?
3. What is the importance of the audience-adaptation stage of message preparation?
4. What are the characteristics of a good central *proposition* for a presentation?
5. What is meant by the concept of *selection?* Of *arrangement?* Of *proportioning?*
6. What are some things to keep in mind when developing transitional material for a presentation?

7. What are some of the benefits of a carefully patterned presentation?
8. What are some of the representative time-honored patterns of organization used in public speaking?
9. Under what circumstances is the scientific problem-solving pattern of organization most useful? The state-the-case-and-prove-it pattern? The psychological-progression pattern?
10. What are the main things to keep in mind about the use of notes during the presentation?

REFERENCES AND SUGGESTED READINGS

HOLM, JAMES N. *Productive Speaking for Business and the Professions.* Boston: Allyn and Bacon, 1967.

MONROE, ALAN H. *Principles and Types of Speech,* 6th ed. Chicago: Scott, Foresman, 1964.

SARETT, ALMA JOHNSON, LEW SARETT, and WILLIAM TRUFANT FOSTER. *Basic Principles of Speech,* 4th ed. Boston: Houghton Mifflin, 1966.

WALTER, OTIS M., and ROBERT L. SCOTT. *Thinking and Speaking,* 2nd ed. New York: Macmillan, 1962.

ZELKO, HAROLD P., and FRANK E. X. DANCE. *Business and Professional Speech Communication.* New York: Holt, Rinehart and Winston, 1965.

CHAPTER SEVEN

STATISTICAL
FORMS OF SUPPORT

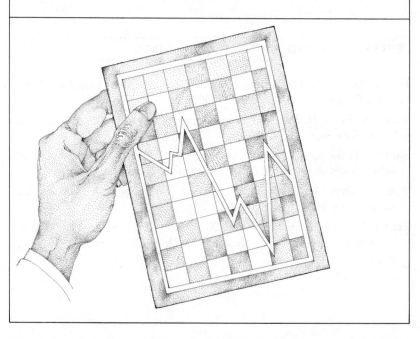

The style that is today the most acceptable for presentational speaking is concise and laconic. "Don't say it; display it" has become the slogan of many who prepare information for presentations. The heavy emphasis upon visual representations stems from the strong need to digest and prepare proposals for brief presentations. Busy, high-level decision makers do not wish to be entertained nor do they demand elegance in the way information is presented to them. They do require that sufficient information is presented for the decision they must make and that the presentation be concise.

One misguided response to the pressure for brevity has been to cut almost all material from the presentation (or the written report) that serves to amplify and prove the assertions. The end result is sometimes a series of laconic statements resembling a telegram more than a speech or essay. While such quick elliptical performances studded with visuals may seem efficient and time-conserving, they often fail because the listeners are confused by them. When the committee that hears a brief and underdeveloped presentation spends several hours in discussion only to discover that it has been confused by the tour de force in brevity, the total time wasted in repairing the damage is much greater than any that was originally saved by cutting the presentation to the bare form of an outline.

"When in doubt cut the material" is beguiling as a general principle of presentational speaking, but it is seldom helpful. The problem of preparing a presentation is much too complicated to be solved by any such simple slogan. One ought to take the slogan "Don't say it; display it" with similar caution. The point is that while presentational speaking must put a premium upon conciseness, the messages must always be clear and contain sufficient information so the listeners can make the necessary decision.

How to support and develop the ideas within the presentation t' becomes one of the most important problems for the person prep a message. Interestingly enough, the beginning writer or speaker ᴜ. reveals his amateur standing by his inability to clarify an idea. (Perhaps one reason why so many presentations delivered by a business leader or professional person are lacking in adequate development of the basic ideas is that so many of the people working up presentations today are untrained in the principles of communication. When one is inept at doing something, he finds it easy to make a virtue out of not doing it.)

The ideas within the presentation must be supported with material that clarifies, proves, and reiterates the basic ideas until the audience can fully understand the message.

AMPLIFICATION

The main use of supporting material in a presentation is for the amplification of the ideas. Often, a single idea needs to be dwelt on for a time for clarity, for conviction, and for interest. Brevity can be tedious. If the presentation consists of abstract topic sentences, each of which could serve as the basis for a paragraph, the audience may lose the thread of the discourse and find the message so abstract as to be incomprehensible. If the speaker succeeds in arousing contemplation in the listener, some time is needed to think about the idea. Presenting the idea from a different angle or using a different form of supporting material can give the auditor that time. The inexperienced student of presentations may overlook the necessity for amplification because he is accustomed to tell things to those who know them better than he does. When presenting new ideas to an audience, a person often assumes without thinking that the listeners know the subject. The danger of overestimating the audience's understanding is greatest when the presentation is made to a group of people whose positions in the organization are equal to or greater than the speaker's. Also, high status makes it difficult for the listeners to ask questions that reveal they are less knowledgeable than the speaker.

THE ROLE OF SUPPORTING MATERIAL

When we discuss the concept of *supporting material,* we must remember that one cannot tell whether a given bit of speech material is supportive or not until it is examined in its relation to the statement to be supported. Just as an architect must examine a column for a building in terms of the beam or rafter that is to be supported, considering weight, aesthetic relationship, and proportioning, so must a speaker evaluate supporting material for a presentation in terms of the point that it is to enhance.

The best way to view the development of ideas, therefore, is in terms of message units. Each unit, to be complete, must contain the point or proposition and the material that amplifies the proposition. Although our discussion of various kinds of supporting material does not always fit the devices into context, the student should remember that material which would be excellent support for one idea might not be logically related to another.

THE CASE OF THE DETERIORATING CAKE MIXES

To illustrate the importance and use of statistical information in presentational speaking we submit the hypothetical case of the deteriorating cake mixes and the sagging sales of Minnesota Mills. Herbert Appleton is a troubleshooter in the marketing research division of Minnesota Mills. He has a relatively unstructured job in a project-oriented division of the company. When a substantial marketing problem arises, Herb and his unit are assigned the task of discovering the causes of the difficulty and suggesting solutions.

On Monday William Archer, vice-president for marketing, called Herb and his boss, Gerald Weaver, manager of marketing research, into an all-day conference. Archer and his assistant laid out the basic problem. Minnesota Mills was receiving a heavy load of complaints about the quality of their cake mixes. Their share of the market was dwindling under the pressure of competition. Herb's job was to draw on the resources of the marketing research division for any men or information required and investigate and solve the problem.

As Herb and his men looked for clues and sifted the evidence, he had to compile and evaluate more and more statistical information. Herb took nothing for granted as he started the case. He did not assume that the only factor in the poor sales record was the quality of the product. He searched for evidence relating to the effectiveness of the advertising and to the impact of the sales force. He checked the quality of the product as developed by the research division and the quality control in the production division. He had to analyze data in light of the fads and fashions of the cake mix world, where new and exotic cakes underwent cycles of popularity and decline. He finally came to the conclusion that the main difficulty was not in the quality of the mixes at the time of packaging but in the deterioration of quality in the interval from packaging to use.

Herb was ready to call together the upper-management group directly involved with the cake mix operation and make a presentation of his findings. Our concern here will be with the problem of statistical analysis and interpretation that Herb faced and the uses that he might make of statistical information in his presentation.

Herb wants to support his argument that the main problem with the cake mixes is the deteriorating quality stemming primarily from an unsatisfactory package. He wants, therefore, the best evidence and reasoning he can develop for his case. An empirically minded research specialist, Herb has a tendency to examine his evidence and reasoning on absolute standards of truth and validity. If the cake mixes are indeed leaving the factory comparable in quality to those of the leading competitor but ending up in the housewife's oven with less quality, that fact weighs heavily with Herb. If his analysis of causes has been exhaustive and if he has pinpointed the factor that is primarily responsible, Herb feels that his responsibility in making the presentation has been fulfilled.

In short, Herb evaluated evidence and reasoning on absolute tests of truth and falsity. If Herb were more knowledgeable about communication principles, he would realize that there is a conflict between absolute tests of truth and validity and those which depend upon relevance and acceptability for a particular audience. On occasion, true and valid supporting material will be ineffective with a given audience, and on other occasions, effective evidence and reasoning will not meet absolute standards of truth or falsity. A person using absolute tests of supporting material will evaluate it on the basis of observations and on the basis of valid deductive forms. The other standard for evaluating material can be called the "response criterion."

Before one accepts or rejects the "response criterion," the mechanism through which reasoned discourse facilitates belief should be examined. Herb will advance the proposition that "The new packaging system should be adopted immediately to preserve quality and increase sales." Several members of the meeting will hear the presentation with considerable skepticism. They have wrestled with the problem of cake mix sales before and it has always defied solution. On the other hand, they want very much to solve the problem and they have no vested interest in how the blame for past failures is assigned. The skeptical but receptive members of Herb's audience suspend judgment while they examine the facts he presents and try to make sense of his reasoning. They respond to Herb's message as reasoned discourse.

In Herb's audience is the sales manager and a representative from the advertising agency. These men embrace Herb's argument immediately because it gets them off the hook. They have been defending their efforts from heavy attack because of the loss of market. Now they can attribute their lack of success to the poor quality of the product. For the advertising and sales personnel the presentation functions partially as reasoned discourse but has powerful overtones of suggestion, and much of their response is unthinking signal reaction to a pleasing conclusion. They are already persuaded and inspect the statistics and other evidence and the reasoning in Herb's presentation to some degree but not with much care or rigor.

In Herb's audience are also two men who were instrumental in adopting the present packaging system. The minute Herb reveals his central proposition they tune him out. They respond negatively to every bit of evidence and reasoning and seek for alternative explanations and other arguments. Although they may believe they are reacting critically, they are responding in signal all-or-nothing fashion without reflection, much as they would respond to a red traffic light.

We can analyze Herb's audience in terms of its tendency to respond to his presentation if he applies only the absolute criteria to his evidence and reasoning along a continuum as in Figure 7.1.

Many difficulties in evaluating reasoned discourse in presentational speaking stem from the failure to understand that a well-constructed argument may function primarily as suggestion. Application of an absolute standard of good evidence and reasoning ignores the nonrational impact of an argument. Herb should concern himself with the validity and truth of his argument but he ought also evalute his

Figure 7.1   Continuum of Response to Message Stimulus

Skeptical Members	Sales and Ad Representatives	Production Management
0		100
Fully reasoned discourse producing symbol response	Partially reasoned discourse producing mixed symbol and signal response	Pseudoreasoned discourse producing signal response

material in terms of its likely effect on his audience. He should restructure his presentation so his argument supports his proposition through signal as well as symbol response.

Certain audience variables determine the blend of signal and symbol response with which they will react when presented with an argument that is impeccable as to truth and validity on absolute standards but which is not adapted to the specific occasion and to the individual listeners. Those who will respond primarily in symbolic terms will be detached, well informed, and have considerable critical-thinking ability. Involvement in the form of vested interests predisposes the listener to signal response as does lack of relevant information. When an audience has little information and is strongly biased, the message unit, although reasonable and true, will often result in a signal response. Suggestion and associated signal response are so important to the outcome of presentations that Chapter 10 is devoted to their consideration.

Once Herb understands the tension that sometimes arises between absolute standards of supporting material and the response criterion, he will be in a better position to develop a presentation that will achieve his goal and solve Minnesota Mills' cake mix problem. Herb is well advised to use absolute truth in factual descriptions such as those supplied by statistical surveys as a starting place. For the good of the organization the management decisions that emerge from Herb's study and his presentations ought to be based upon undistorted representative facts. However, no matter how true the statements of fact and the statistical descriptions nor how sound Herb's reasoning, if the signal response of the powerful representatives from production stop his plan to change their operating procedures, he will have failed.

Herb must remember that everybody has the potential to be thoughtful although everyone may not be in the habit of thinking critically. When he analyzes his audience and decides that there is a danger of signal response to his argument, he should structure his presentation so even those most biased and hostile and least likely to be in the habit of thinking critically will be led to do so.

In selecting his supporting material, therefore, Herb must not only test it in absolute terms, but when he begins to develop his presentation he must test it against likely audience response. His statistical information should meet both absolute and response criteria.

USING STATISTICS AS SUPPORT

Statistics are numerical descriptions of facts. When statistics are appropriate and the numerical descriptions actually represent quantitative and qualitative differences, they provide the most precise information about factual matters that is available to the presentational speaker. Because of the precision of statistical data, they are the single most important type of supporting material used in presentational speaking for business and the professions.

For today's business and professional person the range of events and facts that must be considered is often large, and much information must be compressed into brief form. Statistical descriptions of complicated factual matters provide the precision and brevity required. Take, for example, a statistical sentence that asserts, "Minnesota Mills' earnings from cake mix sales are down 10 percent for the first quarter of the current year when compared with the first quarter of last year." The number of facts covered by the statistic relating to cake mix sales from year to year is very large. The sentence describes one important relational feature abstracted from thousands of boxes of cake mix, their research, development, production, distribution, marketing, advertising, and so forth. The sentence is of great scope. The statistic covers not only many boxes of cake mixes but three months' experience with their manufacture and sale. If the statistic is accurate, it provides a great amount of important information for the management of Minnesota Mills.

Because of the selective nature of statistical statements of fact, they leave out a good deal of information about the events under discussion. For example, the statistic about cake mix sales does not contain information about the geographical distribution of the sales, the changes in container, the delivery record of the distribution division, the time from the point when the mixes were placed on the shelf until they were sold, the distribution of sales according to socioeconomic categories or according to the age of the buyers. The statistic does not contain information about the competition and its activities during the year in question. To be sure, some of the missing information could be supplied by further statistical descriptions. Eventually, however, the question of the quality of the cake mixes would come up. Statistical descriptions yield no information as to the taste of the chocolate or the texture of the angel food of thousands of cakes. The person who relies upon statistical descriptions of facts pays a price for the power and precision of such statements in the loss of qualitative information provided by concrete experience.

Since statistical statements often concentrate upon presenting selected relational information, they are open to distortions and may prove more misleading than helpful. The use of statistical support in persuasive messages to mislead or hoodwink the general public by pleaders for special interests has often been documented. All of us understand and are justifiably suspicious of statistical assertions in such obviously self-serving situations as the television commercial or the paid political advertisement.

Our discussion of statistics will examine both the usefulness of and dangers in supporting ideas with numerical descriptions of the facts.

Statistical indexes of typicality. One of the most important uses of statistical statements is to give an indication of the typical instance in a large population of events or of the general drift of affairs. Thus, when the managers of Minnesota Mills want a quick over-all survey of the entire marketing situation with regard to the firm's cake mixes, they find statistical indexes of the central tendency of marketing habits useful for their purposes. Statisticians can compute one number that reveals a central tendency in a large distribution of numbers describing individual events. Such a number indicates what is most often encountered, most common, usual, normal, or ordinary in the situation under study. For example, if a marketing survey counts the number of days the cake mix boxes are on the grocery shelves, a statistician could add all the times computed in days, divide by the total number of cake mix boxes, and get an average. The arithmetic average, probably the most common indicator of typicality, is the *mean.*

The mean may provide a misleading indication of the typical time a cake mix stays on the shelf. If the observations include a few discount supermarkets that move merchandise within a period of hours, a few such extreme cases would cause the average to be less than the central tendency of most stores. In instances where a distribution of the statistical information reveals a few extremely large numbers at one end or a few extremely small ones at the other, another index of central tendency such as the *median* may be more accurate.

To determine the median the scores must be ordered as to size. The median is discovered by finding the score that is in the middle of the range. The number with half of the scores above and half below is the median. Conceivably, the median time for cake mixes on the store shelf might be twenty-two when the average is seventeen if several rapid-turnover discount stores were included in the distribution. For Herb, discussing the possibility that deteriorating quality results from slow delivery from plant to customer, the median statistic would give a more accurate basis for decision than the mean.

On occasion, neither average nor median is an appropriate indicator of the typical or important central tendency in the information.

The third index of central position is the *mode.* The mode is the value that occurs most often in a distribution. For example, the dress length that occurs most often in a given season is called the "modish" length. The mode does not necessarily have to fall in the middle of the distribution and is not always a single number. On occasion, a distribution may have two or more modes.

Sometimes data fall into categories that cannot easily be arranged in some order. For example, the marketing research division may conduct a survey using four different packages for a chocolate cake mix and discover that the housewives who used the cake mix preferred the packages as indicated as follows:

Package	A	B	C	D
Preferences	15%	10%	7%	68%

The mode in the above instance would be the preference for package D and would be the most useful statistic of typicality. We cannot compute averages because the categories are not arranged in order of magnitude as, indeed, they cannot be.

By careful use of the measures of central tendency such as the mean, the mode, and the median a person making a presentation can convey a great amount of accurate information in a few words.

Statistical indexes of variability.   When Herb tries to give a complete statistical picture of a large number of events that differ as to amount along some important dimension, his audience may need not only to know what is the average, usual, or midpoint event, but they may also need to know how much the events differ from one another and the practical limits of differences. To provide such information Herb's presentation should contain a measure of variability.

The less variability in the scores, the more similar the events under study. If decision makers in an organizational setting wish to deal with a problem such as the staleness of a cake mix, they will find it easier if the events causing the trouble are homogeneous. For example, if the variations about the average time from production to use of a cake mix are small, changes such as cutting the distribution time or improving the packaging to preserve quality for a longer period of time will provide a comprehensive solution. If statistics indicate the average length of time from production to use is 90 days and the bulk of all mixes are used in a period from 75 to 105 days, developing a package that will preserve quality up to four months (120 days) will solve most of the difficulty. On the other hand, if the average is 90 days but the time from production to use shows a substantial variation from 30 to 150 days, the improved 120-day package may not be a satisfactory solution.

One way to discover the variation in events is to take the numerical data and arrange them in a distribution as to magnitude. The statistician can then divide the distribution into one hundred parts so that one percent of the events fall in each part. Each division is called a *percentile*. The median is the fiftieth percentile since it falls at the midpoint. The point where one percent of the cases have smaller values (99 percent have larger values) is the first percentile. The value that falls on a point where 75 percent of the cases have smaller values (25 percent have larger values) is the seventy-fifth percentile.

Students are probably most familiar with the use of percentiles in relation to test scores and grade-point averages. A student may receive a percentile rank describing his position in his high school graduating class. If the grade point of each student in a class of five hundred is computed and then distributed according to magnitude, the resulting distribution forms the basis for discovering percentiles. The first percentile includes the five students withe the lowest grade points, the second the ten with lowest grade points, on up to the last percentile, which includes the five students with the highest grade points. Each individual student can get a rank that indicates his standing in the class. A student whose rank was in the twenty-fourth percentile stood in the lowest quartile of the class, with 76 percent above and 23 percent below him.

Percentiles can be used to discover how tightly clustered the statistical data are around the measure of central tendency and thus indicate how similar are the events described by the median, mode, or mean. The entire *range* of the scores or statistics is the value resulting from subtracting the lowest number from the highest in the distribution. Thus, if the shortest time from factory to use of the cake mix was 24 days and the longest was 184 days, the range would be 160 days $(184 - 24 = 160)$. The entire range is not a very good measure of variations, however, because a few extreme instances could cause considerable fluctuation in the range. For instance, if only very few cases of cake mix ever went beyond 120 days before they were used, the figure of 160 as an index of variation would not be very meaningful. An interpercentile range is often a better clue to how much variation exists in a statistical distribution. If one computed the range of scores between the twenty-fifth and seventy-fifth percentiles, he would have a number indicating how closely half of the statistics clustered about the median. One could compute the distance between the fifth percentile and the ninety-fifth and discover how closely 90 percent of the scores clustered. If the range from the fifth to the ninety-fifth percentile turned out to be 20 with a median of 90 days, the variability of the statistics would be much smaller than if the range turned out to be 40. A package that would conserve a satisfactory level of quality for 100 days would solve the bulk of the problem in the first instance and not in the second.

In a case where an arithmetic average (mean) is the indicated measure of central tendency, statisticians often compute a *standard deviation* as an index to variability. Although to figure the standard deviation one must incorporate the concept of square root for computational convenience, the concept itself is no more difficult to grasp than that of the interpercentile range. Recall that the purpose of the standard deviation is to get some index as to the amount of variation in the statistical distribution. The technique in the instance of the standard deviation is to first discover the average (mean) of the entire distribution and then compute the distance of each individual statistic from the average, add up all the resulting variances, and divide by the total number of scores. The result of such figuring is the average deviation from the mean of all the scores.

When one subtracts the average from each statistic, some of the remainders are plus and some are minus values. Adding them up will always result in a total of 0. To overcome the problem with the figuring of the average deviation the statisticians may ignore the signs. Another way to overcome the problem is to square the values that result from subtracting the average from each score; the process of squaring results in having all positive values for the variation. Squaring the differences, adding them, and dividing by the total number of items result in another figure indicating the size of the variation around the average. The technical name for that figure is the *variance*.

Statisticians seldom use the variance as a way to describe variability, because it cannot be represented graphically. They have discovered, however, that the square root of the variance can be graphed as a measure along a scale of scores and so the most useful measure of variability related to averages is the square root of the variance, a figure that is called the *standard deviation*.

The standard deviation provides an index to the dispersion of values similar to the interpercentile range and is an excellent summary of variability or variety in a set of statistical scores. The middle two-thirds of the distribution will fall in a range one standard deviation above and one below the mean. Approximately the middle 95 percent of the range will fall between two standard deviations either side of the mean. For example, if the distribution of statistics relating to time from production to use of the cake mixes turned out to have an average of 90 days and a standard deviation of five, approximately two-thirds of the cake mixes were used in the period from 85 to 95 days and about 95 percent were used in the period from 80 to 100 days.

Descriptive and inferential statistics. So far in our discussion of the case of the deteriorating cake mixes we have taken the collection of data for granted. Now, we must turn to the question of how were the statistics compiled. Where did the information relating to the age of the cake mixes before use come from? One of two general techniques was probably employed. The investigators may have collected information about *all* the boxes of cake mixes on the shelves of *all* retail outlets that stocked the cake mix over a period of months, the assumption being that the age of cake mixes on the shelves was a good index to the age of the cake mix at use. (Of course, insofar as the housewives stored the cake mixes at home a margin of error would be introduced.) A second method might be to sample only a portion of all the boxes of cake mixes on the shelves of only some of the retail outlets and estimate the character of the total population on the basis of the sample. When an investigator observes every event in compiling the the statistics, he is utilizing *descriptive statistics;* when he observes a sample and infers conclusions about the total population on the basis of partial observation, he is using *inferential statistics.*

All other things being equal, of course, the information provided by observing all events under study is the best. Even so, errors may occur. In examining the use of descriptive statistics one should ask such questions as: Did the compilers collect their information accurately? Were the statistical computations made correctly? Do the statistics support the claim they are alleged to support?

Clearly, Minnesota Mills cannot afford the time and expense of a complete study of all of the events surrounding the manufacture and marketing of a product. Often, decisions must be made quickly and on the basis of partial observations. When statistics are compiled on the basis of inferences from samples, the results may be presented in much the same fashion as they are when statistics are used descriptively, but inferential statistics must be examined with much more care.

Sampling procedures. A sample is a small part of something selected to indicate the nature, quality, or style of the whole. Although a sample can be misleading, decisions made upon methodical sampling tend to be better than those based upon hunch or intuition. A management team can sometimes make wise decisions based on a small and arbitrary sample. If the cake mix is of uniform quality, a small amount of it will reveal its basic characteristics. Thus, if the team wishes to evaluate the quality of the cake mix, they may take several pounds of it to the laboratory kitchens for testing from a half-dozen arbitrarily chosen storage bins. However, if the team is studying a population of events that exhibit considerable variability, such as rate of turnover of cake mixes in retail stores, they must carefully evaluate the sampling techniques employed in making the observations and compiling the statistics.

A random sample results when every event in the total population of events has an equal opportunity to be selected. If every box of cake mix on every retail shelf in the United States had an equal opportunity of being surveyed, the sampling technique would be random. The random sample makes it possible for an investigator to draw precise inferences about the total population of cake mix boxes because it fulfills the assumptions of mathematical statistics that are based upon chance or random probabilities. The random sample is of considerable theoretical importance in any analysis of inferential statistics.

Unfortunately, a random sample is often impractical and another sampling procedure may have to be used. The compilers of statistics may go to every hundredth store on a list of all retail outlets for the cake mix and count the age of every tenth box on the shelves. Such a sample would be systematic and might introduce important biases in the results. For example, suppose that the store's owners typically place the older merchandise in a certain position in order to increase the possibility that a customer will select it. If the boxes are arranged systematically according to age, someone picking the first box and every tenth box thereafter will get uniformly different results than if he picks the ninth box and every tenth box thereafter. Likewise, if the original list is not a random one but based on some other system of collecting and organizing the store names, such as alphabetizing, arranging geographically, or in terms of when they began stocking the product, systematic biases may be introduced into the sample.

The best way to test the distortions introduced into the information by the sampling technique is to compare the actual procedure to the results that would probably have been discovered with a random sample. If the systematic sample has been repeated an infinite number of times, are there retail stores that would *never* have been picked by the procedure? Seldom picked? Are those that are underrepresented or overrepresented different in ways that are likely to affect the results? For example, would the sampling procedure result in more urban supermarkets than a random selection? If so, would the rural store likely be different as to age of merchandise? Would the customers in the rural areas be more or less likely to use cake mixes? To recognize and complain about quality? Questions such as the above ought to be used to examine the information presented as a result of inferential statistics.

Given a random sample, statisticians can draw inferences about the likely results of a complete survey of the entire population. Statistics can be considered the mathematics of chance or of gambling. The notion of *confidence* is closely related to the odds of something happening by chance. That is, a card player who knows the odds against drawing an ace to improve his hand can be more or less confident of doing so and may wisely back up his confidence with a bet. Inferential statistical computations can provide precise numerical descriptions of the odds of something occurring by chance. In analogous fashion, statisticians can compute mathematically a *confidence level* specified ahead of time as to what the possible outcomes of surveying the entire population might be. For example, if the investigators specify a confidence level of being right 90 percent of the time (sometimes called the 10 percent level of confidence), statistical mathematics can provide an estimate of the likely results of a complete study of cake mix age in retail stores on the basis of a random sample.

If the sample is random and the results indicate the average age of the cake mix in the sample is 90 days, the statisticians could compute the odds that the actual average of all the cake mixes in the total population would be 90 days, but the odds against the sample mean being identical to the population mean are so small that the resulting information would not be very helpful. Imagine taking 200 marbles at random from a barrel containing 30 percent black marbles and discovering that your sample had precisely 60 black marbles. The odds against such luck are rather small. One would expect that the percentage would approximate 30 percent but not that it would be precisely the same as the parent population.

Just as a gambler has a better chance of winning when he bets on a horse to finish first, second, or third than when he bets only that the horse will win, so the interpreter of a problem in inferential statistics will increase the probability that the sample mean is an index to a good guess about the population average if he expands the range of outcomes that will qualify. Let us apply the lesson of confidence level and confidence limits to the case of the deteriorating cake mixes. To do so we compute a range of total population means (perhaps from 87 to 93 days) so that the odds are 95 out of 100 that sample results such as those observed for the cake mix (90 days) would come from such a parent population. The statistical argument for the inference is as follows:

1. We took a random sample of cake mix boxes and discovered the average to be 90 days.
2. On the basis of the size of the sample and statistical formulas we conclude that
3. Ninety-five times out of 100, such a sample would come from a total population of cake mixes on grocery shelves in which the actual average age was between 87 and 93 days.

The size of the sample affects the amount of confidence (95 times out of 100 or 99 times out of 100, etc.) and the range between confidence limits. If one keeps the confidence level the same and increases the size of the sample, the range between confidence limits narrows. If one keeps the confidence limits the same (between 87 and 93 days) and increases the size of the sample, the confidence level is increased (perhaps from 5 percent to one percent).

The point is that the use of inferential statistics in presentational speaking requires some care and consideration of the uses for which the statistics are submitted. On occasion, the margin of error may be quite large and still tolerable. If the confidence limits are 87 to 93 at the 5 percent level, the speaker may pick the midpoint and simply assert that in a survey of 200 retail outlets, approximately 10 percent of the total number of stores stocking the cake mix, the average age of the product was 90 days. If the differences among 87, 93, and 90 days are unimportant to the quality of the mix, he would be justified in doing so. If, however, a six-day difference would play an important part in the quality of the mixes, he ought to include the margin of error in his discussion so the listeners could arrive at the best decision on the basis of available information.

One ought not automatically to reject information developed on the basis of relatively small samples. If the study has been carefully done and the sample approximates the ideal of randomness, the statistical information about confidence limits and confidence levels provides precise estimates as to the weight that the information should be given.

Inferential statistics are often presented for public consumption in oversimplified form. The pollster seldom reports in the newspapers that his survey is based upon being right 66 percent of the time nor that the confidence limits are such that between 32 and 36 percent of the people interviewed approve of the way the President is conducting his office. Sometimes a speaker will assert something like "the sale of snowmobiles is up 21 percent." The listener is unable to tell if the conclusion was based upon inferential or descriptive statistics. If the figures come from inferences resulting from sampling, one ought to know how large the sample was. How was it selected? If snowmobile sales, or any other sales, are up "21 percent" they must be up in relation to some base figure. How was the base figure determined? Was it determined for statistics compiled last year? Five years ago? Ten years? If more information about how statistics were compiled is not available, they ought to be discarded. Particularly, such imprecise measures should be excluded from presentation within the organization where accurate information is vital to successful decision-making.

The modern organization assembles large masses of statistics in the normal course of events. Today's management is often inundated by an excess of numerical information because professional researchers and statisticians, buttressed with the latest data processing systems, can provide it in abundance. It is often far easier to gather and present statistical information than it is to determine its meaning and discover the realities that lie behind the numbers. Quite often, the basic information required for wise decision-making is an estimation of relationships. The realities under discussion can often be described in such simple relational terms as *enough, too much, on time, gaining, out of reach, leveling off, losing ground steadily, the weakest region, our strongest line, too slow, ahead of schedule,* and *above-average performance.*

The basic mental process involved in developing relations is that of comparison. One of the most important ways the presentational speaker has of making accurate comparisons is by means of statistical statements. Comparisons make figures meaningful and significant. The basic relationship that statistics describe in comparative terms is that of more or less. The refinements of more or less relate to the concepts of simultaneous observations and to trends through time of consecutive observations.

In the first case, statistics gathered simultaneously in two regions may be compared to see if sales in the South are larger or smaller or the same as sales in the Midwest. In the case of trends, the same statistical surveys could be taken in the same regions at various specified time periods and sales in January compared to sales in March to sales in May compared to sales in August. Comparisons over time of similar measures would indicate larger or smaller amounts of the variable under study through time and could indicate such relations as growing, falling, peaking, leveling off, and cyclical fluctuations.

Investigators get the clearest picture of the realities of a situation when they can count a recurring feature of the environment. Counting and the use of subsequent arithmetical computations assume that individuals can be discerned to be counted or that some recurring feature of continuous events can be discriminated and counted. When a person assigns a number to the length of a table, he may use a unit such as an inch as his standard measure. The quality of length in an object is continuous, but by establishing a standard inch a person creates the equivalent of an individual that can be counted. The only problem arises when the end of the table does not fall neatly at the point where a mark indicating an inch is located on a ruler. However, some arbitrary fraction of the unit may be counted or a simple rule that the counting will stop at the last inch mark will solve the problem of counting individual units when measuring some continuous property like time or length. The clocking mechanisms that tick off seconds provide units that can be counted like the inches on a ruler.

In addition to the necessity of making a decision as to where a unit begins or ends so that it can be counted, statistical information can be a valid index of the relation of more or less only if based on a constant unit that is relevant to the property under study. If one wishes to compare the length of two tables to determine which is longer, the statistics that table A is 100 units long and table B is 50 units long will provide a relationship of more or less that is accurate only if the units are all the same size.

Standard units such as those related to the basic dimensions of time, space, and weight are all carefully established so they are equal and thus result in comparable figures. Because standardized measures are common and yield statistics that are so useful, a person may mistake all statistical information as equally solid and dependable. Often, investigators compile statistical information by counting units that are not as comparable as the standard weights and measures. To return to the case of the deteriorating cake mixes, assume for the moment that despite assurances from the research and development section and from the quality control division that the cake mixes leave the plant comparable in quality with the leading competitor's product, the trouble-shooting team decides to test the product in the field. It purchases a quantity of the leading competitor's product and places it in a neutral package. It then takes a sample of housewives in four major metropolitan market areas and asks the ladies to use both cake mixes, marked A and B, and select the one they prefer. They are told that they will be given a case of the cake mix they choose for participating in the survey. When the final statistics are gathered, the survey may give the housewives a forced choice (that is, they must pick either product A or product B), or it may give them the option of selecting neither and receiving half a case of each. Assume for the moment that the housewives are placed in a forced-choice situation. The survey counts the lady who picks product B after mentally flipping a coin in the same category with the person who is enthusiastically for product B and who wants to know the brand name so she can continue to buy it after her sample supply runs out. In a very real sense the choice of the first subject is not comparable to the choice of the second.

Some statistical data for business and professional organizations are liable to distortion simply because the units are not comparable. One of the most important of these is the basic monetary measure, the dollar. Although people sometimes fail to do so, they ought to correct for changing values of the dollar before making comparisons. The 1970 dollar is to be distinguished from the 1930 dollar. Even last month's value for the dollar will be different from this month's. Thus, the business that compares sales in terms of gross dollar amounts will be misled as to the actual increase in business from quarter to quarter. If the dollar has lost purchasing power in the period under study, an increase in apparent value may simply reflect that fact. On the other hand, if the dollar has increased in value, an increase in gross dollar sales may indicate an even greater increase in business than would seem to be the case.

Even when the units compared are of the same magnitude and are corrected for variations in value, the practice of comparing recent statistics with those compiled in the past often suggests a trend that is not meaningful because of the growth of the population. For example, the latest figures regarding vital statistics will usually indicate an increase when compared with those of several decades ago simply because the population of the United States has grown in size. If one wants information relating to questions such as, has the amount of juvenile drug taking increased in the last ten years, or, has divorce increased in the last decade, trends based on gross statistics may be poor evidence. The total number of divorces ten years ago compared to today would not be as good as the number of divorces per 1000 population. Even better might be the number of divorces per 100 marriages. The latter statistic might indicate a smaller rise or even a drop in divorces where the gross number might indicate a rising trend.

Herb might well be misled if he projected a trend in cake mix sales upward for the past ten years depending upon total dollar sales. Inflation could account for the increase in gross sales and the total amount of cake mix sold might not differ appreciably. Even if an adjustment for real purchasing power indicated a trend toward greater use of cake mixes, the gross sales might be a poor index. The number of cake mixes sold per 1000 population might be a better index to the popularity trend of cake mixes.

Among the most important ways of preparing and interpreting statistical data are the table and the graph. Indeed, one factor in the rise of presentational speaking with its emphasis upon visual aids is that so much information related to matters such as items produced, labor used in production, sales, profits, losses, and time of distribution is statistical. Every student of presentational speaking must have a good grasp of the use of tables and graphs to display comparative statistics and reveal basic relationships.

The summary table. A summary table presents major conclusions derived from analysis of the raw data in such a way that it makes clear important relationships relevant to the purpose of the presentation. Several different summary tables can be developed from the same statistical data for different purposes. We remind the reader of the relationship between supporting material and the proposition it amplifies.

The basic elements of a summary table include the following:

1. The table number, an identifying numeral to facilitate references to the information on the table during the delivery of the presentation.
2. The title, a brief descriptive label that serves to identify the basic contents of the table.
3. The headnote, which may be used as a subtitle to include additional information about the statistical data or refer to the source of the material.
4. The field, entries on the table which represent the summary statistics, the information proper.
5. Column heads, a description of the statistics in each column.
6. The stub, the left column of the table, which describes the rows of data running horizontally across the table, the major summary classifications of the table.
7. Line caption, entries which describe the statistics in each line in the same way that column heads describe each column.
8. Stub head, a statement over the stub of the table, which describes the line captions in the stub, a more general description of the classifications represented by the line captions. As the stub is a column, the stub head is a special case of the column heads.

To illustrate the elements of a summary table, refer to Table 1. The table in this instance is numbered "1," and the title is "Age of Cake

Table 1. Age of Cake Mixes of Minnesota
Mills on Retail Outlet Shelves
A Survey of 200 Retail Outlets in Four Major
Geographical Regions

Region	Average Age in Days
East	75
South	82
Midwest	81
Far West	85

Mixes of Minnesota Mills on Retail Outlet Shelves." The headnote is, "A Survey of 200 Retail Outlets in Four Major Geographical Regions." The field consists of the numbers 75, 82, 81, and 85. The column heads include "Region" and "Average Age in Days." The stub includes the labels "East," "South," "Midwest," and "Far West." The line caption includes each entry in the stub, thus the first line caption is "East." The stub head for Table 1 is "Region."

Statistical summary tables may contain only one main idea, as Table 1, which summarizes the average time since production of cake mixes on retail outlet shelves, or they may be extremely complicated and introduce several summaries. Table 2 indicates a typical way in which greater detail is introduced in a summary table. Table 2 tells essen-

Table 2. Age of Cake Mixes of Minnesota Mills on
Supermarket and Independent Retail Outlet Shelves
A Survey of 200 Retail Outlets in Four Major Geograph-
ical Regions

Region	Average Age in Days	
	Supermarkets	Independents
East	65	92
South	67	101
Midwest	64	95
Far West	69	99

tially the same story as Table 1 except that it indicates another variable; namely, the type of retail store. In addition to adding another column to the field, Table 2 requires an additional explanatory heading for the columns. Instead of using only the heading that includes "Supermarkets," and "Independents," the more general label, "Average Age in Days" is placed as a larger head over the two columns. The more general heading is called a *spanner head.* The horizontal ruling under the spanner head indicates the scope of the more general heading.

Table 3 provides an even greater breakdown of information relating to the statistics summarized on Table 1. Table 3 illustrates the use of

Table 3. Proportion of Supermarkets to Independent Retail Outlets in Cake Mix Survey
A Breakdown of 200 Retail Outlets in Four Major Geographical Regions for Minnesota Mills

Region	Supermarkets		Independents		Both	
	Number	Percent	Number	Percent	Number	Percent
East	30	60%	20	40%	50	100%
South	25	50	25	50	50	100
Midwest	28	56	22	44	50	100
Far West	27	54	23	46	50	100
All Regions	110	55	90	45	200	100

more than one kind of computation in that it presents percents and numbers. To simplify the reading of a table that includes several units, one should place a percent sign after the first figure in the appropriate columns. If the table includes monetary units, the dollar sign may be used in the same way. Percentages are always computed according to some base figure and the last column is filled with entries of 100 percent, which indicates that the percentages in each row are computed to the base of the total number in the last column.

Comparisons are often facilitated by presenting summaries of two sets of data in the same table. Table 4 not only classifies the retail

Table 4. Age of Cake Mixes on Retail Outlet Shelves of Minnesota Mills and Brand X
Based on a Survey of 200 Retail Outlets in Four Major Geographical Regions

Region	Average Age in Days			
	Supermarkets		Independents	
	Minnesota Mills	Brand X	Minnesota Mills	Brand X
East	65	52	92	61
South	67	54	101	65
Midwest	64	49	95	62
Far West	69	70	99	98
Total	66	56	97	72

outlets but also presents two sets of data for each outlet, that relating to the Minnesota Mills cake mixes and that describing the age of the leading competitor, Brand X.

Table 4 furnishes a simple and yet complete example of a summary table for statistical information. Figure 7.2 provides a breakdown of

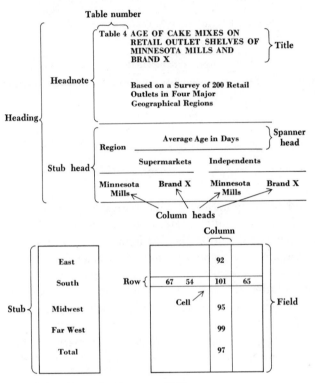

Figure 7.2   Parts of a Summary Table

the three major divisions of a summary table, the heading, stub, and field.

Quite often, the person who is developing a presentation will have extensive statistical data to interpret for his audience. Summary tables prepared for written reports can be detailed and complex because the reader usually has ample time to study and decipher them. The tabular presentation of complicated data in a presentation requires considerably more skill in audience adaptation because at best the tables can only be displayed to the audience briefly.

C. R. Gould, audio-visual coordinator of the Martin Marietta Corporation, an engineering company engaged in highly technical production, starts with the premise that "the best visual aid is a wordless picture" and recommends that a visual aid for a presentation should contain no more than twenty words or symbols. According to that criterion only Table 1, which contains fourteen words and symbols, and Table 2, which contains twenty, would qualify as suitable for a presentation.[1]

What should a speaker do if he wishes to use the information in Tables 3 and 4? A good procedure is to adapt the information for oral presentation by dividing it up and designing simpler tables for the audience. An alternative is to include the more detailed tables in written supplements to be distributed to the listeners following the speech.

Remember that the main purpose of many within-organization presentations is to help establish and clarify basic relationships that will aid a committee of decision makers. Herb will deal with detailed statistical data, but the upper levels of management must have the information reduced to elementary relationships before establishing policy, embarking on a change, or taking action to continue present policies and programs. The reason for the presentation is often to save time for important and busy people by speeding up the process of giving them necessary information more clearly, more effectively, and more rapidly than by any other means. One of the greatest services of Herb's presentation, therefore, is to screen out from a complicated mass of statistical material those elements that need to be brought out to give a representative picture of the facts, and to translate the relevant relationships into clear and simple visual terms that can be quickly and easily understood.

One way to simplify tabular visuals is to prepare rough copies of them and then rehearse the presentation. Eliminating those visuals that contribute little to the support of the main ideas of the speech as well as those elements of the useful visuals that are not referred to can often result in a drastic reduction in the number of tables and in their complexity. C. R. Gould maintains that

> The best way to encourage a technical man to simplify his visual aids is to let him practice a few times with these and eliminate facts that actually are not used or can be conveyed just as effectively by the speaker. On one occasion two engineers preparing for a joint presentation started with 35 visual aids this way. They ultimately took three with them to the seminar and were congratulated for the effectiveness of their message.[2]

[1] C. R. Gould, "Philosophy on Oral Presentations," mimeograph copy of speech delivered to Speech Communication Association Convention, 1967, p. 3.

[2] *Ibid.*, p. 4.

GRAPHIC METHODS FOR PRESENTING
STATISTICAL SUMMARIES

The main purpose of translating tabular statistics in graphic form is to make them more vivid and to present relationships in a way that is easier to grasp. A *graph* is a representation of numbers by geometric figures drawn to scale.[3]

The line graph.   Perhaps the most widely used means of presenting statistical data visually is the line graph. Line graphs are particularly useful for clarifying comparative relationships through time. Since many business and professional presentations deal with information relating to time-based trends—for example, comparing profits, production, wages, or market potential from quarter to quarter or year to year—the line graph is one of the more important tools of the presentational speaker.

If we take chocolate cake mix sales, we can construct a line graph as in Figure 7.3. Drawing a line graph requires that scales are laid out

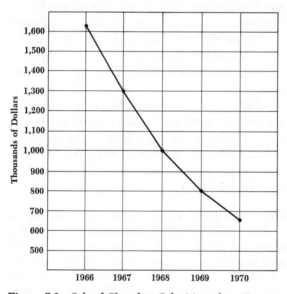

Figure 7.3   Sale of Chocolate Cake Mixes for a Five-
Year Period

[3] The definition is from Helen M. Walker and Joseph Lev, *Elementary Statistical Methods* (New York, 1958), p. 35. This book is a sound and clear elementary presentation of statistics for the student of presentational speaking who wishes more information on the subject.

at right angles to each other. Often, there is little relationship between the horizontal and vertical scales to be selected. The magnitude of a trend can be distorted by compressing or elongating the space allotted to time periods while keeping the scale for the other axis constant. Figure 7.4 presents two line graphs each indicating a decrease in sales of chocolate cake mixes over a four-year period. The graphs have the same magnitude, but because of the difference in scale selected to represent an interval of a year, the lower graph makes the decrease appear much more dramatic.

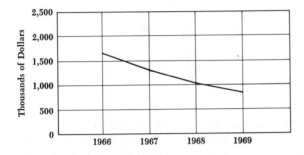

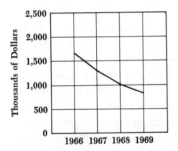

Figure 7.4   Two Graphs Presenting Same Data on
Chocolate Cake Mixes

Placing more than one curve on a graph facilitates the communication of relationships by quick visual inspection. Figure 7.5 indicates the sales of chocolate cake mixes for a five-year period with the supermarket sales compared to the independent retail outlets. The supermarket sales continued to rise, while the sales at independent outlets dropped. The decline of cake mix sales is here revealed to be primarily a function of independent outlet sales. A person preparing a presentation ought not graph more than one comparison for each visual.

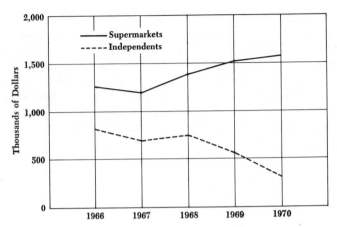

Figure 7.5   Comparison of Supermarket and Independent Retail Outlet Sales of Chocolate Cake Mixes for a Five-Year Period

Occasionally, the comparisons to be graphed are of such widely different magnitudes that equal-interval scales cannot be used. For example, if the presentation about cake mixes required a comparison on the rate of increase in cake mix sales as compared to total income for Minnesota Mills, the share of the total income attributable to cake mixes might be such a small fraction of the total income of the corporation that graphing the two sets of data might not reveal the accurate information. Figure 7.6 indicates the comparison graphed on equal-interval scales (also called *arithmetic scales*). According to Figure 7.6 one might assume that while total sales for Minnesota Mills was rapidly increasing, the cake mix sales have only grown slightly. In terms of dollar volume the graph is accurate. In terms of the rate of increase, however, the graph is misleading. An accurate representation of percentage or rate of increase is provided by a vertical scale which would represent a 10 percent increase in total sales, with the same amount of distance on the vertical axis as a 10 percent increase in cake mix volume. The scale that reveals proportionate increases is called *logarithmic*. A graph that has one arithmetic (equal-interval) scale and another logarithmic (proportional-interval) scale is called a *semilogarithmic* graph. Figure 7.7 presents the same comparative data as Figure 7.6 but in a semilogarithmic graph that reveals that cake mix sales have risen at about the same rate as total corporate sales.

The bar graph. In a bar graph numerical dimensions are visualized in terms of bars of varying lengths drawn to scale. If we take the information presented in Table 1, we can construct a bar graph as illustrated in Figure 7.8.

The bar graph is also well suited to depicting comparative statistics.

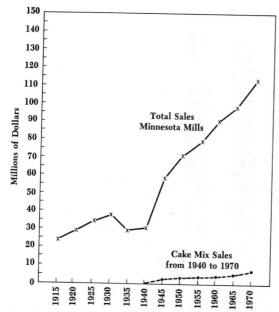

Figure 7.6   Increase in Cake Mix Sales for Minnesota
Mills Compared to Gross Sales

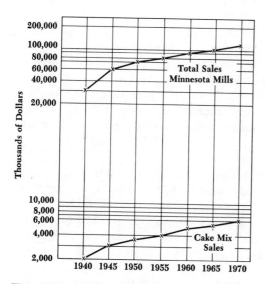

Figure 7.7   Increase in Cake Mix Sales for Minnesota Mills Compared to Gross Sales on
Semilogarithmic Graph

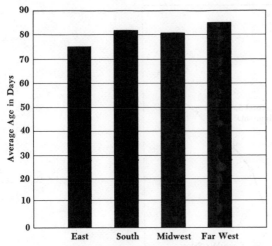

Figure 7.8   Age of Cake Mixes of Minnesota Mills
on Retail Outlet Shelves: A Survey of
200 Retail Outlets in Four Major Geographical Regions

Figure 7.9 displays the proportionate percentage of supermarket to
independent retail stores in the sample.

Bar graphs can present comparisons among many different statistics. Figure 7.10 illustrates a bar graph that compares year-by-year
three different cake mixes and each bar is divided to show further
comparative data.

While bar graphs of the complexity of Figure 7.10 are often useful
in written reports where the reader has ample time to decipher the
various keys and discover the meaning of solid bars versus hatched
bars and the units along the side of the graph, a speaker making a
presentation would not use such a complicated visual. Again, the
principle of restricting the information on each visual to one or two
basic relationships clearly graphed so the audience can quickly grasp
the essence of the information must be applied. Figure 7.8 represents a
good bar graph for oral presentations.

In general the bar graph should have all scale values beginning with
the zero point. Because the relationship is based upon a geometric
comparison, starting the graph at some other point will result in misleading the viewer. For example, if the information graphed on Figure
7.8 were presented as in Figure 7.11 starting at fifty days rather than at
the zero point, the differences among the regions would be exaggerated.

The eye may be misled by graphic material if the numbers that the
bars represent are added at the ends thus exaggerating the length of
the bars, as in Figure 7.12. The best technique is to place the needed

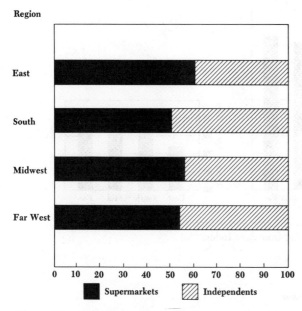

Figure 7.9   Proportion of Supermarkets to Independent
Retail Outlets in Cake Mix Survey: A Break-
down of 200 Retail Outlets in Four Major
Geographical Regions for Minnesota Mills

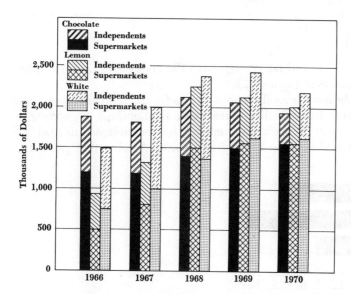

Figure 7.10   Sales of Chocolate, Lemon, and White Cake Mixes
for a Five-Year Period

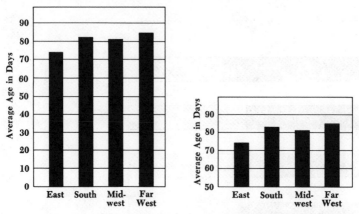

Figure 7.11   Distortion of Comparative Statistical Data Resulting from Not Starting from Zero Index

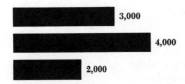

Figure 7.12   Incorrect Labeling of Bars May Mislead Viewer by Making the Bar Appear Unduly Long

figures at the left and far enough from the ends of the bars so distortion is unlikely as in Figure 7.13.

Bar graphs have several obvious virtues for the individual preparing a presentation. Because they reveal basic relationships in geometrical fashion, they can be made large enough for the audience to read and grasp the essential point quickly and easily. A table that presents a

Figure 7.13   Correct Way to Label Bars in Bar Graph

relatively simple relationship often requires some translation by the speaker or listener in gross terms such as "that is approximately twice as much in a ten-year period" or "that is about one-third of the projected sales." A well-constructed graph reveals such relationships as one-half, one-third, and so on, in visual terms.

Other graphic techniques. The pie chart reveals proportional divisions of a whole set of data in such easy-to-grasp form that it deserves special consideration. The pie chart is often used to show the distribution of total income among various sources, or the total budgetary allocation to various divisions or departments.

Although a person might hesitate to use a pie chart in a presentation about cake mixes for fear of being accused of using a mixed metaphor, he might do so to indicate the percentage of sales for various departments within the pastry division. Figure 7.14 shows percentage of

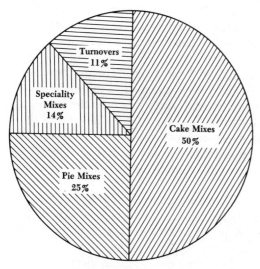

Figure 7.14   Pie Chart of Total Sales of Pastry Division of Minnesota Mills, All Departments

income from various products within that division of Minnesota Mills.

Notice that Figure 7.14 starts with a radius drawn vertically from the center, and the other parts are then laid off clockwise beginning with the largest slice of the pie and continuing with the next largest and down to the smallest component. Unless the data divide logically in another fashion, the procedure used in Figure 7.14 is the usual one.

A person making a presentation to an audience that may be unfamiliar with the data or relatively uninterested in the subject may want to use a *pictograph*. The pictograph represents the statistical information in terms of cartoon pictures, with quantitative relationships shown by areas or heights of pictured figures. Using height of figures to indicate quantity is a distortion, since a taller figure has increased area and suggests greater magnitude.

Pictographs often add interest to a visual and make abstract statistical comparisons more concrete. Drawing symbols requires time and skill and often the added interest may not be commensurate with the expense of preparing good pictographs. When pictographs are used, the symbols must be simple and depend primarily upon their outline. Often, the symbols are prepared in silhouette rather than including detail in the drawings. The data must be such that gross differences in the size of the pictures will convey the intended message. The pictograph is relatively inflexible and can only be used with very simple data. Most of the data on Figures 7.1–7.14 could not be easily illustrated with a pictograph. (Pictures that would readily distinguish between chocolate cake mixes and lemon cake mixes are not easy to come by.)

The use of graphs for presentational speaking. The decision as to whether to use a table or a graph to present statistical information and comparisons is one that needs to be made with an eye to the audience, the graphic resources available to the speaker, and the amount of time available for the speech. As a general rule, the graph will serve the speaker's purpose better than a table because it is less difficult to decipher and presents relationships visually in terms that can be readily understood.

On occasion, to be sure, an audience that is used to interpreting statistics in tabular form will appreciate the added information that tables can provide. Tables do require less time to prepare and less skill and artistry.

Graphs must be large enough so they can be easily deciphered by all members of the audience, a problem that is easily solved by use of the overhead projector. With the projector, a pencil can serve as a pointer to indicate crucial parts of the graph and their relationships.

The presentational speaker should be highly selective in deciding what statistical informaton to present in graphic form. Only a few of the more important data should be developed into visual aids and incorporated into the speech.

Each graph ought to contain only one or two basic comparisons and ought not be shown to the audience for more than twenty or thirty seconds at one time. Important graphs may be shown again a second or third time.

All in all, the graph is one of the most important and useful tools for the presentation of statistical data in business and professional speaking. Every student of presentational speaking should become adept at developing, interpreting, and using graphs as visual aids.

SUMMARY

Statistics are numerical descriptions of facts. Because of the precision of statistical data, they are the single most important type of supporting material used in presentational speaking. One of the most important uses of statistical statements is to give an indication of the typical instance in a large population of events or of the general drift of affairs. The arithmetic average, probably the most common indicator of typicality, is the *mean*. When a number of statistics are ordered as to size, the *median* is the number that is in the middle of the range. The *mode* is the value that occurs most often in a distribution.

In addition to typicality statistical information can include estimates of how much the events under study differ from one another and the practical limits of differences. The most important measures of variability include range, interpercentile range, and standard deviation.

When an investigator observes every event in compiling statistics, he is utilizing descriptive statistics. When he observes a sample and infers conclusions about the total population on the basis of partial observations, he is using inferential statistics.

Inferential statistics depend upon sampling procedures for their usefulness. A random sample results when every event in the total population has an equal opportunity to be selected. A random sample makes it possible for an investigator to draw precise inferences about the total population. A systematic sample is illustrated by the technique where every *n*th name on a list is selected for a survey. Systematic samples may introduce important biases in the results of the study and must be carefully evaluated against the ideal of the random-sampling procedure.

It is often easier to gather and present statistical information than it is to determine its meaning and discover the realities that lie behind the numbers. Quite often, the basic information required for wise organizational decision-making is an estimation of relationships. The basic mental process involved in developing relations is that of comparisons. Comparisons make figures meaningful and significant.

Comparisons to be useful must be based upon counting units that are relatively constant and comparable. Unless the units compared statistically are equal on some scale of magnitude, the factual descriptions that result will be distorted.

Among the most important ways of preparing and interpreting statistical data are the table and the graph. A summary table presents major conclusions derived from analysis of the raw data in such a way that it makes clear important relationships relevant to the purpose of the presentation. The main purpose of translating tabular statistics in graphic form is to make them more vivid and to present relationships in a way that is easier to grasp. A graph is a representation of numbers by geometric figures drawn to scale. The main types of graphs used to present information are the line graph, the bar graph, the pie chart, and the pictograph. As a general rule, the graph serves the presentational speaker better than a table and is one of the most useful and important ways to present statistical information in business and professional situations.

QUESTIONS FOR DISCUSSION AND REVIEW

1. What is the difference between evaluating evidence and reasoning on the basis of absolute tests of truth and validity and on the basis of the audience-response criterion?
2. What factors in a listener predispose him to respond to an argument in symbolic terms?
3. What are the statistical indexes of typicality? How may they best be used?
4. What are the statistical indexes of variability? How may they best be used?
5. What are *descriptive statistics? Inferential statistics?*
6. What is meant by the concept of *random sample?* By *systematic sample?*
7. What are some important ways in which inferential statistics are sometimes presented for public consumption in oversimplified form?
8. What requirements of counting must be met before statistics can be used to describe the relationship of more or less?
9. What are some things to remember when preparing statistical tables for a presentation?
10. What are some representative methods of presenting statistical information graphically? What are the strengths and weaknesses of each?

REFERENCES AND SUGGESTED READINGS

HUFF, DARRELL. *How to Lie with Statistics.* New York: Norton, 1954.

SMITH, G. MILTON. *Guide to Statistics for Psychology and Education,* 3rd ed. New York: Holt, Rinehart and Winston, 1962.

WALKER, HELEN M., and JOSEPH LEV. *Elementary Statistical Methods,* 2nd ed. New York: Holt, Rinehart and Winston, 1958.

WILLIAMS, FREDERICK. *Reasoning with Statistics: Simplified Examples in Communications Research.* New York: Holt, Rinehart and Winston, 1968.

WITTICH, WALTER A., and CHARLES F. SCHULLER. *Audiovisual Materials: Their Nature and Use.* New York: Harper & Row, 1967.

CHAPTER EIGHT

NONSTATISTICAL FORMS OF SUPPORT

Nonstatistical forms of support for the contentions in a presentation may be divided into two main categories: (1) evidence and (2) clarification. *Evidence* is supporting material designed to furnish grounds for belief or to make evident the truth or falsity, rightness or wrongness, wisdom or folly, of a proposition. Evidence is a technical legal term that refers to material furnished by lawyers in support of their briefs. In the courts evidence may consist of both testimony of witnesses and factual exhibits such as pistols, knives, clothing, and so on. *Proof* is the sufficient marshaling of evidence to achieve conviction or acceptance of the proposition from the judge or jury. Evidence carries weight as proof with the members of the audience. For the student of presentational speaking, evidence includes both oral and written testimony (verbal evidence) and things such as prototypes of new products, models of buildings and bridges, and demonstrations. Our emphasis in this chapter will be upon verbal evidence, which includes, in addition to the statistical information treated in Chapter 7, case studies and the testimony of eyewitnesses and experts.

Clarification is supporting material designed to enlighten the listener. Clarification is primarily aimed at achieving understanding. Clarification consists solely of verbal devices. *Understanding* is achieved when sufficient clarification results in a meeting of the minds among those involved in the communication.

The distinctions between clarification and evidence and between understanding and proof are pedagogical ones, to enable the student to grasp the similarities and differences in various communication techniques. In actual practice the psychology of the audience is such that listeners will tend to respond in a unified way to all supporting material. That is, some will be convinced by clarification as well as by evidence and others will be led to understanding by evidence as well as clarification. One important difference should be noted, however. Herb Appleton's presentation may be accepted by the sales manager because he likes what he thinks Herb is saying even if he does not understand it and may be rejected by the production manager because he dislikes what Herb is saying even though he understands it.

NONSTATISTICAL EVIDENCE

The case study. As we saw in Chapter 7, the virtue of numerical descriptions of facts is that they have precision and scope. Statistics suffer, however, from lack of qualitative material, human interest, and concreteness. Statistical descriptions of factual situations tend to be cold, dull, and dry. Some businessmen and professionals deal with situations that are so idiosyncratic that statistical descriptions of central tendency or range of variability are essentially meaningless. The most useful complement for statistics where they are appropriate and the best substitute for them when they are not is the form of evidence known as the case study.

The *case study* (sometimes called real-life example) is a detailed observation and analysis of a given event. Case studies used for evidence in support of an argumentive position are always based upon observations of actual events and should not be confused with hypothetical case studies such as the ones we have been using in this book for clarification. Hypothetical cases are fictions dreamed up by the communicator to help clarify his ideas and gain understanding. We deal with hypothetical cases later, in our discussion of clarification.

When case studies are used to supplement, clarify, and humanize statistical descriptions, they ought to be selected so they complement the basic statistical analysis. Several cases that are typical of the most common or usual events integrated with such statistical indexes as averages, means, or modes will help support the statistical evidence. Conceivably, a case or two illustrating the extremes at each end of the range of events will help support the argument that is based primarily upon statistical grounds. To return to Herb Appleton's presentation based largely upon statistical evidence, he might supplement the statistics with a case study of a supermarket that was typical of all those surveyed in terms of the age of Minnesota Mills' cake mixes and their turnover. If he felt it necessary and if he had time for the development of several more cases, he might have included a small rural independent outlet and a large high-turnover discount store.

The problem of submitting cases as evidence for a proposition when statistical evidence is inappropriate is more difficult. Should Minnesota Mills contemplate a reorganization of their corporate structure from a pyramid form of organization to a more fluid project-based structure, they might find that the only precedents for such a change in companies of similar size in a milling industry are furnished by five firms. A careful examination of the five cases in which companies have changed to the new organizational structure might provide the best evidence for the decision. Each case study would contain statistical evidence relating to corporate profits, labor turnover, and so on. Although the details may include statistics in this instance, the form of support would be the case study.

Case studies are often appropriate in clinical professions such as medicine, social work, psychology, and psychiatry. Careful case studies of welfare clients may prove to be the best evidence for a change in the welfare program of a given city.

Case studies must be based upon careful and accurate observations. If the features of the case that are crucial to the decision are falsified, then the actions based upon the evidence may be unwise. Even accurate case studies may be poor evidence for a given proposition, however, if they are not typical of the category they represent. While case studies serve to humanize conditions and provide understanding of the qualitative detail of a problem, they do so at a considerable sacrifice of scope and generality. The danger of drawing a conclusion from too few cases and applying it indiscriminately to new situations is thus increased when arguing from case studies.

Testimony. The most convincing evidence is often that of the senses. If a person sees for himself, he is often convinced. Direct verification of factual assertions is the ultimate test of truth or falsity. Thus, in the law courts witnesses testifying to what they have personally experienced are evaluated as a source of good evidence. In scholarship the primary document is one that contains the account of a person who can testify from his own experience. The lawyer or scholar developing an argument to prove a proposition about something that he does not know firsthand must often turn to the words of those who have directly observed the facts in question. The testimony of eyewitnesses thus becomes another important form of evidence.

The person developing a presentational speech is often in a position where he must depend upon testimony of observers for his information. Herb studying the deteriorating cake mixes cannot witness personally all of the facts he must deal with. He must depend to a lesser or greater degree upon the eyewitness reports of the people making investigations for him.

As Herb evaluates the case of the deteriorating cake mixes and searches for a satisfactory solution, he must weigh and test the words of those reporting to him for their relevance, truth, or falsity. Herb will read many reports, study eyewitness accounts of many different persons, as he tries to find out what is in fact going on in the cake mix division. Herb would be well advised to divide his sources into two groups: those who are reporting what they have witnessed personally and those who are giving him hearsay reports. The first source is generally the best source. Next, he should divide the eyewitnesses into those who have special training and competence in the area under study and those who are untrained. The testimony of an expert in marketing research might be evaluated differently than the quotation of an advertising copywriter depending upon facts discussed by two witnesses.

In examining the testimony of various eyewitnesses Herb should consider such matters as: Was the witness in a position to observe the relevant facts? Was the witness motivated to make adequate observations? Perhaps, the person conducting a survey of cake mix boxes on supermarket shelves visited the supermarkets assigned for the survey but grew tired of the drudgery of checking and "dummied up" the results. Herb should also ask if the witness was willing and able to tell the truth. Was the witness strongly biased? The quality control manager who heatedly asserted to Herb that "The quality was there when the packages left the plant. I know because I've been down there eight hours a day for the last month checking myself" has a strong bias to defend himself and his department. Herb must take that bias into account in evaluating the testimony. On the other hand, should the quality control manager admit reluctantly that "I've got to say in all honesty that we've had some trouble keeping up the quality the last couple of months, but we've had a lot of new people and some things have slipped through that shouldn't have," Herb would be justified in weighing such testimony a bit more heavily.

Eyewitnesses may also distort the facts in their descriptions for reasons less obvious than self-interest. Observers may temper their remarks because they do not want to displease the listener. They may soften or heighten a description to meet the expectations of the person making the investigation. Herb may get testimony from some witnesses that represents what they think Herb wants to hear rather than precisely what they have observed.

Once Herb has analyzed the testimony of eyewitnesses and tested it for truth, he must decide whether to submit the testimony as part of the evidence when he makes his presentation. If he decides to do so, he must be extremely selective because of the time limitations. Herb has three options in the way he uses testimony of witnesses. The most complete, convincing, and time-consuming way to use testimony in the presentation is to

1. Name the witness (John Gallager of quality control)
2. Qualify the witness by summarizing his expertness, bias or objectivity, and knowledge of the facts (John was in charge of checking quality for the three months of the winter. He was on the floor as a quality control checker for the five years before his promotion last January. Certainly, John stands to gain nothing by admitting that his department has slipped up badly the last three months. John spent a good deal of his time on the floor supervising the quality control people.)
3. Quoting the words of the witness directly (John said, and I have his statement here, "I know that we let slip by twenty-three cases of Chocolate Pecan Delight that were returned by the retailers in the second week of January alone.")

A second way to use testimony is to name and qualify the witness and paraphrase the testimony in briefer form. "John Gallager of quality control spent a good deal of his time on the floor supervising his people the three months of last winter. Certainly, he would not testify that his people missed twenty-three cases of poor quality Chocolate Pecan Delight cake mixes in one week of January unless it was true."

A third way is to simply name the witnesses with little or no qualification and assert that their testimony will support your contention. "Not only does Gallager testify to poor quality control, but Harry Draper of sales, Bill Mitchell of customer services, and Mary Abbott of the test kitchens all told me the same thing."

Another form of evidence from testimony relates not to the question of whether a thing is true or false or whether factual descriptions are accurate but to what inferences or conclusions can be drawn from the facts.

In the organizational context, as indeed in most areas of a highly structured urban culture, the drawing of inferences from complicated factual descriptions is a job for experts. When the top management of Minnesota Mills wishes to know about a new tax law, they call in their lawyers for an expert opinion. When they wish to decide what the audience analysis studies of television shows mean, they call in their ad agency's media expert to give them a conclusion or an inference from the facts. Thus, Herb might assert in his presentation that "Jack Mills in the lab tested our current Chocolate Pecan Delight package very extensively and he is of the opinion that the package will hold up the quality for about ninety days without appreciable deterioration."

The final form of evidence from testimony also consists of expert opinion. When an expert gives advice as to what to do in a given situation, the fact that he is an authority may serve as proof for an audience. The tax expert may testify that under the circumstances Minnesota Mills ought not expand and diversify by merging with Consolidated Electronics, because in his expert opinion the merger would result in an appreciable increase in corporate taxes. The media expert may testify that placing commercials on prime time television on Monday night is unwise for Minnesota Mills and that they should sponsor daytime dramatic serials. Jack Mills may testify that improving the packages is a good plan because increasing the package's ability to conserve quality for a longer period of time will be easy and relatively inexpensive.

Herb should take into account many factors when deciding the weight to be attributed to the testimony of experts. Is the specialist highly rated by his peers? Does he have a field of specialization that is appropriate to the group's problems? The political campaign organization that hires a print media expert may find its television campaign badly advised. Finally, we all tend to respond to authorities as human beings. Is the expert given to rash, thoughtless statements? Is he emotionally unbalanced? Is he biased? Will he talk frankly? Sometimes members of the medical profession fail to talk frankly and explain in comprehensive fashion the advice they give their patients. Does he relate well to other people? Sometimes, unfortunately, the advice of a highly competent authority is not accepted simply because he is not liked as a person.

The general preoccupation of the contemporary audience with a man's "image" is undeniable. The real concern within an organization as to whether or not an expert is a "good guy" is similarly an influential element in the situation. We may not feel competent to judge a man's ability in his profession, but we do feel that we can judge him as a man. If advice comes from someone we like, and trust, if he is also a person who has established his competence by past performance, his advice is likely to be accepted.

The basic strength of the modern corporation is its ability to utilize narrowly and highly trained specialists. Minnesota Mills can undertake such a complicated project as launching a new cake mix because it has among its employees specialists in milling of flour, nutrition, home economics, marketing, production, advertising, distribution, sales, and so on. The corporate structures make it possible for all of these experts to focus their energies on the development of a new product. Thus, by having talented people do a small part of the task very well and by integrating these specialized functions, the entire project can reach a level of excellence that no one man no matter how great his genius could hope to match.

The utilization of expert opinion becomes one of the most important and difficult tasks for the modern organization. Under ideal conditions a group of experts such as the one that will hear Herb's presentation should take the information he provides and integrate it with other evidence and clarification in order to formulate expert conclusions. They ought then to participate in a rigorous give-and-take discussion testing one another's advice. Too often, the expert's opinion is accepted without question.

Often, the testing of expert advice does not go beyond the previously mentioned estimates of the source's competence and credibility. Rating source credibility ought to be only preliminary to the testing of the content of the advice. One way to evaluate the substance of the advice is to check the accuracy of the factual material submitted as evidence. Another is to examine the way the argument moves from premises to conclusions. Chapter 9 examines reasoned discourse in greater detail. The criteria for sound reasoning suggested in that chapter ought to be applied to every important recommendation even though the source of the advice is a highly regarded expert on the subject in question.

Under ideal conditions, when the decision-making group has gathered the relevant factual information, heard the authorities draw their expert conclusions, and listened to the recommendations of the specialists on all questions relating to their specialties, the next step should be the previously mentioned free-for-all discussion in which everyone tests and challenges everyone else's conclusions and recommendations. A major difficulty in achieving the ideal condition is the tendency for experts to be defensive about their special prerogatives. If someone challenges an electronic engineer about electronics, he tends to brush off the challenge on the basis that only a fellow engineer is competent to discuss technical problems, for example. What often happens, therefore, is that a norm of behavior is established in an organization that "if you do not challenge my expertness by questioning my professional recommendations, I will recognize your authority in your area of specialization and not challenge you."

EVIDENCE AS SUPPORTING MATERIAL

The three major forms of evidence useful for the student of presentational speaking are statistical descriptions of facts, case studies of actual events, and testimony. Evidence performs two functions for the speaker. The first and primary function is the description of reality. This is provided by numerical statements about facts, detailed case study accounts of facts, and eyewitness descriptions of the facts. In short, the starting place for evidence is observation and description of physical and social reality. Herb Appleton needs to know what the situation is in terms of the problem he is investigating. Do housewives in appreciable numbers complain about the quality of the cake mixes? Does it take an average of ten days to process an order? Evidence provides the answers to questions such as these. The second use for evidence is to evaluate the agreed-upon reality, draw conclusions interpreting its significance, and submit recommendations. Testimony is the form of evidence that accomplishes the second function.

Presentational speaking in business and the professions puts a premium on sound evidence because the response of the environment often provides a clear-cut evaluation of success or failure. If Herb Appleton's recommendation is implemented and if cake mix sales continue to fall, he will be judged responsible for the failure. A mistaken or warped analysis of the facts can lead to group and organizational disaster. Under such circumstances the more absolute criteria for truth of factual statements and rigor in testing and using evidence take on added importance.

CLARIFICATION AS SUPPORTING MATERIAL

Hypothetical cases. Hypothetical case studies resemble real cases in all respects save that they are fictitious. The speaker creates imaginary situations to illustrate a point, clarify a complex analysis, or present abstract and esoteric principles or theories in concrete terms. Just as a good novel may illuminate human nature and human experience even though it contains characters who do not resemble any real persons living or dead and its plot consists of incidents that never happened, so can a good hypothetical case clarify a speaker's ideas. Since hypothetical cases are fictitious, they are not evidence and thus cannot be considered as proof. Hypothetical cases can, however, dramatize a central tendency or a general trend if they are developed by people who know the real facts intimately. If a speaker is using a hypothetical case in order to make concrete the general information already presented in statistical form, this should be made known to the audience. The case is then more than a fiction and becomes a technique to enable the audience to grasp the significance of the evidence it exemplifies. Often, a hypothetical case can reveal the implications of statistical data more accurately than a real case because a truly typical real case might be difficult to find.

Hypothetical cases are also useful for clarifying and adding interest because the speaker can tailor them to his purposes. The hypothetical case is often the best choice to clarify a concept because it does not require as extensive a search of materials as does the real case study and because the speaker may add or subtract details depending upon the point to be made and the time available without fear of distorting the facts. The hypothetical case is probably the most useful clarifying device available to the presentational speaker.

Analogy. Another important technique useful in refining and clarifying ideas for an audience is the *analogy*. An analogy is a similarity between two individuals, facts, things, or events upon which a comparison can be based. Analogies may be found by comparing and contrasting events drawn from the same class. Thus, an analogy might be found between the sales pattern of the Chocolate Delight Cake Mix and the Lemon Taffeta Cake Mix. Top management officials might discover an analogy in their experience with the merger with Timkin Toy and the proposed merger with Consolidated Electronics. A literal analogy is one in which the similarity is discovered to hold between two individuals, facts, things, or events drawn from the same class. Analogies can also be invented by rearranging unlikely individuals, facts, things, or events into patterns that reveal an unexpected or unusual similarity. When the ad agency copywriter named the new lemon cake "taffeta," he invented a similarity between the cake and a piece of cloth and asserted in his copy that the cake was "rich as taffeta." The fictitious or invented similarity between two things that are not, in fact, similar (the copywriter did not seriously suggest that anyone try to make a dress out of the lemon cake) is called a *figurative analogy*.

In an important sense the basic process by which man orders his perceptions, forms concepts, and categorizes his experience is by discovering similarities among events. In much the same fashion the most creative and ingenious attempts to communicate difficult emotions, feelings, and idiosyncratic experiences are often figurative analogies.

The prediction of future events from past experience is often based upon a literal analogy. The management of Minnesota Mills may discover after careful comparison and contrast of the two situations that the proposed merger with the electronics firm is, indeed, similar to the merger with the toy firm. They may then reason that they can predict a set of disastrous consequences resembling those that followed from merger with Timkin Toys should they merge with Consolidated Electronics. Reasoning by analogy, therefore, is to argue from known similarities to unknown similarities.

Thus, a literal analogy is an extended treatment of similar elements in two cases. If possible, the case or situation to be clarified should be compared to a similar case or situation that the majority of the audience know intimately. When Herb Appleton's friend who used to work with Herb at Universal Business Machines asks what it is like to work at Minnesota Mills, Herb can clarify his answer by pointing out similarities in fringe benefits, salary schedule, management style, working conditions, and physical equipment between Minnesota Mills and Universal Business Machines.

The figurative analogy has much less validity as a means of prediction. An executive may argue that for Minnesota Mills to merge with an electronics firm is like a major league ball player going on an African safari to hunt lions with his baseball bat. He may say that Minnesota Mills is in the big leagues as a milling company and has hit its share of home runs. He may urge Minnesota Mills to keep on doing what it knows best. He may suggest that if a ball player takes off for Africa with a ball bat trying to hit lions instead of baseballs, he's likely to get badly mauled. He may conclude, "As I see it, we'd be a lot better off if we didn't go hunting any lions like General Electric on a safari run by a little two-bit outfit like Consolidated Electronics and stick to hitting more home runs in our own ball park." The figurative analogy about ball players and lions compared to a merger of Minnesota Mills and Consolidated Electronics may add interest to the meeting and clarify the rigidity of the speaker's position, but as a bit of argument against the merger it does not have the stature of a literal comparison of the Timkin Toy and Consolidated Electronics capital structure, product lines, growth potential, and so on.

Figurative analogies are used sparingly in contemporary presentations. The spare shorthand style of today's business speaking does not lend itself to inventing colorful and unusual comparisons. Figurative analogies must be used with skill and good taste or they degenerate into the laughable as did the analogy about mergers and lion hunts. However, the paucity of figurative analogy in business and professional speeches is perhaps unfortunate. Used with discretion, they add spice and sparkle to what might otherwise be a relatively grim and dull message. Often, a good figurative analogy will clarify a difficult argument or concept more effectively than can any other rhetorical device.

Literal analogies cope directly with the realities of a situation. The speaker must exercise considerable care in their use, however, because unless contrasts as well as similarities are examined and weighed, predictions may be based upon a few superficial similarities while crucial differences are ignored. A typical argument from literal analogy states that for the past ten years there has been an upward trend of some variable and therefore, unless something is done, the trend will continue. The argument takes for granted that conditions affecting the variable in the next ten years will be the same as those in the past, an unwarranted assumption.

Figurative analogies are particularly useful in those presentational situations where a speaker is talking to an ingroup to inspire it to greater efforts, to build *esprit de corps,* a sense of group identity.

Narratives. Another important clarifying device is the *narrative.* Narratives are stories of events or experiences either true or fictitious. They may be long or short and deal with past events, present situations, or future possibilities. Generally in the presentation, narratives are used to clarify and to add interest. On occasion, however, the purpose of a narrative may be primarily amusement.

Good narratives for presentational speaking contain characterization, conflict, suspense, and a point directly applicable to the topic under discussion. A story requires characters to play the various parts. Stories usually concentrate on one central character who is sympathetic and draws the audience's interest. Usually, the main character has a clear object in view and his attempts to achieve his goal dictate the selection of incidents for the story. As the character strives to gain his objective, he meets obstacles that he does not expect. Some of the obstacles are of natural origin and some may be placed in his way by an antagonist, a bad guy who is working against the hero, and the result is a conflict which arouses suspense. In a good narrative the forces of good and evil ought to be equally balanced so the hero has a fighting chance, but a slight tipping of the scales in either direction can carry the day.

Characterization can be quickly accomplished by naming the characters in a narrative, supplying a few brief distinguishing comments, putting the characters in action, and having other people in the story respond to the characters in certain ways. Early in his presentation Herb might say the following in order to provide characterization for a narrative:

I have here in my hand a typical letter of complaint, one of 127 received last week, blasting our cake mixes. Apparently what happened was this. Mrs. Phil Templin, an attractive young matron and a newcomer to the village of Cedar Rapids, Iowa, was entertaining her bridge club for the first time. She was in a bit of a dither as to what to serve for refreshments until she saw our ad for Chocolate Pecan Delight in the June *Harper's Bazaar.* Early the morning of the party she walked two blocks to Ernie Silverthorne's Grocery and bought the two packages of Chocolate Pecan Delight that remained on his shelf.

She carefully followed directions and baked and frosted the cakes. That afternoon, she proudly served them to what apparently were the seven best cooks in Cedar Rapids. The result was a new taste experience, but not a taste treat. I think Betty Templin might have survived the disaster if Gladys Bockleheid hadn't smiled sweetly after a bite and said, "You must have made this yourself, dear. A cake like this couldn't come out of a package."

That evening when Mrs. Templin simmered down to the point where she could write us a letter, this is what she wrote. . . .

Conflict and suspense can result from any number of obstacles. Herb Appleton trying to solve the problem of cake mix sales might come in conflict with members of the distribution department. He might find it difficult to get adequate funds to make his investigation, or might run into difficulty from someone within his own team who begins to goldbrick or sabotage the operation. If we were to introduce conflict and suspense into our case study of the deteriorating cake mixes, it would soon take on the characteristics of a narrative.

Narratives may recount a factual event. True stories carry conviction and are often more impressive than fiction in a presentational speech. Quite often, however, actual events do not fall neatly into a good narrative pattern and the speaker may wish to modify the details of the story to improve its narrative quality. When telling of actual events, the speaker may base the story upon his personal experience or he may recount events as an experience of someone else. His conscience limits the amount of distortion he will introduce to make a good story. The personal-experience narrative is one of the most widely used and effective clarifying and amplifying techniques. A personal experience, if it is told well, can amuse, illustrate, clarify, convince, and present the speaker in an attractive light as a person of insight and humor.

A danger in using personal-experience narratives is that they may make the speaker appear egotistical and self-centered. A secondary problem is that personal-experience stories often require more time for the telling than the point they make will justify. Speakers tend to include unnecessary incidents and expressive detail in relating narratives.

An *anecdote* is a short narrative concerning a particular happening of an interesting or amusing nature. When the anecdote is amusing, it may also be called a *joke*. Serious anecdotes and jokes both tend to have a sudden and unexpected conclusion. In a joke the sudden surprise "twist" at the end is called the punch line because it is the point that should arouse a humorous response. In the more serious anecdote the twist at the end should reveal an insight or a point to be applied to the topic under discussion.

Parables are narratives about events seemingly unrelated to the topic but with an unusual appropriateness when the speaker points out the application. A famous lecturer of the turn of the century, Russell Conwell, gave a speech called "Acres of Diamonds" thousands of times. The basic narrative that formed the spine of the lecture was the story of an ancient Persian named Ali Hafed who was wealthy but grew discontented when he heard that with one diamond the size of his thumb he could purchase his entire country and that if he had nine diamonds he could place his children upon thrones through the influence of his great wealth. Ali Hafed sold all of his holdings and taking the proceeds traveled over the world searching for diamonds. He wandered the earth without success until he had reduced himself to poverty. He then drowned himself in the bay at Barcelona in Spain. Meanwhile, the man who bought Ali Hafed's farm led his camel one day into the garden for a drink, and as the camel drank, the farmer noticed a flash of light from the sand in the bottom of the stream. He had discovered the diamond mine of Golcanda which exc Kimberly itself. When delivering the lecture in Philadelphia drew the lesson from his parable that "you have 'acres of di Philadelphia right where you now live." He told his audience that "the opportunity to get rich, to attain unto great wealth, is here in Philadelphia now, within the reach of almost every man and woman who hears me speak tonight, and I mean just what I say."[1]

Another form of narrative is the *fable*. Fables are short stories designed to teach a moral and often have animals or inanimate objects as characters. The common phrase "sour grapes" comes from Aesop's fable about the fox who called the grapes he could not reach "sour."

Narratives as clarification are helpful because they add interest and excitement to a speech. They also serve to develop an appealing image for the speaker as an amusing and likable person. Generally, they serve as a positive suggestion to put the audience in a good mood to listen attentively and to predispose it to accept the speaker as a person.

Narrative material in the form of jokes and amusing personal experiences provides one of the major vehicles for humor in the presentational speech. Humor is a popular, useful, and hazardous technique of presentation. It is a form of indirect suggestion and is discussed in detail in Chapter 10.

Clarification by stylistic devices. An interesting paradox of business and professional communication results from the claim of many organizations that their communications should be utilitarian. Business and professional people often praise brevity, clarity, and objectivity as the best characteristics of good communication. They often, therefore, shun elegance, aptness, or beauty of language in oral and written reports, memorandums, and presentations. The paradox is that the same people who talk down stylistic flourishes in messages seem to crave verbal elegance. They often repeat the apt slogan or a memorable aphorism. They may hang a particularly striking maxim on the wall of the office or print it on their letterheads. An extreme example of this paradox is the archetype of the modern presentation, the television commercial. It exploits every avenue of visual communication, aims at being persuasive in the most economical fashion, yet best illustrates the advantages of stylistic artistry. Almost without exception television commercial copy relies upon the catchy jingle with reiteration and

1 Russell H. Conwell, *Acres of Diamonds* (New York, 1915), pp. 3-9.

restatement or a swinging slogan and alliterative word play to reinforce the message.

Certainly one of the basic devices for amplification of oral messages and clarifying their meaning is the use of reiteration. Reiteration is the device of repeating the same idea in another way either by presenting another case, supplementing the case with testimony, making the same point with narrative material, or simply repeating the idea in slightly different words.

Another of the highly effective devices of oral communication is repeating elements of the message in a rhythmic or patterned way. The child is charmed by a story or poem that repeats the same phrases or comments by characters over and over again. Music and poetry illustrate the charm of echoing sounds. The refrain in a song and the repetition of the last line of each stanza in certain poetic forms is a common form of repetition.

While reiteration and repetition may be ineffective in a written message, seeming to constitute unnecessary verbiage, these are necessary and useful parts of the spoken communication. Reiteration serves to give the audience time to absorb an idea and see some of its many implications and ramifications. Since the listener cannot go back over the material and read it again and again as can someone studying a written paragraph, the speaker can provide for somewhat the same effect by reiterating and repeating an idea several times.

Perhaps more important, reiterating an idea by submitting another form of support that makes the same point or supplying another illustration (either in the form of a case study, an analogy, or a narrative) may add layers of meaning to the bare outline or statement of the point. The presentation is analogous to motion pictures and television in the calculated juxtaposition of images and supporting material to develop complex concepts. One important film technique is that of the montage. Sergei Eisenstein, an early Russian cinematographer, was one of the masters of the montage technique. He viewed montage, the juxtaposition of different images in rapid succession, as the essence of the film. Eisenstein felt that by suggesting a complicated meaning from different approaches, now a shot of a line of soldiers' rifles at the ready and the bayonets fixed, cut to a crowd of frightened fleeing civilians, cut to a herd of charging cattle, cut to rifles firing, and so on, he could shape meanings within the audience. Eisenstein felt each image could push and mold the meanings within the viewer into closer and closer approximations of what the film director wanted him to perceive. In somewhat the same way a speaker can develop an idea in greater and greater complexity by reiterating a variety of illustrations.

In Conwell's "Acres of Diamonds" after the parable of Ali Hafed, he told the narrative of the man in California in 1847 who owned a ranch but heard that gold had been discovered in southern California so he sold his ranch to Colonel Sutter and left never to return. Of course, Colonel Sutter subsequently discovered gold on the ranch worth $38 million. Conwell next told the story of a man who owned a farm in Pennsylvania but wanted to go into the coal-oil business. The farmer had a cousin in Canada who was in the oil business. He wrote his cousin asking for employment. The cousin said he could not hire him until he was more knowledgeable on the subject. The farmer set about studying oil. When he was well informed, the cousin hired him and the man sold his farm for $833. The new owner of the farm went out to arrange for the watering of his cattle and discovered that the previous owner had put a plank across the brook at a sharp angle to hold back a scum through which the cattle would not drink. The man who sold out and went to Canada had for twenty-three years been damming back crude oil, and his farm subsequently became the center of a rich oil field. Conwell next told the story of a man in Massachusetts who left his homestead to go to Wisconsin in search of copper with the Superior Copper Mining Company. He was a graduate of Yale in mineralogy and a tutor at the time he left for Wisconsin. The new owner of the mineralogist's homestead discovered silver on the property.[2]

Conwell reiterated essentially the same idea by telling four different narratives and each reiteration added a dimension to the idea, in montage-like fashion. As a result, he was able to develop the point he was making.

In its simplest form reiteration consists of saying the same thing *in other words*. Quite often, simply rewording an idea will add a nuance that the audience finds enlightening.

Restatement is a repetition of the same words. The restatements that follow in quick succession serve primarily as emphasis. The use of restatement for emphasis is illustrated by the person making a presentation who says, "Gentlemen if we want to hold our share of the market in the next decade, we are going to do three things: first, we are going to have to develop our human resources; second, we are going to have to develop our human resources; and third, we are going to have to develop our human resources."

Restatement may also occur after some other material has intervened. Restatement then becomes something of a refrain commenting upon the previous material and reminding the audience that a number of items relate to the same basic notion. Thus, a speaker might begin with the assertion, "We must develop our human resources." He could then tell a personal-experience narrative and conclude with, "We must develop our human resources." Next he might develop a case study of a firm that failed because of lack of adequate personnel and conclude

[2] *Ibid.*, pp. 10–15.

that section of his presentation with, "We must develop our human resources."

Another stylistic supporting device is to borrow particularly apt sayings, sentiments, or verbal pronouncements from philosophers, poets, theologians, and novelists. In one sense the use of quotations is a form of testimony. But primarily, quotations function as stylistic devices of support. The speaker is using the talents of another to provide him with his material, but the function is much the same as if he himself had originated the material. (Of course, we must recognize that some positive suggestion about the speaker results from his quoting Aristotle or Confucius or Emerson.)

A final important stylistic way to support and clarify ideas in presentational speeches is by the use of distinctive phrases, catchwords, and terse sayings. An *aphorism* is a brief apt statement that embodies a general truth such as, "Nobody can make your mistakes for you." The test of a good aphorism is how often it is repeated and appreciated subsequently. Barnum's assertion that "there is a sucker born every minute" has proved itself an aphorism according to that standard. Other examples of aphorism would include: "The greatest enemy of communication is the illusion of it." "See it big and keep it simple." A *maxim* is an aphorism that contains advice as to how one should conduct himself. Organizations thrive on maxims and often display them prominently in offices, on letterheads, and on buildings. Examples of maxims would include: "Don't say it—display it." "Never say it—write it." "Talk it over—jot it down."

Aphorisms and maxims are often used to inspire to greater effort or to add meaning and significance to the organization's efforts. They are excellent for presentations of an inspirational nature.

A *slogan* is a catchy phrase that becomes a motto for a party, group, product, or manufacturer. "Better things for better living through electricity" might be a slogan for an electrical manufacturer. "Progress is our product" is another slogan for an industrial firm. Slogans serve both to build commitment from the members of the group using them as their motto and as positive suggestion for persuading the hostile or apathetic outsider to view the group more favorably or to buy its product.

Closely related to slogans are organizational names and titles. The importance of a good name or title to the person or the enterprise is widely recognized. New parents often spend hours trying to find a suitable name for their child. Automobile manufacturers search for model names with great care. Movie stars change their names to make them more attractive and euphonious. Every organization searches for a name for new programs and projects with considerable diligence because of the positive or negative suggestion inherent in a name.

Thus, industrial firms may call a new program "participative management" or "sensitivity training" or a "work improvement program." A
person developing a presentation relating to a change in established
routine or a new project or department must pay considerable attention to the development of suitable titles and slogans.

One interesting feature of stylistic development in organizations is
the use of acronyms as a naming device. An *acronym* is a word formed
from the initial letters of the words making up the official title of a
project, department, or organization. Thus, the Congress of Racial
Equality becomes CORE.

On occasion, organizations begin with an acronym that relates to
the purpose of the organization and then create the title by working
backward from a persuasive set of letters. The result is that urban
development organizations, charitable groups, and so on have acronyms like HOPE, ASK, and HELP. A group is well advised when
developing a title for a project or program to take considerable care to
assure that the inevitable acronym is desirable in itself, no matter how
desirable the full title may be. Some of our colleagues thought that the
title of a leading organization in speech and communication should be
changed to the Society for the Advancement of Communication Arts
and Sciences until they examined the acronym SACAS more carefully.

Closely related to acronyms is the practice of using the initial letters
of a name as a shorthand device. Thus, the Students for a Democratic
Society become the SDS and the Young Americans for Freedom become the YAF. Letters, numbers, and acronyms become, in some technical organizations, a form of positive suggestion. Long technical titles,
often abbreviated to the capital letters of each word, serve to remind
the listener of the importance and complexity of the project, program,
position, or organization. The space exploration program of the United
States illustrates the use of technical jargonese, for descriptive and
persuasive purposes very nicely. The Lunar Exploration Module is
really only a small drone space capsule connected to the main space
ship, but the words of Latin derivation in the phrase "Lunar Exploration Module" lend an aura of science and mystery that a name like
"Moon Search Buggy" would never manage. The Lunar Exploration
Module became a LEM in the everyday parlance of the insiders.
When the time came, however, for the LEM to star on television, its
name was changed to "Eagle."

Other more mundane examples of technical terms and titles for
persuasive purposes are furnished by the television commercial. If
ingredients in patent medicines, soaps, and toothpastes can be given
esoteric names that suggest great scientific and technical knowledge
and at the same time illustrate onomatopoeia, the persuasive impact is
often increased. Thus, a toothpaste that contains *fluoristan* or *chloro-*

phyll or a soap powder that has *enzyme action* may seem more mysterious and powerful than products with mundane ingredients like *sugar* and *fats*.

SUMMARY

Nonstatistical forms of support may be divided into evidence and clarification. Evidence is designed to furnish grounds for belief. Proof is the sufficient marshaling of evidence to achieve conviction or acceptance of a proposition. Evidence consists of both oral and written testimony and things such as prototypes, models, and demonstrations. Clarification is designed to enlighten the listener and is aimed primarily at achieving understanding.

The case study is one of the most useful forms of nonstatistical evidence. Cases may form the bulk of the evidence in support of contentions for which statistic information is inappropriate or they may be used to supplement statistical evidence.

Testimony may relate primarily to facts observed and their interpretation or to recommendations as to policy or programs. The best testimony as to facts always comes from eyewitness accounts. When experts testify as to inferences to be drawn from facts or as to policy, their ability and training must be evaluated as well as their biases, familiarity with the facts, and willingness to give good advice.

Hypothetical case studies resemble real cases in all respects, save they are fictitious. Hypothetical cases are not evidence in the same sense that real cases are, but they can serve to reveal the implications of statistical data and they are extremely useful for clarifying and adding interest to a speech.

Another important device for clarification is the analogy. A literal analogy is one in which a similarity is discovered to hold between two individuals, facts, things, or events drawn from the same class. A figurative analogy is a comparison invented to show a similarity between an unexpected or unusual pair of events. Literal analogies may be used as a basis for predicting future events and as a form of reasoning from the known to the unknown. Figurative analogies are not to be used as reasoning but do serve to instruct and amuse an audience. If figurative analogies are apt and well constructed, they can often illuminate and clarify a complicated concept or situation.

Narratives are a class of important clarifying devices that include true and fictitious stories. True stories may be personal experiences of the speaker or historical events that he testifies are true. Fictitious stories may include anecdotes, jokes, parables, allegory, and fables.

A final way to clarify ideas in a presentation is by stylistic devices such as reiteration, restatement, quotations, aphorisms, maxims, slogans, and names.

QUESTIONS FOR DISCUSSION AND REVIEW

1. What is meant by the concept of *clarification?* Of *evidence?*
2. What are some of the advantages and disadvantages of the hypothetical case study when compared to the real case study in providing understanding and proof?
3. What are some of the uses of testimony to provide amplification for presentations?
4. In what way does a witness's image affect the audience's response to his testimony?
5. What is the difference between a figurative and a literal analogy?
6. How might analogies be used for clarification and proof?
7. What are some things to keep in mind when considering using narrative material in a presentation?
8. What is the difference between reiteration and restatement?
9. What is an aphorism? A maxim? A slogan? An acronym?
10. How might a person go about testing the evidence presented by testimony?

REFERENCES AND SUGGESTED READINGS

BETTINGHAUS, ERWIN P. *Message Preparation: The Nature of Proof.* Indianapolis: Bobbs-Merrill, 1966.

MILLER, GERALD R., and THOMAS R. NILSEN, eds. *Perspectives on Argumentation.* Chicago: Scott, Foresman, 1966.

MILLS, GLEN E. *Reason in Controversy: On General Argumentation,* 2nd ed. Boston: Allyn and Bacon, 1968.

NEWMAN, ROBERT P., and DALE R. NEWMAN. *Evidence.* Boston: Houghton Mifflin, 1969.

WALTER, OTIS M., and ROBERT L. SCOTT. *Thinking and Speaking.* 2nd ed. New York: Macmillan, 1969.

CHAPTER NINE

REASONING
AS A METHOD OF
PRESENTATION

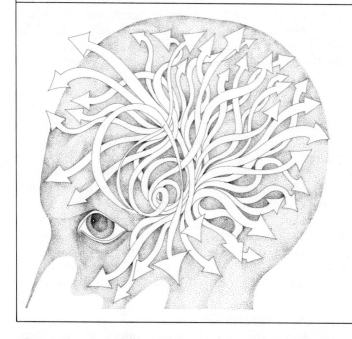

The reader is already well along in his study of reasoned persuasion because of the previous chapters on methods of support. However, these chapters were concerned with evidence and clarification primarily, and the problem of *interpreting* evidence in a sound fashion—i.e., reasoning about it—was not treated in detail. The present chapter examines the application of the critical-thinking abilities of people to the formulation, transmission and reception of messages, and in particular, of presentations. It attempts to demonstrate that good presentational speaking is, and should be, carefully reasoned. Methods of implementing sound reasoning in purposeful communication both to inform and to persuade are explained and demonstrated.

THE PROBLEM OF IDENTIFYING AND EVALUATING
REASONED ELEMENTS IN A MESSAGE

A valuable bit of advice to the person who would speak or write accurately and be understood comes from Ralph Nichols, an authority on the teaching of listening. Nichols tells the thoughtful communicator, "Illustrate, don't explain." Explanation tends to become abstract and dull, while providing an actual case tends to be interesting and considerably more specific. Therefore, to be as specific as possible and minimize reader boredom we begin by examining a case study of the difficulty of identifying and evaluating reasoned elements in a message.

In May, 1960, the famous "U2 Spy Plane Incident" occurred. On the first of May the Soviet Union announced that it had shot down a U.S. plane within its borders. The United States denied that any plane destroyed by the Russians was there for the purpose of spying. On May 7 the Russians announced that they had an American U2 plane, brought to earth six hundred miles inside the USSR, and its pilot, Francis Gary Powers.

Powers was a prisoner of the Soviet Union for twenty-one months. Upon his release and return to the United States his conduct as a "patriotic" spy was much discussed and disputed. Finally his employer, the Central Intelligence Agency, and a congressional committee agreed that he had conducted himself appropriately, and assured Mr. Powers that he would receive $50,000 in back pay.

Among the reactions to the news that Francis Gary Powers had been cleared of possible misconduct was the following newspaper editorial:

SPYING ONLY FOR PROFIT?
Francis Gary Powers emerged from his sessions with the Central Intelligence Agency and congressional committeemen with a slightly improved reputation—and with assurances he'll get his $50,000 in back pay. But his appearance still did not answer all of the questions that had been raised about his performance as a U2 pilot and his conduct while a prisoner of the Soviet Union.

The slight improvement in his reputation stems from the CIA statement commending his conduct, the board of inquiry's acceptance of it, his own testimony explaining it, and congressmen's favorable reaction to him.

The CIA cleared up—at least for the record—one controversial facet of Powers' conduct when it asserted that his contract did not require him to commit suicide. The poison needle he carried was to have been used, the CIA said, only if he were "subjected to torture or other circumstances which in his discretion warranted the taking of his own life."

In addition, the CIA contended that Powers and other U2 pilots were under contract to "surrender without resistance and adopt a cooperative attitude toward their captors" if evasion did not appear feasible and capture appeared imminent. The CIA said that under their contract the pilots were free to tell the full truth about their mission, with the exception of certain specifications of the aircraft, and even to admit their CIA employment and nature of their mission.

In its statement, the CIA also cleared Powers of any blame for his failure to destroy his aircraft. The CIA accepted Powers' story that he had been unable to set off an explosive charge in the plane after he had opened the canopy over the cockpit. It contended that a study of the debris of the plane and testimony of the Russian witnesses at Powers' trial in Moscow supported the pilot's own story.

It might still be argued that as a patriotic American, Powers should have committed suicide to prevent the plane, or its contents, or his person from falling into Soviet hands. But he was a "spy by contract," not because of patriotic motives. So perhaps no more should have been expected of him than performance according to the letter of his contract.

Even though Powers now has been cleared of any contract violation, we suspect that the CIA still is not telling all it knows about this episode. And we hope it is not. It did concede that it had additional information "from confidential sources"—whatever they may be—but the job of an agency such as the CIA is the collecting—not the making public—of information essential to the security of the United States.

It is to be hoped, however, that the CIA also enlists Americans who are more heroic figures than Powers and who have a higher purpose than simply spying for personal profit.[1]

The first question that probably comes to the mind of the reader trying to think critically about the editorial is, "What does it say?" This is an excellent question. Before any judgment can be made about the quality of reasoning in an argument, the point to be supported must be located, with some precision. As is often the case in spirited controversy, the conclusions reached in the editorial are indirectly stated and consequently are less than obvious.

Once a point made by the editorial writer is located and phrased in clear simple language, the search for the reasoning used to justify the point can begin. Here the problem of the consumer is to set aside the irrelevant and locate the small, hard core of common sense that relates to the conclusions the writer would like us to believe.

When a view as controversial as the one in this editorial is printed, criticism is generated more or less automatically. "Letters to the Editor" are a well-accepted means of critical response in the press of the Western world. So, before suggesting a system of analysis appropriate to tasks such as evaluating the sample editorial, let us look at the letters that appeared in the *Minneapolis Tribune* six days later.

[1] *Minneapolis Tribune*, March 8, 1962, p. 4.

TO THE EDITOR:

Referring to your "slightly" biased editorial of March 8, "Spying Only for Profit?" I fail to see any merit to your incongruous comments, unless it be the fact that you took up space which might otherwise have contained something even less enlightening.

The circumstances in which Francis Gary Powers finds himself may or may not be the result of imprudent judgment on his part, but we, the people (you included), must give this man the benefit of the doubt in view of the CIA and congressional findings.

What right, then, do you have to try to agitate the feelings of a public for whom this man was risking his life? Certainly he was spying. He was spying for you and me! The fact that he was doing so for "personal profit" as you put it, is of little significance, really. You stated that he was a "spy by contract," not because of conviction and not because of patriotic motive. Who are you to make such an asinine statement? How do you know what his motives were, or are? Are you less dedicated to your job because you earn a salary?

Powers was cleared of irrational and un-American behavior, and in accordance with our judicious way of life he is free to continue his job. Apparently he was not interested in being a dead hero, and what's more, he was not required to become one. I'm taking issue here, not with the justification or condemnation of Powers' actions, but rather with your right to stir up public opinion against his vindication.

I am not disputing your right to your opinion. I'm disputing your use of the editorial page to air your dissentious perspective of an unfortunate situation of which, I'm sure, you know very little more than has already been publicized.   *Dr. K. L. Strauss, Fairmont, Minn.*

TO THE EDITOR:

Certainly $25,000 a year is not an unusual sum to pay a civilian spy during peacetime for a very dangerous job. And it is unbelievable that the CIA should make suicide mandatory unless absolutely necessary for national security reasons.

If Powers had failed to follow instructions by cooperating with the Russians it is possible the incident may have caused even more serious reactions than it did.

On top of this, it strikes me as poor grace for a writer who is snug in the bosom of Minneapolis to get sarcastic about anyone who is doing a job that only one in a million would tackle or be qualified to do.

        D. H. Kotz, Mpls.

TO THE EDITOR:

I take serious exception to your implications regarding suicide. Although you qualify your statement with "it still might be argued," the conclusion you leave is that a "patriotic" spy would have used the needle.

For most patriotic Americans there is a higher authority that forbids self-destruction. We are not our own. We are bought with a price. We are to glorify God with our bodies, which are God's, not our own. The cowardly escape of temporal suffering compares with eternal punishment which suicide invites.   *H. C. Gravrock, Pastor, Mineota, Minn.*

TO THE EDITOR:

Your editorial on Francis Gary Powers was simply nauseating. It was very surprising to see how brave you are, writing from behind your marble facade. I wonder how patriotic you'd be at 68,000 feet over Russia.

I don't think the people believe that Powers was any less patriotic than anyone else. Whatever Powers' motives were, it takes courage, fortitude, bravery and all the rest to be a spy on such a mission.

You state that he spied for profit. This is certainly not clear at all. Did you interview Powers? Did you ask him? Are you judge and jury? Don't we all work for some profit? Are you serving the public interest here? I doubt it.

In Powers' behalf, he was a good flier, had 1,000 hours of flying time, fulfilled his contract according to the CIA, refused to divulge names of fellow U2 pilots, bore up well under intensive questioning, attempted to destroy his plane twice, and spent 21 months in a Russian prison. I think his record stands by itself.   *F. M. Gary, Minneapolis*

TO THE EDITOR:

There is, no doubt, much more to the Powers story than can be printed. If this were not the case we would not have an effective secret service.

However, your editorial on the subject is a most smug, pompous and unfairly accusing bit of writing, I think.

Powers was engaged in this work to earn a living. To call it "spying for profit" is a sneaking innuendo. Did you write your editorial for "profit"? or did you write it in the course of earning your living?

It is to be hoped, you say, that the CIA can enlist Americans who "are more heroic figures than Powers." Who are you to cast such a literary stone?   *G. McKnight, Wayzata, Minn.*

TO THE EDITOR:

When you state that Powers emerged from his session with the CIA with a slightly improved reputation you are insinuating that his reputation had been damaged. By whom?

Certainly not by the public. Certainly not by the facts. The press is guilty of condemning this man before the facts were known. I, for one, resent this insidious method of reporting.

Spying is an unsavory business but a necessary one. We can be thankful there are those who will accept such perilous assignments. We all accept our contracts for profit. Some are less glamorous than others, but who are we to judge the motives of those entering on an assignment?

How would you have conducted yourself under such circumstances? I hope as well as Powers. *T. Lorenz, Mpls.*[2]

Within the spirited series of letters from these responsive readers is their interpretation of what the editorial said *to them,* and the reasons and evidence causing them to disagree. However, in order to extract the "hard core of common sense," that is, the reasoned content of criticism, we must first set aside the colorful suggestive elements in the letters. Calling the editorial "biased" and labeling the comments therein "incongruous" is persuasive but nonlogical. Attacks upon the editorial writer as a person—for example, "Who are you to make such an asinine statement?" and ". . . it is poor grace for a writer who is snug in the bosom of Minneapolis to get sarcastic about . . ."—are irrelevant to the argument, though capable of stimulating vigorous response. Elements of suggestion are the parts of a message other than conclusions, reasoning, and evidence. Emotive or "loaded" language is a type of suggestion, and extracting reasoned discourse from a message requires substituting "report language" for "loaded words." This is not to say that only the reasoned content is important. It is to say that the quality of reasoned communication can be effectively assessed only if suggestive elements are as much as possible set aside. Otherwise, these interfere with a systematic scrutiny of the thoughtful, sensible ingredients in communication.

One possible extraction of the major reasoned elements in the letters and editorial follows. First, let us state the points in the editorial as the letter writers interpreted them, with the reason and evidence the editorial writer supplied in their support.

EDITORIAL CLAIMS AND SUPPORT
1. Powers' reputation was damaged by his conduct as a captured U2 pilot
   Because (no evidence given)
2. Powers should have committed suicide
   Because he might thereby have prevented his plane from being captured
3. Powers was not motivated by patriotism
   Because he was paid $25,000 a year

Using the same process of setting aside suggestive elements and seeking out major claims with logically related support, the letters to the editor can be found to challenge the reasoning of the editorial as follows.

[2] All letters to the editor quoted here appeared in the *Minneapolis Tribune,* March 14, 1962, p. 4.

LETTERS TO THE EDITOR CLAIMS AND SUPPORT

1. We are obliged by our system of justice to consider Powers innocent

    Because he was cleared by the CIA and the committee of inquiry

2. The editorial is unfair to Powers

    Because an individual cleared in a fair trial should not be condemned without new evidence

3. It was proper that Powers should have been well paid

    Because people are normally paid for their work according to its difficulty and risk

4. Powers should be assumed to be patriotic

    Because undertaking high risk for one's country is consistent with patriotism

5. Powers should not have "used the needle"

    Because human beings should not commit suicide

The above condensation of reasoned discourse is far from comprehensive. Even so, if the reader will accept as illustrative this version of the communicative interaction, he will probably admit that the extracted version clarifies the disagreement between the letters and the editorial. Reducing an argument to a skeleton of rationality is termed *briefing*, and the product of the briefing process is labeled, logically, the *brief*. So the extraction above produced a brief of the editorial and a separate brief of responses to it.

In the format of a brief a claim is stated as a complete sentence, followed by its support. Either the word "because" or the word "since" links the support to the claim, to remind a reader that support is proof for the claim. The skeleton nature of the brief permits easy scrutiny of the relationship between any claim and the reasons and evidence given for it, and among the claims themselves.

Briefing is not only an aid to identifying and evaluating reasoned elements in a message. In planning a presentation, building a brief is the short cut to a tightly organized, well-supported message. It is infinitely easier to refine and rearrange skeletonized thought units than to juggle whole paragraphs. Minimizing elements of suggestion during structural planning is beneficial also. Once the wording and sequence of claims and the nature of support for each are reasonably fixed, the elaboration into the complete talk is much more orderly than would otherwise be the case. If the editorial and letter writers above had gone to the trouble of briefing their messages as a first step, a resulting sense of order and progression would have increased their impact. When a serious persuasive purpose is to be served by any unit of communication, briefing is an efficient means of selecting and arranging materials.

THE PROPOSITION AS A KEY ELEMENT IN PRESENTATION

What has been referred to as a "claim," a point to be proved by a message unit, is more generally known as a "proposition." A presentation typically has a central proposition and one or more subordinate propositions. When the subordinate propositions are supported and accepted, they in turn become support for the central proposition. Great importance attaches to the formulation and arrangement of propositions. Language choices become critical.

The decision to use relatively abstract or relatively specific language is a particularly difficult one. To improve our ability to structure propositions for optimum effectiveness in a particular situation we need to know how to word a recommendation in a relatively more abstract or in a relatively more concrete form.

Language and abstraction–concreteness. Abstraction–concreteness is an important dimension of language. Because complete knowledge of all events is impossible to transmit or obtain, any sample of language will fall somewhere on the continuum between abstraction (bits of information sacrificed for applicability to a large number of events, e.g., "Many fools run for public office") and concreteness (number of applicable events sacrificed for inclusion of many bits of information, e.g., "Mr. Gulch, who couldn't pass the eighth grade and who spends 90 percent of his income on drinking and gambling, is running for the state legislature from the sixteenth district"). Truth–falsity is another dimension.

As we move to more abstract expression, we include:
1. More events.
2. Less information.
As we move to more concrete expression, we include:
1. Fewer events.
2. More information.
Thus, we might say:
1. Abstraction is less about more.
2. Concreteness is more about less.

Purpose and propositions. Although purpose and proposition are both related to desired audience response, the former tends to be more abstract and may be outside the control of the persuader. In Radio Moscow programming, the purpose of, for example, improving Americans' attitudes toward the Soviet Union is more abstract than propositions about education, family life, and so on, which might be used in developing the message.

Support of a proposition is more concrete than either the purpose or the proposition. Although relatively more abstract material may appear to support a proposition, it is not support unless it is made more concrete than the proposition. For example, the proposition "Taxes on business are unreasonably high" is *not* supported by the generalization "government is robbing the entrepreneur."

Moral and propositions.   A proposition is likewise not a value abstracted from a message by a member of the audience (listener or reader). For example, a persuadee listening to a persuader with an intent no more abstract than seeking blood donors might conclude: "It is good to help those in distress." Such a value resembles the moral sometimes appended to stories for children.

A proposition is related to a message unit by being only as abstract as is necessary to summarize the unit. It should be as concrete as possible without being as concrete as the support.

To summarize:

1. The purpose of a message is the manner in which the persuader wants the audience to respond to the over-all message—his intent.
2. Propositions summarize the significance of message units as concretely as possible.
3. A moral is considerably more abstract than either purpose or proposition; it draws a conclusion that is a judgment of value from the message.

The dimensions of concreteness–abstractness are shown diagrammatically in Figure 9.1.[3]

THE EFFECTIVE WORDING OF PERSUASIVE PROPOSITIONS

Reasoned elements in a message depend upon clearly worded propositions. The proposition or claim is a concise and precise statement of what the persuader wishes the receiver to believe or to do as a result of his persuasion. Eight criteria of a good proposition are helpful guidelines toward realizing maximum benefit from thoughtful use of propositions to this end.

A good proposition is a complete declarative sentence.   While fragments of sentences may have headline value, a phrase only sug-

[3] The above material, from "Language and Abstraction–Concreteness" through and including Figure 9.1, is taken from "Abstraction–Concreteness and Propositions," an unpublished paper by Lois Bursack, written at the University of Minnesota in 1968.

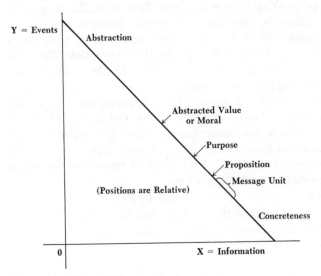

Figure 9.1   Slope of Abstraction–Concreteness

gests an idea while a sentence says something about it. "Recognize Red China" is unsatisfactory as a proposition because it fails to specify who, when, and how, details that are important in determining response to the recommendation. "The United States should extend official recognition to Red China as soon as possible" provides a substantially more complete base for discussion.

"Inefficient committees" suggests in a vague and general way that the speaker will indict the use of committees in some manner but it fails to tell us, for example, whether he will criticize the committee system in general, or committees as used for certain purposes in an organization. "Poor planning makes committees inefficient in Research and Development at ABC Corporation" pins down the point he may wish to make much more satisfactorily.

A good proposition is as concrete as possible. Some complete declarative sentences are little better than fragments. "We need loyalty oaths" is indeed complete as a sentence, but it fails to meet the requirement of specificity or concreteness. Before the desirability of loyalty oaths can be considered seriously, they must be placed in a limited context of real people and situations. "Loyalty oaths should be administered to all public school teachers at all levels of education" is much more concrete than the first loyalty oath statement and much more likely to contribute to a meeting of minds of people discussing issues involved.

A properly worded proposition expresses a single idea. The principle of concentrating upon one idea at a time to maximize clear thinking and minimize confusion explains this criterion for writing propositions. "Air pollution and organized crime are major problems in U.S. cities" is a double proposition because two essentially unrelated topics are combined. Such a duality should be divided into two separate statements. A series of single claims is easier to present and easier to follow than a shorter list of multiple propositions.

The temptation to write multiple propositions is great when the ideas involved are closely related. "If you want to lose weight safely, don't go to a 'fat doctor' who prescribes sacks of potent pills that are dangerous, but rather see your family doctor." This statement seems to many at first reading to be a single idea. It incorporates many nonessential elements that prevent clear reception of the message. Actually, only one idea is needed for the argument. "Your family doctor can help you plan a safe weight reduction program" covers this area of discussion and permits the persuader to talk about "fat doctors" as evidence that at least most overweight people should turn to family physicians for help.

Propositions should be written in report language. The double proposition about losing weight cited above contains several terms that violate this criterion. For example, "fat doctors" and "sacks of potent pills that are dangerous" are connotative phrases and tend to produce an immediate, unthinking response of rejection. "Report language" in contrast is carefully selected to be objective and avoid triggering prejudices and emotions.

Sometimes, loaded language almost totally obscures issues by arousal of intense emotive reaction. When done intentionally, this phenomenon is known as "slanting." By careful choice of words a proposition may be slanted vigorously in either a positive or negative direction. For example, the contention that "the employers are participating in union activities" in a mimeographed meeting notice was phrased, "The phony and slimy attempts by the bosses to besmirch and discredit the Union and the health and welfare corporation in their mumbo jumbo questionnaires as well as their forced 'captive employee' office calls are criminal." When slanting becomes extreme, as in this instance, the actuality referred to is almost totally inaccessible. A similarly drastic positive slanting could produce this version of the same proposition: "Company officials are generously offering free advice and aid to employee self-help projects in the interest of providing more beneficial services to their loyal members." Again, reading the positively slanted proposition provides little information concerning the facts of the case.

Extremes in slanting are not likely to occur in presentations designed to be reasoned and thoughtful. However, the zeal that produces eloquence often generates either an unconscious loading or a slanting that seems justifiable and necessary to its author. "The high price of food is caused by unwarranted farm price supports." "The cities of St. Paul and Minneapolis should purchase the inefficient Twin City Rapid Transit Company." In these propositions the words "unwarranted" and "inefficient" can be said to "beg the question." Accepting them predisposes acceptance of the propositions, regardless of the merit of arguments pro and con. Loading factors like these create difficulties as great as the problem of answering the well-known trick question, "Have you stopped beating your wife?"

Propositions should omit reasons and explanation.   Since the claim or proposition is the most economical statement of intended belief or action, reasoning, evidence, and elaboration are never included. But these tend to intrude, as shown in this example: "The great humanitarian stance of many members of the New Left is fallacious because it is the result of fear, hate, and lack of citizen responsibility on the part of its advocates."

The major defect in the example is inclusion of the "because" clause, which consists of material in support of the proposition. A second defect is intentional or accidental loading caused by including the unnecessary adjective "great." If this proposition were reworded to put it into acceptable form, it would read simply, "The humanitarian stance of many members of the New Left is fallacious."

Figurative or colloquial language is inappropriate in a proposition. Many a heated discussion has been unproductive because its subject was expressed in figurative or colloquial terms. "Communism is like a colony of ants" is an attractive analogy that evaporates when one attempts to ascertain precisely what it means. "Only a cat on the near side of the generation gap can turn on modern youth" is a statement couched in slang that fluctuates in meaning from person to person, time to time, and place to place.

Even subtle figurative usages blur the meaning in an otherwise definite proposition. Consider "Philosophy courses are more than a mental exercise" and "The U.S. will be doomed unless it reverses its traditional self-view as the world's savior." Mental exercises are a loose entity, and reversing a traditional self-view is difficult to envision, particularly when it is of the United States as world savior. Metaphors make these propositions unclear.

The reason any figure or colloquialism is undesirable in a proposition is that the statement is more abstract with it than without it. Since good propositions are as concrete as possible, the use of colloquial and figurative language in them is seldom if ever justified.

A well-worded proposition assumes a definite burden of proof.   As a statement of intent, a proposition in persuasion must necessarily specify a belief or an action that is not currently acceptable to its receivers. If the objective of a communicator is something his audience already believes or would do anyway, without his message, he cannot be said to be persuading, and no purpose is served by his act of communication. The obligation to word a proposition so it requires a change of belief or action is called "burden of proof."

Burden of proof is always in terms of a particular topic, audience, and situation. Typically, the persuader first studies the current attitude of the audience toward his recommendation. Then he estimates how far he can reasonably expect to "move" it (change its attitudes and beliefs) with his appeal. He then words his proposition to express this calculated goal. If his is an action recommendation, he designs the nature of the requested act by deciding what he can reasonably expect his audience to be willing to do, once it has understood his message. He words his claim to state this action objective.

An ever-present pitfall is the tendency of many persuaders to assign themselves an excessive burden of proof. A recommendation should be examined thoughtfully to assure that, for a particular audience and circumstance, its burden of proof is substantial but not beyond reason. Trying to do more than can be done accomplishes little. And since the persuader defines his own goal, failure from overestimating one's persuasive potential can be particularly punishing.

Propositions should be worded positively. One good reason for avoiding the word "not" in a proposition is the tendency people have when told *not* to do something, to want to do it. Probably this explains why positive suggestion is generally conceded to be more persuasive than negative suggestion. Wording a recommendation in the affirmative thus removes at least one roadblock to its acceptance.

But is it possible to word all claims positively? By and large it is possible, although in a few instances converting a negative wording to a positive form may be prohibitively awkward. Let us see how some sample propositions, originally worded in the negative, can "accent the positive."

"The United States should not expand its space program" becomes "The United States should restrict its space program to present levels."

"Capital punishment is not a deterrent to crime" can be worded "Capital punishment should be abolished."

"Society is not to blame for the decay of our democracy" although figurative and abstract can be worded affirmatively "Forces other than society are to blame for the decay of our democracy."

With ingenuity almost all negative propositions can be changed to positive wordings with negligible distortion. In addition to the benefits of positive suggestion, the change avoids some confusion should the recommendation be disputed. When one argues against a "not" proposition, he contends that the negative position is not the case, and "not not" phrasings muddy the arena of argument. It is much cleaner and neater to advance an affirmative position and make it possible for the contrasting view to be designated by a single negation.

PLANNING THE REASONED CONTENT OF A PRESENTATION

Hit-or-miss arranging of logically related information is the result of myopic planning procedures. The author of such a message is unable to see beyond one piece of information and its interpretation. He cites an example and draws a conclusion, gives some numerical data and another conclusion to interpret the numbers, and after projecting a trend into the future, he concludes once again. Each fragment may be closely reasoned while his over-all impact is negligible, because the parts are not clearly interrelated. He makes a series of effective sub-points but the big picture fails to emerge. For evidence and reasoning to attain a cumulative effect, the ingredients in a reasoned appeal must be articulated so that one point builds upon another, and these in turn serve as foundation for a third. The structure of the presentation should be assembled without a missing or unneeded building block.

Essential Information	Reasons and Support for Reasons	Qualified Proposition
		Exceptions
Necessary Explanation 1. 2. 3. 4.		

Figure 9.2   Unit Plan for Rational Presentation

To build a logic-tight structure that incorporates a variety of sub-points and supporting materials requires a *system* for arranging in a visible and orderly fashion every element needed to advance a major point. The layout presented in Figure 9.2, which often requires an outsize sheet of paper, permits the builder of a message to see the relationships among all parts of his argument.[4] He can then eliminate

[4] The Unit Plan for Rational Presentation is an adaptation of the model of argument in Stephen Toulmin, *The Uses of Argument* (Cambridge, England, 1958), chap. 5.

the nonessential, emphasize the relatively more important, and improve the integration of all elements in a complex rational unit. The skeleton of the unit plan reveals the basic strategy of the system. After a few suggestions for applying the layout, we will look at a sample structure that shows how diverse elements in the network of reasoning become unified.

HOW TO USE THE UNIT PLAN FOR RATIONAL PRESENTATION

Perhaps the most important suggestion for using the unit plan effectively is this: Begin with the proposition. The claim or proposition states the desired outcome of the presentation in terms of an action response or a specific belief. Above all else, effective persuasion is goal-oriented, so specifying the intended result rather precisely at the beginning of planning creates a frame of reference in which all materials used can be related and focused.

"Qualifying" the proposition increases its precision. The difference between "each and every" and "by and large" claims is shown by the qualifiers used. "Probably" and "certainly" are qualifiers, as are "always" and "usually." A properly worded proposition always incorporates a qualifier that is carefully chosen to assume a sufficient burden of proof without going beyond available means of support. The good qualifier makes a claim both believable and provable to the contemplated audience.

When the message builder is satisfied with his qualified proposition, he sets about accumulating essential information. He asks himself what evidence will best contribute to the credibility of his proposition in the minds of his listeners. Attempting to be extremely selective, he notes on his planning sheet a minimum number of facts and assumptions. Later, if more information is needed, he can collect only what is required to complete his pattern. The selective, "bare bones" approach to listing items of essential information is recommended because of a universal tendency to assemble unneeded information and the confusion caused by a surplus of little-related facts.

The next step is to check out the adequacy of essential information by filling in the middle column, "reasons and support for reasons." Reasons interpret information. Whenever a reason is not self-evident, support for it is supplied, attached to the reason by "because." If essential information is adequate, and the reasons are properly structured, the qualified proposition will follow as a conclusion, without other basic elements of communication having to be supplied.

As the arrangement of proposition, reasons, and information is gradually improved by selecting better evidence and rearranging and rewording reasons and their support, the planner asks himself repeatedly, "What will be unclear or difficult for my audience?" By assuming the point of view of a listener, he finds that certain explanatory materials add significance and make basic points easier to grasp. He notes these items as "necessary explanation" in his plan.

Now the author of the message turns back to his starting point. Can the qualified proposition be improved so that it states his point better and has more persuasive potential? Usually, the process of building a unit of rational presentation changes the author's perspective of his assignment enough so that he finds it desirable to reword his proposition. The perfect proposition is not likely to be achieved. Other things being equal, the more a proposition is rewritten, the better the final product will be. Particularly, simplicity and clarity are enhanced by rewriting.

Finally, the plan is completed by noting any exceptions that might invalidate the conclusion. Often there are possibilities, usually of an unlikely nature, which if true would negate the entire line of reasoning in the unit. The thoughtful planner may or may not wish to include them in his presentation. But he certainly makes them a part of his plan, to protect against being unpleasantly surprised by an unanticipated and damaging exception at the time of the presentation.

To make the unit concrete we are including in Figure 9.3 a sample structure designed to argue that cigarette manufacturers should be permitted to omit health warnings on their packages. Read the plan in the order of its preparation: first the Qualified Proposition, then the Essential Information, then the Reasons and Support for Reasons, and finally, the Exception and Necessary Explanation items. The parts of the structure will fall into place neatly, each related to every other part, and to the whole.

Most presentations incorporate several units of approximately this level of complexity. Occasionally, a single unit will encompass the evidence and reasoning involved. More often two or three, or as many as four or five such layouts, are necessary. These become the central themes and the foundation pillars on which the presentation rests. When these are arranged so that interlocking takes place, the resulting structure is indeed impressive. The unit plan is a specialized form of the brief, one that has great utility as an aid in preparing closely reasoned presentations.

The speaker with a completed unit plan will proceed to implement it by first selecting a pattern of organization (Chapter 6), then evolving it into a speech of presentation by arranging and balancing his statistical and nonstatistical means of support (Chapters 7 and 8), incorporating appropriate devices of suggestion (Chapter 10), and finally, deciding upon audio-visual materials to be utilized (Chapter 11). The well-built unit plan protects the speaker against loose ends

Essential Information	Reasons and Support for Reasons	Qualified Proposition
1. Liquor bottles carry no warning. 2. Cola bottles carry no warning. 3. Cigarette packages carry a warning. 4. U.S. agencies should be consistent in requiring warnings on harmful products.	1. Liquor is potentially harmful because of alcoholism, heart trouble, loss of control. 2. Cola is potentially harmful because it is addictive and causes diabetes. 3. If cigarettes should carry a warning, then cola and liquor should also. 4. But cola and liquor carry no warning: Therefore: Qualified Proposition	Cigarette manufacturers should probably be permitted to omit health warnings from their packages. **Exception** Unless cigarettes are substantially more harmful than other products without warnings.

Necessary Explanation

1. The federal government has no obligation to protect citizens from any and all harmful products.
2. Information about the damage done by harmful products is unreliable and scarce.

Figure 9.3   Unit Plan for Rational Presentation of Argument that Cigarette Manufacturers Should Probably Be Permitted to Omit Health Warnings from Their Packages

and unsupported conclusions. It guarantees that all major points are dealt with sensibly and arranged in a proper sequence. Unity, coherence, and selective emphasis are the consequence, yielding a speech that is easy to follow and understand.

A PATTERN FOR PROBLEM ANALYSIS AND SOLUTION

Underlying every presentation is the analysis of a problem. Problem-solving is accomplished through reasoning, so the reasoning in the presentation becomes a part of the over-all problem-solving process. Just as guides to the use of reasoned communication are necessary if the presentation is to be efficient and systematic, so a more or less standardized pattern for analysis of the basic problem is essential to guarantee that vital elements in the situation are not misinterpreted or overlooked.

People analyze problems poorly for two reasons: They lack good habits of critical thinking, and their desire to solve the problem quickly causes them to embrace any possible solution as the best solution. Efficient problem solvers force themselves to follow a fixed sequence of steps. They know that no intuitive short cut is safe. They form the habit of meticulously "checking off" each item in order, the way the airline pilot and copilot go through their checklist before a flight. They resist the impulse to become anxious and involved, maintaining their objectivity and thoroughness despite pressures.

The easiest way to improve in problem analysis and solution is to adopt a particular system, learn it thoroughly, and make it a habit. The following pattern is applicable to the great majority of problems, is readily remembered, and if each step is completed carefully before proceeding to the next, will insure that significant variables in the situation are not neglected or omitted.

PLAN FOR PROBLEM SOLVING[5]

1. What should be?
2. What is?
3. Describe differences between 1 and 2, being specific. (What? When? Where? How much?)
4. List possible causes of differences.
5. Test possible causes, beginning with most likely.
6. Verify probable cause by attempting to disprove it.
7. Design corrective action, considering side effects.
8. Make decisions to implement corrective action.

To illustrate the application of the above steps we will return to the case of the deteriorating cake mixes in Chapters 7 and 8. Herb Appleton, analyzing the problem for Minnesota Mills, accomplished Step 1 (What should be?) by projecting the sales increase of the past two years into the present and future and by assuming steady increases in consumer satisfaction and concomitant decreases in consumer complaints. These projections were what should have been.

Step 2 (What is?) produced a concise, quantitative summarization of the status quo, often defined as "the mess we're in." Herb tabulated and graphed the actual decreases in sales, the dwindling flow of letters praising the product, and the rapidly increasing number of complaints about spoilage, taste, and texture of the cake mixes that came directly to Minnesota Mills and through their outlets.

---

[5] The problem analysis and solution pattern here is practical and sufficiently comprehensive for the analysis of presentational speeches. For other problem-solving procedures, see John Dewey, *How We Think* (Boston, 1933); *A Programmed Introduction to PERT* (New York, 1963); Charles Kepner and Benjamin Tregoe, *The Rational Manager* (New York, 1965); and Ernest G. Bormann, *Discussion and Group Methods: Theory and Practice* (New York, 1969).

Differences between "What is?" and "What should be?" could be calculated directly from Herb's worksheet, and answers to the four subordinate questions of Step 3 could be supplied concisely. What? The decrease in sales of cake mixes, increase of consumer complaints, decrease in customer compliments. When? Over the past two years. Where? In all geographical regions of distribution. How much? Here Herb could take a recent month and give the difference between projected and actual sales; then by using earlier months, show the rate of decline. Numbers of letters of appreciation and complaint actually received as compared to the normal expectation could be statistically compared in similar fashion. Finally, by projecting the "what is" and "what should be" trends into the future, Herb could show "how much" more serious the uncorrected problem would be in days to come.

Listing possible causes of the differences described in Step 4 is, in a way, the most difficult of the steps in problem-solving. The ongoing movement toward an answer must be interrupted for the widest possible free association and "mulling over" in an effort to identify each and every element in the situation that might contribute to the difficulty. Here Herb consulted the range of expertise in Minnesota Mills, from manufacturing, quality control, marketing, advertising, and shipping. The list of possible causes included advertising, competition, inflation, poor quality control, deterioration of the product, packaging, inefficient distribution, and changes in consumer preference. Only when he was convinced that whatever might conceivably have aggravated the Minnesota Mills cake mix predicament was on his list did Herb proceed to Step 5.

Because complaints emphasized inferior quality of the cake made from Minnesota Mills mixes, Herb decided that quality control and product deterioration were the more likely causes, so he started the testing procedure with them. His evidence indicated that the mixes were leaving the factory with uniform high quality. As reported in Chapter 7, he also found that it was taking considerably longer for the product to reach the consumer than was intended. Supermarkets moved the cake mixes to the customer in less time than did small, independent stores, supermarket sales held up, and supermarket customers had fewer complaints. Herb's investigators collected the oldest packages of cake mix from small stores in several localities and brought them back to the factory for testing. Sure enough, their quality fell far below accepted standards. Further testing established that after 90 days in the package, the quality of the cake mix deteriorated rapidly, at an increasing rate. Quality control was eliminated as a cause, and product deterioration was verified.

Of the other possible causes, none were found to be significant, except inefficient distribution and packaging, which became a possible contributory factor in cake mix deterioration. The Minnesota Mills laboratory devised accelerated aging tests and was able to show that a better package could delay the onset of noticeable deterioration at least 30 days. When it was discovered that the present package was adopted two years before, packaging emerged as the most likely basic cause of deterioration, which in turn was the most likely cause of falling sales and consumer dissatisfaction.

Now in Step 6 the assumption that packaging caused the cake mix problem was challenged in every way Herb and his associates could devise. Daily quality control checks were made on current output, a new collection of packages of varied ages from another sampling of grocery stores was tested, and the lab did further experimentation on the effects of packaging on product deterioration. All results supported the original hypothesis that inadequate packaging was the variable that contributed most to loss of quality of product. Because he was unable to disprove this conclusion, Herb proceeded to Step 7.

The Minnesota Mills laboratory in the process of testing different packages had come up with a design that would advance the point of significant deterioration 30 days. This was judged to be adequate, since 97 percent of the mixes were in the consumers' kitchens in 110 days and the new, safe threshold time was 120 days. Materials for the new package were available, the box manufacturing process was the same, but there was one undesirable side effect, increased cost. Each new box cost .1 of a cent more.

At this point in the problem-solving process, Herb developed and made his presentation. He recommended that the new packaging be adopted immediately, the cost to be absorbed for the time being by Minnesota Mills. With the approval of the Board of Control the way was clear for the details of the change to be settled by the managers involved, and the implementation of corrective action could take place.

Problem analysis and solution is a rigorous, systematic and exacting business. It includes ingenuity and creativity, as in discovering and testing possible causes, but always within the fixed structure of eight inevitable and sequential steps. Results are the payoff, for this sometimes painful discipline outproduces the use of hunches and intuition by a wide margin. The best solution is usually so much better than the second or third best that one cannot afford the chance of missing it.

Our advice on problem analysis and solution obviously extends far beyond the making of a presentation. Systematic problem-solving becomes a style of management, and for many of us, a way of living. Human potential can be realized when it is channeled in an orderly and purposeful manner. We are recommending that our readers attempt to use our system—or another—in the making of day-to-day decisions. And, of course, one of the vital problems to be solved is how to go about making a presentation.

REASONING AND MOTIVATION

At this point in the discussion of reasoning in presentation, it is necessary to confront a popular belief that poses a dilemma. Are motive appeals and appeals to critical thinking incompatible? Can common sense and personal desire coexist? Do logical and nonlogical messages activate separate segments of the human psyche or does the receiving mechanism process all incoming signals in a single integrating and blending operation?

Probably most people envision reasons and motives as distinct and separate phenomena. The notion that a man tends to become thoughtful about something he wants fervently does not occur to most of us. Still, we know that in many instances only rigorous problem-solving can lead us to our heart's desire. And we *do* "reason about our wants." This suggests strongly that reason and desire cannot be separated and that their constant interaction is the usual rather than the exceptional case.

Our position with respect to the reason-motivation dichotomy is simple and clear: The dichotomy does not exist. The presentation, as we noted at the beginning of this chapter, is a predominantly rational form, *but in the frame of reference of the listener's motives.* This interaction was described several decades ago by William Norwood Brigance, who summarized his analysis by writing ". . . arguments which appeal to 'human reason' without touching human wants will be ineffective."[6] Thus, reasoning is seen to be one method of triggering motives, a thoughtful, reflective method useful in meeting the needs of people. Indeed, rational units are often the most effective motive appeals.

If we grant that being reasonable is an effective means of helping people get what they want, we then ponder what is meant by "being reasonable." Since modes of critical thinking vary from culture to culture, we must conclude that logics are relative. Whatever provokes a listener to pause and reflect is, for him, logical. In North America people tend to become thoughtful about assertions of cause and effect. In the Middle East similar statements have little meaning, since there causation is not a significant part of problem-solving procedures. In Japan the possibility of losing face promotes considerably more reflective thinking about a business problem than does the prospect of losing money. Hence, loss-of-face logic is more reasonable than profit and loss—to the Japanese.

[6] William Norwood Brigance, *Speech Composition* (New York, 1937), p. 182.

Necessarily, what is reasonable to the listener *is* reasonable, by definition, as we explained in the previous chapter. The implication for the communicator is clear. He must understand the habits of critical thinking possessed by his receiver and know the values assigned to preferred patterns. Only then can he be "reasonable" in a way that makes the most sense to his listener.

Because perception is congruent with people's needs, the ultimate extension of meaning for the concept "reasonable" is that nonreason may be perceived as reason. This does indeed occur. When a person's prejudice drives him furiously enough, he becomes capable of seeing an emotional, unsupported argument as carefully reasoned and conservatively stated. Truly, one man's suggestion is another's reasoned discourse, and vice versa. Hence, "good" reasons that are not important to the receiver of the message are functionally bad reasons, since they fail to generate reflective thought.

CRITERIA OF REASONED APPEAL

It is useful to the maker of a presentation to have definite means of assessing the quality of his reasoned materials. This takes the form of three criteria. The first is derived from knowledge of members of the audience and of their systems of logical thought. The second and third are absolutes, in that they can be applied to a message independent of its intended receivers.

1. *Will the selected evidence and its interpretation be thought-provoking to this particular audience?* Concerns of the listeners are weighed and shrewd guesses made as to their problem-solving behavior in response to stimulation from the message. To the extent that the audience will probably be intrigued by information, topics, facts, and conclusions, the message is judged to satisfy the first criterion. Habits, needs, interests, desires, and goals, the entire motive structure of people who will be responding, enter into this evaluation of the rational elements in the presentation.

2. *How concrete and specific is the reasoned content?* Truly, concreteness is the basis of rationality. The more specific and definite a presentation is, the more reasonable it may be said to be. "Facts of the case" presentations are the most concrete, and nothing gets people thinking like involving them in real situations where they need to make decisions. Examples and illustrations, given in detail, contribute to this desirable characteristic of a message.

The Slope of Abstraction–Concreteness (Figure 9.1) showed the advantages of wording propositions as concretely as possible, but more needs to be said about concreteness as a characteristic of language. Often a key term is selected from a choice of several words that differ in their definiteness. Almost always, the wise choice is the more specific of the varied options. The concrete term represent fewer meanings, insuring that the audience will read into it a somewhat uniform interpretation.

Semanticists have made much of this point with their "ladder of abstraction." The "ladder" consists of a series of words, any of which could be used to designate the same object, person, or situation. The words differ predominantly in definiteness. The higher-level words are more general in that they represent a greater number of objects, people, or situations than do the lower-level words. The higher-level words are said to be more abstract and the lower-level words more concrete.

Let us assume that the author of a presentation wishes to refer to a costly error in production involving the setting of machine controls for an experimental product. The key term he is looking for is the one to designate the cause of the malfunction. Here is the ladder of labels, any one of which might be used to complete his sentence: "The cause of the difficulty was ＿＿＿＿＿＿＿＿＿."

ABSTRACT
An unfortunate circumstance
Human error
Inefficiency
Sloppy management
Poor communication
A breakdown in communication
Use of erroneous instructions
Failure to proofread typed instructions
Joe Doake's failure to proofread typed instructions.
CONCRETE

Each term below the top of the ladder conveys more information than the one above it, because it is narrower and more specific. It informs the audience better about what happened. A communicator is always wise to seek out the lowest possible levels of abstraction in his choice of language. Fewer misconceptions will be the result and audience members will be more thoughtful in their responses because they perceive his point more precisely.

3. *Is the reasoned appeal valid and true?* A message is true when its verifiable elements correspond to reality, and a message is valid when its form violates none of the generally agreed-upon patterns of sound thinking. Using representative and comprehensive statistics and avoiding fallacies are matters of validity. False information, such as assuming a consensus that does not exist, is a matter of truth. The truth test is generally understood, although many slight distortions are difficult to detect and confirm. But criteria of validity in reasoning are many

and complicated. The following tests of validity will be useful in producing soundly reasoned presentations.

1. Is all wording simple and clear?
2. Are opposing points of view recognized?
3. Are units compared really comparable?
4. Are statistics representative?
5. Are bases of all percentages supplied?
6. Do examples and illustrations represent the situation fairly?
7. Are generalizations adequately supported?
8. Are quoted authorities reliable and qualified?
9. Is concealment and other deception avoided?
10. Are all relevant facts of the case acknowledged?
11. Is appropriate documentation supplied?

Truth and validity are criteria to be continuously applied during the planning and the building of a message. But when the presentation is substantially complete, a reworking in an effort to make all parts of it even more true and valid often pays rich dividends.

SUMMARY

Reasoning is undoubtedly the dominant method of presentation. Yet effective use of the critical-thinking process does not just happen. It requires knowledge of the structure of sound argument and hard work in building it from the basic materials of evidence, clarification, and interpretation.

Briefing, the operation that reduces points and their support to the bare essentials, is seen to be necessary to either the logical analysis of a message or the planning of one that is unified and well articulated. Propositions, the points to be made, are key elements in the brief. Moral, purpose, proposition, and message unit can be appropriately related on the Slope of Abstraction–Concreteness (Figure 9.1). Wording of propositions is found to be highly critical, although it is often done ineptly. Eight suggestions for effective wording of propositions can be used to insure their clarity and persuasiveness.

A complete presentation usually consists of several fairly complex units, in a logical sequence and closely interrelated. Since a unit involves more evidence and reasoning than a claim and its direct support, a more comprehensive guide to preparation of the message is necessary. The Unit Plan for Rational Presentation (Figure 9.2) is a format that encompasses varied evidence and related reasoning, plus qualification of the proposition, recognition of possible exceptions, as well as explanatory materials that may be required.

The reasoned content in a presentation is part of an over-all problem-solving process. A plan of problem analysis and solution is useful because it provides a sequential, systematic procedure of investigating, exploring and solving difficulties that arise. The presentation can be no more successful than the related problem-solving that precedes it.

Finally, establishing criteria of a reasoned appeal requires a balancing of perceptual standards peculiar to the specific audience and more universal standards of good reasoning that are largely independent of topic and listeners. These evaluative criteria to be applied to any presentation to determine its successful utilization of the method of reasoning are: (1) Will the selected evidence and its interpretation be thought-provoking to this particular audience? (2) How concrete and specific is the reasoned content? (3) Is the reasoned appeal valid and true?

QUESTIONS FOR DISCUSSION AND REVIEW

1. How are evidence and reasoning related and interdependent?
2. In what ways do "loaded" and "report" language differ?
3. What are the techniques of extracting and evaluating the reasoned content of a message?
4. What are the differences among purpose, moral, proposition, and supporting material?
5. What are the characteristics of a properly worded persuasive proposition?
6. What is meant by the concept *burden of proof* and how is it important to a presentation?
7. What are the parts of the Unit Plan for Rational Presentation and and what is the function of each part?
8. In what ways are problem analysis and solution a single process and in what ways are these separate processes?
9. Are an individual's motive interests and critical-thinking abilities necessarily in conflict? Explain.
10. How does the nature of the audience enter into the formulation of criteria of reasoned appeal?

REFERENCES AND SUGGESTED READINGS

ABERNATHY, ELTON. *The Advocate*. New York: McKay, 1964.

DIMNET, ERNEST. *The Art of Thinking*. New York: Fawcett World Library, 1962.

FEARNSIDE, W. WARD, and WILLIAM B. HOLTHER. *Fallacy the Counterfeit of Argument.* Englewood Cliffs, N.J.: Prentice-Hall, 1959.

MILLS, GLEN E. *Message Preparation.* Indianapolis: Bobbs-Merrill, 1966.

SMITH, DONALD K. *Man Speaking.* New York: Dodd, Mead, 1969.

CHAPTER TEN

SUGGESTION
AS A METHOD OF
PRESENTATION

SUGGESTION AND REASONING COMPARED

The human being is a suggestible animal. If he is told to believe or do something when he has no impulses or reasons to the contrary, he believes or does it. Behavior resulting from suggestion occurs without deliberation, often with little recognition that any change has taken place. Controlling people by suggestion is basically a button-pushing procedure. Response to suggestion often approximates the automaticity of a conditioned reflex.

In the presentation, elements of suggestion supplement reasoned arguments. Properly controlled, suggestion clears the channels and paves the way for favorable reception of recommendations and supporting materials. Improperly used, suggestive elements contribute roadblocks to favorable response that neither source nor receiver may fully understand. Much of the artistry in the successful presentation consists of developing verbal and nonverbal suggestive support to enhance the impact of the "hard core of common sense" that is the reasoned content.

The extreme state of suggestibility is hypnosis. A person in a fairly deep hypnotic trance reacts to suggestions as does a machine to programmed instructions. The unhypnotized person thinks about most messages to some extent, but he will probably be unthinking in his reaction to certain stimuli in most speeches.

The process of persuasion is diagrammed in Figure 10.1 in a way that shows both the differences between reasoning and suggestion and their interaction.

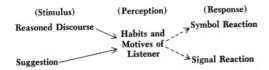

Figure 10.1   Channels of Persuasion (SOURCE: Ernest G. Bormann, William S. Howell, Ralph G. Nichols, and George L. Shapiro, *Interpersonal Communication in the Modern Organization* [Englewood Cliffs, N.J.: Prentice-Hall 1969], fig. 10.)

Response to either suggestion or reasoned appeal depends upon the habit and motive structure of the individual member of the audience. The nature of perception of the stimulus shapes the outcome. If the receiver perceives the stimulus as something unrelated to his interests (habits and motives), little or no response results. However, if the listener finds himself interested in the stimulus, he will either respond thoughtfully or automatically.

If a person responds thoughtfully, his response is a *symbol* reaction, one that takes some time and is consciously mediated. If he responds without thinking, automatically, his response is a *signal* reaction, one that is quick and largely subconscious. Both signal and symbol responses occur continuously during an act of communication. When they are harmonious, each reinforces the other, and when they are contradictory, favorable response to a message is inhibited.

The dotted arrows in Figure 10.1 leading to the responses "suggest" that often an intended suggestion produces a symbol response, and the intent to reason with a receiver may trigger a signal response. The ultimate decision about the nature of response to a message comes from observation of the receiver rather than from knowledge of the source's intent.

An example will make the functioning of suggestion concrete. Let us suppose someone is driving across western North Dakota on a hot August afternoon. He is tired and hungry and preoccupied with the problem of deciding whether to stop overnight at Minot or drive on to Williston. As he slows to conform to the speed limit of a village, a large sign before a tiny restaurant enters his field of vision. It states simply, "EAT." He brakes his car and drives nearer to the curb. A small sign in the restaurant window says, "Air-Conditioned." He parks, enters the restaurant, has a hamburger and a cup of coffee.

Probably, his stopping for refreshment was not a conscious decision. The familiar signs "EAT" and "Air-Conditioned" triggered habitual, automated response patterns. Because he was without impulses or reasons to the contrary, he "reflexed" suggestion to action. Meantime, his conscious mind was free to examine the pros and cons of stopping early for a good night's sleep or pushing on to cover more miles in the cool of early evening.

The example is of further interest because two kinds of suggestion are involved. The "EAT" sign is *direct suggestion,* telling you what to do. The "Air-Conditioned" sign is *indirect suggestion,* hinting that you will be cool and comfortable while following the directly suggested recommendation. The categories of direct and indirect suggestion are further explored and illustrated in this chapter.

Insufficient attention has been paid to the mechanism of suggestion in presentations and other forms of spoken communication. In Chapter 1, five elements of presentational speaking were listed: (1) presentation of recommendation, (2) presentation of self, (3) adaptation to standard human obstacles, (4) adaptation to particular circumstances, and (5) adaptation to the motives of individual receivers. All five central elements depend heavily upon the use of suggestion in their implementation. However, numbers 2, 3 and possibly 5 would seem usually to be more dependent upon the skilled use of suggestion than upon good reasoning. Truly, the person who would excel in the making of presentations must become proficient in the controlled application of many forms and devices of suggestion.

To conclude our introduction to suggestion as a method of presentation, we should observe that its advantages spring from bypassing the critical thinking mechanism of the receiver. Among the desirable consequences for a speaker of getting an uncritical response from the audience are these:

1. The method of suggestion gets past defenses. When evangelist Billy Graham tells a university audience that he knows the Psychology Department has come to study him, he causes that audience to "drop its guard" and be more receptive. When he tells the story of labor

leader Walter Reuther speaking to the National Association of Manufacturers with brutal frankness and being rewarded with a standing ovation, his listeners become more inclined to listen to Dr. Graham's message without prejudice, reading frankness into his speech.

2. Suggestion skillfully used is efficient, colorful, memorable, and impressive. Instead of noting that the corporation's new venture is unprofitable and difficult to terminate, the speaker may say, "We are the flies that captured the flypaper." The Antiballistic Missile program that was proposed for the United States in the late 1960s was damaged by the suggestion in the statement, "The ABM will be our Maginot Line in the sky."

3. Positions established by suggestion are difficult to attack. Suggested concepts are "nonlogic," and logical analysis is thus often irrelevant. Reasoned refutation of suggestion tends to be cumbersome and complicated. How would one be reasonable in answering this:

> Obey that impulse! You may be robbing yourself of happiness and success by not following your hunches! Are you missing out on the richer life and greater achievement that *could* be yours—simply because you fail to act on your "inner flashes" before they cool off?

4. Good suggestion has a universal "human interest" appeal. A clever columnist wrote a piece about a spell of hot weather in Minneapolis, relying upon the suggestive power of hyperbole, extreme exaggeration. The title of his column showed hyperbole: "Conversation Droops Too, When Tongue Hangs Out." Here are two paragraphs about some effects of a recent heat wave.

> Political oratory sank to a new low in the hot spell. Children's screeching rose an octave and had more penetrating power. Buses gave off more nauseous fumes. Lake levels dropped so far you could wade across Lake Calhoun. Ice cubes in drinks were actually warm.
>
> As you recall, a high pressure area came to town, stayed five minutes and then retreated. Humidity was so high that you could collect a glass of water by merely setting out the glass. Mosquitoes were so fagged that when they hit on your arm they just sat there without the ambition to probe.[1]

Writer Sherman suggested common experiences through his vivid pictures which caught and held interest. Although his absurdities were pure fantasy, his readers enjoyed them, and recollections of the "hot spell" were intensified and elaborated thereby.

The above four advantages of using suggestion skillfully constitute an incomplete list. As we proceed with discussion of various forms of suggestion, the reader will see how the more exciting, titillating, shock-

[1] John K. Sherman, "Conversation Droops Too, When Tongue Hangs Out," *Minneapolis Sunday Tribune,* August 2, 1964, p. 6.

ing, and surprising factors that enliven a message and hold rapt attention are suggestive in nature. Breaking away from literal, earthbound reasonableness can help to transform a presentation from "clear" to "eloquent," from "understandable" to "fascinating."

NONVERBAL TECHNIQUES OF SUGGESTION

In Chapter 2 we discussed influences coming from elements of context, human and inanimate, formal and informal. Mainly, we dealt with remote factors, such as status relationships deriving from the organizational hierarchy (formal) and from personal traits and abilities (informal). Now we will emphasize immediate, controllable circumstances that affect the outcome of the presentation. However, both immediate and remote circumstances operate suggestively, and, ironically, the speaker may be as unaware as the listener of how they function or the extent of their influence.

Researchers are at long last studying the little understood and grossly neglected factors of physical relationships and delivery of a message by a speaker. Training in interpersonal communication in the last decade has developed a "nonverbal dimension." How the speaker looks and sounds, the location and arrangement of his audience, lighting and ventilation, what comes before and after his presentation, visual aids and their use, all these and many other elements independent of the words he says contribute substantially to his success or failure. Now it is as necessary to study suggestion originating in nonverbal arrangements and behaviors as it is to learn the disciplined use of evidence and reasoning.

We will examine the nonverbal, suggestive constituents of the presentation by separating the details of arrangement from the delivery of the speech. We will call physical relationships and environmental conditions "proxemic" items and those associated with the behavior of the speaker will be classed as "personal."

PROXEMIC ELEMENTS IN THE PRESENTATION

Proxemics[2] refers to the way available space is utilized by living

[2] The books that generated interest in the proxemic dimension of interpersonal communication were Ray L. Birdwhistell, *Introduction to Kenesics* (Louisville, Ky., 1952), and Edward T. Hall, *The Silent Language* (Garden City, N.Y., 1959). Hall's later book, *The Hidden Dimension* (Garden City, N.Y., 1966), further developed and applied proxemic concepts. See also Weston LaBarre, "The Cultural Basis of Emotions and Gestures," *Journal of Personality*, 16 (1946), 49–68; Michael Watson and Theodore V. Graves, "Quantitative Research in Proxemic

organisms. In presentational speaking, proxemic elements, then, include the characteristics of an immediate environment and the physical relationships of the people who inhabit it. Planning the proxemics of the presentation should be a central concern of those preparing for the event.

There is little appreciation of the amount of influence general comfort, pleasantness, and appropriateness of surroundings have upon a presentation. When one adds the dimension of *arrangement* of the people who interact in communication, with resulting ease or difficulty in seeing and hearing each other, a host of important variables are involved. Fortunately, people preparing for a presentation can easily control physical conditions and relationships. In most cases speakers fail to manage these ingredients of the presentation properly only because of ignorance of their effects upon the communication process.

An optimum environment for a presentation includes a tastefully decorated room, acoustically perfect, large enough for the intended audience, and no larger. Comfortable chairs should be easy to turn and rearrange, and table space for each person should be conveniently located. Room lighting should be shadowless and continuously controlled from bright to dim. Audio-visual equipment should be built in, with tape recording and playback, sound motion picture projection, overhead projector, flip chart, and blackboard immediately at hand. The room should be soundproofed to the extent that noises from outside can never be loud enough to cause distraction.

Only in an environment that approximates the above can a high quality of production for the presentation be achieved. "High quality" in production can be described by two adjectives, "smooth flowing" and "inconspicuous." A presentation flows smoothly only when there is no delay caused by any visual or audio or mechanical failure or ineptitude in any other part of the performance. Production is inconspicuous when it looks easy and natural. If ever the listeners find themselves thinking about *how* a point was made, or admiring an elaborate visual or the tricky timing required to integrate the flip chart and overhead projector, then production is deficient. Whenever production calls attention to itself, that attention is diverted from the subject of the presentation. Effective production focuses total attention on the content of the message.

Smooth-flowing, inconspicuous \production is a powerful technique of suggestion. Many a proposal has succeeded because it was presented skillfully rather than because of its intrinsic merit. The quality of production is assigned to the content of the message through the

---

Behavior," *American Anthropologist,* 68 (1966), 972; and Edward T. Hall, "A System for the Notation of Proxemic Behavior," *American Anthropologist,* 65 (1963), 1003–1026.

psychological phenomenon known as *transfer*. Transfer is the mechanism through which much suggestion produces its effect, and more will be said about it later.

An important proxemic consideration is the physical relationship between speaker and audience. It is the custom in American and in European cultures to locate the speaker apart from his audience, elevate him, and place him behind a large speaker's stand, or podium. Does this contribute to his effectiveness? Usually not. The amount of interaction between human beings is increased by proximity.[3] Increased interaction means better communication. The notion that a speaker gains esteem by being set apart and elevated is unfounded and obsolete. Rather, his esteem grows through his being more easily seen and heard by his audience. Since a speaker communicates non-verbally with his whole body, little benefit can come from hiding most of it behind the podium. Further, speakers have a universal impulse to grasp the speaker's stand and hang on, thereby eliminating the possibility of movement and gesture. In short, placing the speaker behind a podium on a platform suggests separation from the audience, implying a lack of common interests that is difficult to surmount.

Exceptions to the rule that a speaker should be as close to the audience as possible occur where transmission of the message is subordinate to other elements in the occasion. For example, the annual report made by the president and his executive committee to all employees may be as much dedicated to emphasizing the status and prestige of top management as it is to communicating information about the company. The imposing spectacle of well-dressed, distant, elevated executives may promote feelings of awe and respect. Since the information they impart is available in printed form, communication of content is not vital. In this and other ritualistic situations, including most meetings of stockholders, impressing the audience by phsycial separation of listeners and speakers may be advisable. However, there is little speaker-audience interaction in such environments and the possible development of rapport is thwarted.

A useful guide in handling the speaker-audience physical relationship is found in a simple formula: $R = 1/D$. R is the amount of overt, or observable, response in the audience. D is the distance between speaker and audience. So the formula tells us that the amount of overt response a speaker achieves from an audience is inversely proportional to the distance between him and that audience, other factors being held constant. Since overt responses correlate well with the attention and interest necessary to success in a presentation, a speaker is well

[3] For a review of research relating to spatial arrangement and its effect, interaction and communication, see Robert Sommer, "Small Group Ecology," *Psychological Bulletin*, 67 (1967), 145–152.

advised to get on the same level as his listeners, be as close to them as possible, and talk directly to them, with maximum eye contact.

Common-sense observations support our formula metaphor of $R = 1/D$. When the speaker is close by, he is more easily heard and seen, which means that his subtle nonverbal cues will be better understood. He can more easily control attention and overcome distractions. The speaker who is close to his listeners gets better feedback. He sees the nods and smiles and other expressions of agreement, as well as the frowns and grimaces that tell him something is wrong. Only by being near can he develop circular response, where he reacts to the audience and they react to him in a way that builds approval for him and thus maximum support for his recommendation.

PERSONAL, NONVERBAL TECHNIQUES OF SUGGESTION

Let us assume that a speaker has planned appropriately the proxemic factors in his presentation. How can he conduct himself *personally* in utilizing suggestion to harmonize with and enhance his message? Proxemic considerations have placed him close to his audience, with no barriers between them. In this intimate situation, how should he talk and act?

The image he would like to create in the perception of his listeners serves as a guide to his speaking behavior. His message will be more favorably received if he is seen as a sincere, active, alert, informed, confident, warm, and friendly person. What speaking behaviors suggest these characteristics?

Vigorous, dynamic, informal, direct, and unaffected speaking help to generate such a perception. Good posture, much eye contact, lots of movement and gesture, and a strong voice with many changes in pitch, volume, and tempo suggest confidence and sincerity. A natural, easy, conversational manner and an obvious interest in the reactions of his audience convey to them the impression that he is a warm and friendly person, a "nice guy." He will find that his own facial expression is his most flexible and useful tool of nonverbal communication. He should let his reaction to what he is saying "show in his face" freely and continuously, and he should carefully avoid the "deadpan" delivery affected by many speakers.

Two specific nonverbal techniques can be helpful to the presentational speaker, the *kinetic* and the *empathetic*. The kinetic technique consists of always striving for activity and variety. It is based on the established principle that a moving object commands attention better than does a stationary object. The kinetic speaker is above all else *active*, "pumping in" vocal energy and variety, using many gestures of varied sorts, walking about, and particularly, showing an expressive countenance. The suggestive effectiveness of being kinetic is illustrated by the positive connotation in our culture associated with the speaker who is "dynamic."

The empathetic nonverbal technique has two distinctly different dimensions, the response of the speaker to the audience and the control of audience response to the speaker.

Empathy is the tendency of human beings to imitate what they see and hear. Much of the pleasure experienced in the theater comes through empathy. The person who becomes involved with the play empathizes with a character by mimicking his movements with bodily tensions. These tiny, largely unobservable movements produce sensations in the playgoer that have come to be described as "feeling in" with the scene on the stage.

The speaker needs to empathize with his audience. By watching them closely and trying to be highly sensitive to their reactions, he can learn to feel the changing currents of response. The "feeling in" of a sensitive speaker with his audience provides a valuable source of feedback.

The second empathetic technique, using empathy to control the response of the audience, may be thought of as empathy in reverse. The speaker knows that his audience will empathize with him, so by acting out what he wants them to feel or do, he can increase the probability that they will feel or do it. For example, if he wants his listeners to relax and rest for a minute, he can relax his body and voice and assume a casual manner. When he wants their close attention, he can "look serious," lean forward, tense his body, increase the intensity of his voice, and his audience will lean forward and frown in their concentration.

The speaker will find this use of empathy to control response particularly helpful in creating a particular mood to suit his purpose. Here, like an actor, he can show the vocal and physical symptoms of the mood, and his audience will begin soon to feel it, through the automated process of suggestion.

VERBAL TECHNIQUES OF SUGGESTION

While the nonverbal elements discussed above clearly "bypass the critical faculties" of an audience, it is less obvious that language can stimulate the nervous system to unthinking response. However, such is the case, and we will set about seeing how this can be so.

The two basic kinds of verbal suggestion are *direct* and *indirect*. Direct suggestion, like the restaurant sign "EAT," tells the receiver what to believe or what to do, in so many words. It is explicit. Indirect suggestion, like the sign "Air-Conditioned," is implicit. The proposition it suggests is concealed. It does not tell the receiver in so many words what it means to him. That he discovers for himself.

Verbal techniques of direct suggestion.   Direct or explicit suggestion occurs in presentation in three forms: positive, negative, and autosuggestion. Positive suggestion recommends a belief or course of action as directly and affirmatively as possible, as "Buy Buick," "Smoke Luckies," and "Fly Northwest to Hawaii." Negative suggestion tells the receiver *not* to do something, and is identified by its negative wording, as "Thou shalt not steal" and "Don't put beans up your nose." Autosuggestion is a form of self-persuasion. The salesman who looks at himself in his shaving mirror in the morning and shouts "Boy! Am I enthusiastic!" is using autosuggestion, as is the computer programmer who tells himself, "I can get the bugs out of that program. I *know* I can!"

Positive suggestion, clearly and forcefully worded, has substantial persuasive impact. Just telling a person that something is so moves him perceptibly toward belief. When the receiver lacks reasons for disbelief, the effect is multiplied. Also, a high-prestige source further increases the power of positive suggestion, as does a judicious amount of repetition. Belief is easier than doubt, and more comfortable. And all of us, to some degree, have been trained to do what we are told. Is it any wonder that positive suggestion is an effective means of persuasion?

Negative suggestion is less effective than positive suggestion. A major weakness results from its calling attention to an undesired belief or behavior. Human nature being what it is, many of us are tempted to try the forbidden fruit. The sign "DO NOT OPEN THIS DOOR" guarantees that someone *will* open it, and soon. The denied possibility is often made irresistible unintentionally, as when the mother tells her teen-age daughter, "Don't kiss boys. It will feel so good you won't be able to stop!" Comparison of positive and negative suggestion forces us to conclude that a speaker is wise to rely upon positive suggestion and avoid negative suggestion. Truly, suggestion is strongest at its "positive pole."

Autosuggestion is a highly respected source of motivation and its effect is often designated as the "Power of Positive Thinking." The speaker making a presentation can use this "power" by leading members of his audience to envision their roles in his proposal. By suggesting to Fred that his job will be made easier, and to Joe that his assembly line will produce more at less cost, the speaker will be telling these men something they will wish to believe. Belief has been found to correlate with desire. Fred and Joe will repeat the attractive promises to themselves, and through autosuggestion will increase their faith in the recommended beliefs.

Verbal techniques of indirect suggestion. Whenever a communicator hints at a point but avoids saying it outright, he is using indirect suggestion. The mechanism of indirect suggestion is generally misunderstood in that many people believe an implication must be subtle in order to be indirect. To the contrary, an indirection can be of any degree of complexity, extremely obvious or very difficult to decode. An example of an effective use of obvious indirect suggestion is the instance of the departmental secretary who spilled a bottle of ink on the floor. Her note to the night janitor read:

Dear Janitor:
   I think ditto fluid will remove this stain.
   Thank you.
                         The Secretary

The methods of indirect verbal suggestion are so many and varied that one is tempted to conclude that it is impossible to enumerate them. Without attempting to be comprehensive, we will select five major categories useful in presentational persuasion, discuss them, and illustrate their application.

1. SIMPLE IMPLICATION

The secretary's note to the janitor is an example of simple implication. By being indirect, she was spared the necessity of making a possibly embarrassing request. In this situation as in many other delicate human relationships it seems more diplomatic to avoid the bluntness of asking directly for what you want.

Simple implication, then, is somehow talking around a point in a way that would seem to assure that a receiver "reads into" a message the desired meaning. The "reading into" process reveals the built-in hazard of using any form of indirect suggestion: When you rely upon other people to guess what you actually mean, you can be sure that wrong guesses will occur. To phrase it in scholarly language: "Response to indirect suggestion is more variable than to direct suggestion." To avoid distortion of the implied point, two precautions are indicated, (1) resist the temptation to be clever, and (2) suggest your point in several ways, thereby making it easy for your audience to conclude correctly.

Are there guides that help the speaker decide when to be direct and when to use implication? When an audience is hostile to your proposal, indirect suggestion is a way of avoiding the jolt of direct confrontation. A young speaker talking to a more mature and experienced audience is well advised to be indirect, while in the reversed situation a highly respected older person talking to a group of his juniors may well be predominantly direct. Direct suggestion may be necessary when immediate action is the goal, while planting seeds for a long-range program is often better accomplished by fairly subtle indirection. It is possible and usually desirable to introduce an idea in such a manner that the listener perceives it as his own, through implication.

2. COUNTERSUGGESTION

Contrasuggestible people are those who can be relied upon to do the opposite of what they are told. A few of the population are predictably contrasuggestible every day of their lives, but all of us have this perverse, contrary tendency to some degree. When the communicator uses what would appear to be direct positive or negative suggestion with the intent of precipitating an opposite response, he is resorting to countersuggestion.

The roofing salesman tells his prospect, "That beautiful roof for your house is a major investment. Don't you think you had better call your wife and talk it over with her?" If the salesman has correctly identified the contrasuggestible customer, the prospect will reply, "I don't need to check with anybody. Where do I sign?"

"Charlie, you probably better not take on this account. It means a lot of business and more men to supervise, and you're busy now." "We can get along without modern data processing. We'll just move a little slower and work longer hours." "Keep at it, Jack, the end isn't in sight but after another month, it may be." "Dear, I understand and I'm not complaining. I know you can't afford to buy me a mink stole." Other examples will come to the mind of the reader, illustrating how wide is the use of countersuggestion.

The danger in using countersuggestion is the "boomerang effect." Occasionally, the receiver accepts the suggestion literally and the persuader has brought about the opposite of his intended result. Satire is countersuggestion, and it is a risky literary device because many people "take it straight" and thus act upon a message that is completely contrary to the one the sender intended.

Before countersuggestion is used in a presentation, the people and situation involved must be thoroughly understood. Both circumstances and motives must point strongly in the direction opposite to the apparent recommendation. Then, if a wording can be contrived that would invite these listeners to react against it, countersuggestion may be judged sufficiently free of risk to try. When it works it is conclusive, for the people who were influenced have formulated their own position in the crucible of opposition, so they regard it affectionately and cling to it tenaciously.

3. WORD MANIPULATION

Choosing one's language provides unlimited opportunity to build suggestion into a message. Words are slanted, positively or negatively, causing persons to accept or reject the thing talked about. Consider the contrasting impact of referring to the Mayor's assistants as his "executive staff" or as his "henchmen." Changing "War Department" to "Department of Defense" is a typical, purposeful switching of labels. Attempting to control responses of receivers by linguistic variables used in conveying a message is the form of indirect suggestion we term "word manipulation."

The "henchmen" and "Department of Defense" examples illustrate, respectively, negative and positive name-calling. We illustrated hyperbole, intentional overstatement, and exaggeration earlier. Understatement, the technique of concluding much less than the situation justifies, is a powerful persuasive device. When an audience expects a sweeping conclusion and is given a restricted, conservative understatement, it rewards the speaker by trusting him more.

Figurative language in the form of analogy, metaphor, and simile can be effective suggestion. Saying that "Fighting communism is like killing a snake. You cannot do it by chopping off its tail" supplies little logical analysis about United States policy in the Far East but it may influence attitudes concerning involvement there. Simpler than analogy, metaphor and simile add visual imagery and interest. President Lyndon B. Johnson told U.S. troops in Vietnam that he wanted them "to nail the coonskin to the wall." When Neil Armstrong, the first man on the surface of the moon, stepped from his landing craft, he said, "It's a small step for a man, a giant leap for mankind." A mausoleum salesman happened upon a tested statement that sold his product, "You don't rot. You just dry out, like a prune." Figurative language increases impact by converting a matter-of-fact statement into something colorful and memorable.

The next word problem we consider has intentional and unintentional aspects. Ambiguity and vagueness are ever-present characteristics of language which usually inhibit purposeful communication, but which can also be used suggestively to produce intended responses that further the purposes of a communicator.

Ambiguity is the linguistic circumstance in which a word or phrase has two or more discrete and legitimate meanings; for example, "Modern youth are revolting." Typically, the sender intends one and the receiver selects another. Communication breaks down without either party suspecting that the other used a meaning different from his own.

Vagueness is a lack of definite meaning. Vague language, speaking figuratively, has a high "fog index"; for example, "The situation is under advisement." A typical response to a vague statement is "What did he say?" accompanied by a frown.

Unintentional ambiguity and vagueness are barriers to communication, and as such are usually to be avoided. But there are times when the cause of the speaker can be helped by their purposeful use. To avoid taking a clear-cut position on an issue one can create vagueness by combining incompatible objectives, for example, "We must proceed with all deliberate haste," by devising a puzzling paradox, "We do not advocate irresponsible experimentation. But at this time not to experiment would be irresponsible," and by adding qualifying conditions until the original position is diluted beyond recognition, as "We will bring the boys back from the war, as soon as our allies are able to replace them, and providing the enemy withdraws and of course, assuming that peace talks make satisfactory progress." Intentional vagueness may well be the major method of avoiding commitment.

Language used to obscure rather than convey meaning is appropriately labeled "gobbledegook." An example that combines ambiguity and vagueness calculated to confuse and frustrate the reader is taken from an editorial written during the war in Vietnam:

> The current bargaining tool being used by the United States at the Paris Vietnam talks is something that might be called "counter de-escalation," the threat of not reducing U.S. participation in the war as fast as Hanoi thinks the American public thinks President Nixon is planning. This is no less intricate than the differences between State and Defense Department interpretations of enemy intentions. The view from State has been the decline in infiltration and a relative lull in the fighting the past two months are "significant." Pentagon spokesmen stress "cautious" interpretations of the same facts, suggesting that the lull may be only a breathing space.[4]

In the above paragraph contradictory elements, tricky and complex uses of language, and an ambiguous interpretation of the same evidence by equally prestigious agencies contribute to confusion. Often, creation of confusion is a highly effective "stalling" technique. Confused people are reluctant to act because they do not know what to do. Hence, word manipulations serve to block critical thinking through purposeful vagueness and ambiguity.

However, it is easy to be ambiguous or vague unintentionally and the safeguard against uttering gobbledegook is to always strive for concreteness and specificity. Never say "Steps will be taken immediately" without supplying what and when. Soothing statements like "You can rest assured that all possible avenues are being explored" mean next to nothing until the audience is informed of what precisely is being done, and by whom. The sweeping, unsupported assertion, couched in appropriately slanted language, has great suggestive power but at the cost of inhibiting thought.

The illustrations given above demonstrate that word manipulations can be deceptive or enlightening, constructive or destructive to the

---

[4] "Vietnam: 'Counter De-escalation,'" *Minneapolis Tribune*, August 31, 1969, p. 2C.

welfare of the individual and the group. In a final word on this controversial topic, we would leave with the reader the conviction that ingenuity in language can contribute to both clarity and impact of communication. It is choosing the less effective alternative to ask "Are we ready to change?" When you could say, "Do we have the gumption to break away from the shackles of custom?" Typically, the language used in organizational communication is lifeless. Bringing a ruddy glow to its cheeks is a worthy project in itself.

4. HUMOR

All skilled speakers use humor as a device of suggestion and for many it is a major method of communication. Yet the use of humor has received less study and has been less written about than any other rhetorical method. Perhaps the academic community considers the use of humor to be undignified. The effectiveness of the method is its claim to dignity, in the opinion of the present authors. We hasten to pay tribute to the two scholars who have become the leading authorities on contemporary humor, Bennett Cerf and Bergen Evans, and to recommend to our readers that they extend their understanding of the utility of "being funny" through studying articles and books written by these men.

Humor is, necessarily, pure suggestion. No critical deliberation lies behind the guffaw. But because everybody craves to be amused, a point made in a context of tasteful fun is viewed more receptively than one that is deadly serious. Over recent decades public speaking has steadily become less formal. Conversational style is suited to humor, with the consequence that jokes appear where before they were unknown, in sermons, commencement addresses, presidential inaugural speeches, and funeral eulogies. The humor content of public address is on the rise. It behooves those of us who would master the art of the presentation to become serious students of humor.

Humor can be used in the presentation to establish rapport, to control attention, and to improve retention.

The best way to begin a presentation, or for that matter any public speech, is a matter of dispute. Two theories conflict. Theory A says that a speaker should begin with one of his strongest, most dramatic points and not bother about devices to gain attention. The material will be so interesting, this theory holds, that attention will come automatically.

Theory B points out that some time is required at the beginning of a speech for those assembled to stop thinking about what they have been doing and get acclimated to new conditions. Particularly, if the speaker is a stranger, they will tend to wonder about him as a person before concentrating on his subject. Bill Gove, a popular speaker in the area of sales training and a leading exponent of Theory B, contends that the audience will not start listening to your subject until it has made up its mind about *you*. So Bill spends a brief interval at the beginning on related human interest and humorous materials, until he sees the audience settle back and begin to relax. Then he starts to talk about the content he wants it to remember.

At the time of this writing, Theory B seems to be supported by observation and experience more than does Theory A. A "get acquainted" period does seem to occur, and humor is an effective agent to bring about the pleasant interaction between speaker and audience that we term "rapport." And, humor is perhaps the best antidote to social tension.

However, building rapport with an audience is not just a matter of telling funny stories. Selection of opening material is extremely important. Humor consists primarily of human interest experiences and jokes and both must suit the occasion and the audience, be fresh rather than trite, be adapted to the situation, and be used sparingly. The time to turn off the humor is while people are anxious for more.

A relevant criterion for selection of humor is, does it suit the source? A speaker must learn for himself what kinds of stories and jokes he can relate effectively and what kinds he cannot. For example, some speakers find it easy to get "belly laughs," while others excel in quiet, chuckle-producing humor. Further, the stereotype of the speaker limits the stories he can tell and dictates his language in telling them. The college professor or clergyman cannot use certain material acceptable to the American Legion commander or the sales trainer. The audience sees the speaker in his professional role, and while he may "stretch the stereotype" a little to indicate that he is a "regular guy," if he goes too far his listeners will be alienated and they will punish him for his indiscretion.

Humor is perhaps the best single method of establishing rapport for a very good reason. It is difficult to dislike the person who makes you laugh. In addition, the pattern of informal social interaction in our culture utilizes amusing related materials to open a conversation. After chuckling together, the participants turn to serious matters. Using humor to gain a fair and sympathetic hearing encourages a warm acceptance and conforms to the habits of relating to one another socially in Western cultures.

Let us consider the human being listening to a presentation. Two factors cause problems for the speaker who would like to receive universal, fair, favorable, and undivided attention. The first is the fact that attention is intrinsically unstable and sporadic, and the second is the fact that the listener has to "work at" paying attention and he is not inclined to work very hard.

The act of attention is normally intermittent. A person attending to a speech actually concentrates on that stimulus for periods of fifteen to forty-five seconds. Then he "tunes out" the speaker and thinks about something else. Later, he "tunes in" on the speaker, and depending upon what the speaker is saying, his burst of attention may be shorter than the one before. If the periods of attention to the speaker get longer and the periods away get shorter, the speaker is winning the battle for attention. If the reverse occurs, the speaker loses, and when the listener fails to come back at all, he has lost absolutely.

A classic error made by speakers is assuming that because they have attention at the beginning of a presentation, that attention will continue. Nothing could be further from the truth. Attention must not only be *gained,* but it has to be *maintained.* Control of attention is a continuing problem, from the beginning to the end of a speech.

How do the professional speakers manage an almost complete control of attention? By a combination of feedback and humor. Bill Gove watches every member of his audience for signs of disinterest or distraction. When these appear, Bill changes the scene. He stops driving and hammering home his points and provides a relaxing interlude with a bit of related humor, and perhaps a little bantering interchange with some members of the audience. A few moments later, back to work.

The changes of pace and varieties of material shown by successful speakers argue that an ongoing speech resembles alternating current more than it does direct current. The alternations are accomplished by narratives, illustrations, and changes of topic as well as by insertions of humor. But whatever the nature of an element of variety, humor adds to its effectiveness. The restorative relaxation of laughter readies a person for a period of close attention better than any other experience.

When the "alternating current" pattern of a presentation is established, the audience often finds the experience pleasurable and an interesting phenomenon of attention takes place. What was originally "voluntary" attention, requiring conscious work, turns into "involuntary" attention, the kind that sustains itself without effort. When audience and speaker become involved in a common project, it becomes rewarding to both. Such involvement should be the goal of every speaker. Chapter 12 explains further the concept of speaker-listener interdependence.

To phrase it figuratively, humor can provide pegs on which to hang the key points of a speech. The humor is recalled later, and perhaps to the surprise of the person remembering the funny story, there also is the concept he acquired along with its peg.

Using humor to carry speech content demands a delicate balance between being funny and being serious. The response of laughter is so rewarding to the speaker that he may well overdo the use of amusing sidelights and obliterate the point he wanted to emphasize. He then becomes a crowd-pleaser, using humor as a crutch and assigning a low priority to his message. His listeners remember his jokes but cannot recall what he talked about.

Because people forget so much so easily, the most valuable speech material is that which tends to lodge in the mind. We are not sure what it is that people remember best, but in all probability, very close to the top of the list, are real-life stories about what happened to people. If these have humor in them, so much the better, and most of them do. The great speakers spend their lives collecting just those experiences that illustrate the points they want to make. They know that if the story is a good one, and if it is an example of the related point, later both it and the point associated with it will be recalled and retold.

In addition to the "piggy-back phenomenon" described above, retention of materials in a presentation is aided by anything that influences positively the quality of attention paid to the speech. Since humor is a major means of raising attention levels, it also operates indirectly but significantly to increase the amount remembered.

5. SHORT CUTS TO ACCEPTANCE VIA INDIRECT SUGGESTION

Study of successful presentations reveals techniques or devices that are used generally and that seem to contribute substantially to winning acceptance. Indirect formulas, the hidden short cuts to acceptance, are one category of considerable importance. These procedures are true indirect suggestion, for they operate effectively only when the recipient of the message does not know they are being used. If a receiver identifies a particular short-cut technique being addressed to him, it loses much of its effect. This dependence on concealment will become obvious as we discuss kinds of short cuts and give examples of their use.

A. Common Ground

The mind of a listener is prepared for agreement when early in his presentation a speaker talks about beliefs shared by those present. Such "common ground" may include praise of past accomplishments, reiteration of goals and objectives, endorsement of leadership, dedication to progress and improvement, and so on. Each fact and value judgment on which audience and speaker agree becomes a building block in the foundation on which the speaker can rest his proposal. Because the use of common ground shows the speaker to be much like them, members of the audience become inclined to accept both him and his ideas.

Language can constitute common ground. If the speaker uses the vocabulary, colloquial expressions, and verbal stereotypes of his audience, they perceive him to be one of them and without thinking about it, lower their guard against his recommendation.

An effective variant of the common-ground technique is the "together" device. People have an impulse to conform, to go along with the crowd. If the speaker can show that his recommendation is part of a trend, that the rush has started to "get on the bandwagon" his listeners will feel that they, too, should become a part of the movement. The "together" appeal works best as a subordinate theme. Ideally, "the trend" and "everybody is moving in this direction" concepts are casually mentioned from time to time but are never permitted to assume the role of a major reason for change.

Ways in which common ground can be utilized in a presentation are limited only by the ingenuity of the speaker. He should prepare a list of all agreements he can think of that might be mentioned to reinforce habits of agreement and select items from the list.

B. Yes Response

Closely related to the use of common ground is a technique of encouraging tendencies toward agreement through providing opportunity for affirmative responses. If a person answers "yes" to each one in a series of questions, he becomes more likely to say "yes" to the next question. A habit of either affirmative or negative responses is easily established, and the maker of the presentation should take care to encourage only yes responses by the way he words his statements and his rhetorical questions.

In Chapter 6 the rhetorical question was cited as an excellent way to make a transition to the next topic. With thought and planning, transition questions can be so worded as to insure predominantly positive answers. Here is a list of a half dozen such questions that might occur along the way as the presentation proceeds.

1. Are we acknowledged to be leaders in our field?
2. Have we introduced more well-accepted new products than any of our competitors over the years?
3. Is demand for our product increasing?
4. Does our top management support reasonable risk-taking?
5. Are there gaps in our product line?
6. Would it be desirable to have our product line more complete?

The link between the "yes response" technique and "common ground" appears in the above questions. Each "yes" opens another area of shared interest. Coordinating yes response and common ground devices in this manner is easy and the effect is cumulative.

C. Transfer

The most varied of the short cuts to acceptance is transfer. Transfer is the effect of stimuli unrelated to the topic of the presentation upon readiness to accept or reject a recommendation. The nonverbal suggestive elements of environment and production mentioned earlier operate through transfer. For example, distractions produce negative transfer and a pleasant speaking manner transfers positively. Here we are concerned with verbal incidents that might influence audience response positively or negatively and that are separate from evidence and reasoning used to develop the topic.

Positive transfer occurs when the speaker chooses his illustrations from the interests of his audience. Using an analogy from tennis to a group of golfers would probably cause negative transfer. Positive transfer is associated with providing opportunity for audience questions and answering them carefully; negative transfer comes from cutting them off. Unnecessarily technical and complicated language builds hostility through negative transfer, while easy-to-understand, layman's translations of technical terms generally transfer positively.

Contingent situations lead to positive or negative transfer. If an audience is slow in arriving, the speaker can proceed with his talk regardless, or delay his beginning, probably by talking informally with the audience about related matters, until the audience is assembled. The latter choice transfers positively, because it shows the speaker's concern for his listeners.

What a speaker says about his audience transfers to his topic. If he credits his hearers with expertness and defers to them in their specialization, positive transfer takes place. When a speaker goes "beyond the fact" in awarding merit to his listeners, we term his act "flattery." Unless it is outrageous, flattery tends to transfer positively, due to the ability we all have to enjoy hearing nice things said about ourselves.

The speaker's attitude toward himself as reflected in his words is a rich source of transfer. If he assumes the authority of his position and expertness but is careful not to exceed or exploit it, he transfers favorably. But either pretension beyond position and achievement, or excessive humility (the "humble bit"), is apt to transfer negatively.

In discussing humor we stressed the importance of quality and relevance. Through transfer an improper or irrelevant story can reduce the impact of good evidence and reasoning, while these can be equally enhanced by pointed and pertinent humor.

Pronunciation, grammatical correctness, and language appropriate to the occasion have great negative or positive transfer potential. How much if any slang and profanity to use is a related and difficult problem. This decision is another contingency, made after considering the norms of current practice and the peculiarities of a particular situation.

To insure that he will maximize positive transfer and reduce negative transfer to a minimum, a speaker must scrutinize whatever he plans to do or say and ask himself, "How could that possibly affect the reception of my message?" If a planned behavior has even a possibility of creating an adverse effect, it should be replaced with one of greater positive potential.

D. Multiple Options

A person preparing a proposal tends to be trapped in a rut. He attempts to perfect a single possibility and channels all of his efforts to support this one goal. By doing this he becomes vulnerable. If there is some aspect of his recommendation that fails to win approval, his listeners have but one choice, to reject the whole package. In short, he has made a "something or nothing" proposal when he might as well have argued for "something or something else."

The "multiple options" approach consists of preparing two or more versions of a recommendation. These need not differ drastically and, ideally, each should be acceptable to the maker of the presentation. The posture of the speaker becomes more comfortable. He can say, "There are two or three ways of going about this. I'm not sure which is best. Let me tell you about the possibilities."

With multiple options the tendency of the audience is to concentrate upon choosing among the possibilities or attempt to combine them rather than deciding to accept or reject the entire proposal. When the strategy is successful, speaker and audience work together as a team to decide what is, indeed, the best recommendation. Typically, the listeners become so involved that they find it difficult to reject the version they decide is best. After all, they selected it!

Probably, the multiple-options strategy is less well known than the other short cuts to acceptance. But it may well be the most powerful of them all. Our readers are advised when next they prepare a proposal to submit it in two or three versions and observe how many listeners assume without question that one of the proposals will prevail.

E. Team Play

To differing degrees all people like to work with others, to be a part of joint effort, to collaborate on a worthy cause. Man is a social being. When he has an opportunity to join a team and play an interesting game, he usually wants to do it.

The speaker who uses the "team play" approach assumes the role of enlisting helpers to join him in building a better world. Many advantages accrue to this posture. The proposal becomes the center of interest rather than the maker of the proposal. Each listener begins to think in terms of what he has to contribute. A task-oriented interpersonal relationship develops among members of the audience leading to a sharing of skills and ideas. A "gung ho, let's get on with it" attitude gains momentum. When the recommendation of the speaker becomes a project for the group, success is at hand.

Participative management is an application of the team-play device.

Individuals play needed roles in group efforts. Work becomes a game, with rewards to both the collective and the individual participant. Both satisfactions and output increase. From the point of view of getting the job done, the basic advantage comes from the employees becoming more interested in the job they are doing, for its own sake. Their achievement-motivation increases, causing their energies to be focused on the task more effectively.

What happens in good participative management occurs when the team-play approach is skillfully applied in a presentation. Resources of the group focus on the recommended project and the resulting momentum will do much to implement the proposal.

THE USE OF SUGGESTION IN THE PRESENTATION OF SELF

Aristotle, who wrote one of the first important treatises on persuasive speaking, asserted that "Persuasion is achieved by the speaker's personal character when the speech is so spoken as to make us think him credible . . . his character may almost be called the most effective means of persuasion he possesses."[5] Twentieth-century scholars have made extensive researches into the phenomenon of the persuasive power of human personality. Some studies have gone beyond personal character to ask more general questions about the positive suggestion inherent in attributing a message to a source such as the president of Minnesota Mills or a professor at Harvard University. In Chapter 2 we discussed the implications of position status on the credibility of the source of a message. A class of studies that can be categorized as *source credibility* investigations has demonstrated the general principle that a prestigious source will affect the perception of a message.[6]

A number of other studies have examined the factors involved in personal proof by using the technique of the semantic differential tests first developed by professors at the University of Illinois to study meaning. For example, David Berlo, James Lemert, and Robert Mertz made a factor analysis of the verbal descriptions of speaker credibility and discovered three factors accounted for most of the variability in the selection of descriptive labels to apply to respected authorities. The three factors were safety, qualification, and dynamism.[7] Kim Giffin, in

[5] Aristotle, *Rhetoric*, trans. W. Rhys Roberts, 1356a.

[6] See, for example, F. S. Haiman, "An Experimental Study of Public Speaking," *Speech Monographs*, 16 (1949), 190–202; C. I. Hovland, I. L. Janis, and H. D. Kelley, *Communication and Persuasion* (New Haven, Conn., 1953); and Kenneth Anderson and Theodore Clevenger, Jr., "A Summary of Experimental Research in Ethos," *Speech Monographs*, 30 (1963), 59–78.

[7] David K. Berlo, James B. Lemert, and Robert Mertz, *Dimensions for Evaluating the Acceptability of Message Sources*, mimeographed report, Michigan State Uni-

expanding the work of others into the concept of interpersonal trust, suggested that the first two factors discovered by Berlo, Lemert, and Mertz were analogous to the trustworthiness and competence features emphasized by Hovland, Janis, and Kelley.[8]

A third group of studies deals with the interpersonal dynamics of leaderless group discussions that result in certain members rising to leadership or becoming influential within the group.[9]

In our discussion of techniques that are useful for the presentational speaker to build an impression of good character we draw upon the research results when possible. Much of the research has served primarily to support insights already well known but some new information is available and some modifications of old theory are now indicated.

Biographical detail is a source of suggestion. Just as the historical record shapes the future, so do the reminiscences, memories, and legends about the biography of the speaker affect the audience's response. If a person sees a twisted pile of steel and wire on the porch and inquires about it, he may be told that it is some discarded junk from the basement waiting to be carted to the dump ground. His response to the artifact may then be to dismiss it and attend to other matters. If, however, he is told that the thing is the product of one of the most gifted contemporary artists and that it was recently purchased at auction for $10,000, he may well respond differently. He may circle it, view it from all angles, and it may now evoke in him a feeling of aesthetic pleasure, of amusement, of anger, or of disbelief because of the biographical detail attributed to the person who fashioned the object. Someone may glance at an individual at another table in a restaurant without noticing him until told that the person is an astronaut who has walked on the surface of the moon. The bit of biographical information may well cause considerable interest in and study of the individual.

Stereotypes inferred from assumed biographical detail. If a person has had a series of unpleasant experiences trying to buy a second-hand automobile and if his most intimate acquaintances report similar experiences, he may infer certain biographical details about an indi-

---

versity, 1966. See also Erwin P. Bettinghaus, *Persuasive Communication* (New York, 1969), chap. 5.

[8] Kim Giffin, *The Trust Differential,* mimeographed report, The University of Kansas, 1968. See also Kim Giffin, "Interpersonal Trust in Small-Group Communication," *Quarterly Journal of Speech,* 53 (1967), 224–234.

[9] Our discussion on rising to positions of influence that follows relies heavily upon studies of leadership emergence in leaderless group discussion at the University of Minnesota. The Minnesota studies are summarized in Ernest G. Bormann, *Discussion and Group Methods: Theory and Practice* (New York, 1969).

vidual when he discovers that the person is a used-car salesman. As a result, the prospect approaches the salesman with a set of expectations that influences his response to the sales pitch.

A number of professional fields require such long periods of education and training that certification requirements are standardized. Thus, a medical doctor, a professor of mathematics, a certified public accountant, a dentist, and a lawyer, to name but a few professions, will have gone through a prescribed course of study and certain practical apprenticeships. When a speaker is called an M.D., therefore, the audience will expect that he has graduated from medical school, served a period of internship, and perhaps a residency.

Just as members of a given culture will have stereotypes for certain important functionaries such as medicine men, priests, seers, fakirs, physicists, astronauts, movie stars, and football quarterbacks, so will they understand the importance of certain key institutional, organizational, or corporate positions. While the king, chief, or president of Minnesota Mills may be personally unknown to the listeners, the biography of anyone who reaches such a position can be partially inferred. An individual does not rise to the top of a modern corporation without certain skills and drives, and without having served an organizational apprenticeship.

The biographical information inherent in identifying a speaker as a medical doctor or the president of Minnesota Mills, therefore, serves as suggestion, either positive or negative for a given audience, topic, position, or profession. The fact that a speaker is a physician may prove to be positive suggestion (believe the speaker) for some audiences and enhance his presentation if the topic is how to avoid heart attacks and may be negative suggestion (do not believe the speaker) if the subject is "Why doctors are underpaid."

A host of studies have demonstrated that in the absence of other information and controlling the variables of topic, audience, and situation, the source of a message can be rendered more persuasive by positive suggestion that the speaker is certified as a competent authority in the area under discussion or that the person has risen to a position of importance in an institution that deals with the topic in question. For example, in one study the investigators discovered that when students were asked to rank ten religious, political, and social groups in terms of general credibility, the three top-ranked categories were medical doctors, physicists, and civic leaders. The three low-ranked groups were labor union members, high school dropouts, and sexual deviates.[10]

When only a very general label qualifies the source as a person with

[10] Alvin Goldberg, Lloyd Crisp, Evelyn Sieburg, and Michele Tolela, "Subordinate Ethos and Leadership Attitudes," *Quarterly Journal of Speech,* 53 (1967), 354–360.

experiences that render him credible and competent to discuss the topic, as in the categories discussed above, the resulting suggestion tends to be relatively weak. Much more persuasive is the demonstrated trustworthiness, competence, and likability of a person who has worked with every member of the audience in close interpersonal relationships over a period of time.

Interpersonal relationships and speaker influence. If we know the speaker and he has been a responsible person, if his advice has been good and his friendship unselfish, we will weigh his words favorably. While patients might respond positively to a presentation from a stranger who is introduced as a medical doctor, they will respond more favorably to a person they have known very well for years and who has proved to be a good doctor.

One ought not, of course, overlook any avenue of positive suggestion when developing a persuasive presentation, and if a speaker can have someone who is known and trusted by the audience introduce him and comment on his qualifications and character so much the better. Our concern here, however, is with the elements of a presentation that go beyond reputation established prior to the speech. What can the speaker say and do that will make the audience trust him as a friend and respect him as an adviser on the topic of his presentation?[11]

Nonverbal suggestion to enhance personal influence. The speaker should strive to conduct himself so that he projects an image of a person in control of the situation. If his manner, including eye contact, gestures, vocal inflections, and so on, give the audience the impression that the speaker is extremely nervous, embarrassed, or unsure, the impact will often be negative. If he is unable to meet the problems posed by a presentational speaking situation, why should the audience suppose that the speaker is more able under other conditions of stress? On the other hand, the speaker who projects an image of calm confidence and assurance, who seems sincerely and honestly convinced of the wisdom and truth of his message or product, will benefit from the suggestion. Successful salesmen often testify that the first person to whom they sell a new product is themselves, on the assumption that unless they are sold they will not be able to sell anyone else.

In general, positive suggestion results from nonverbal cues for the audience that the speaker is audience-centered rather than self-centered. If the speaker appears to lose himself in the importance of the topic, the occasion, and, above all, if his interest in his listeners seems strong, then he is more often trusted, believed, and liked than

---

[11] The distinction we make here between prior reputation and suggestion during the course of the speech is essentially the same as that made in Winston L. Brembeck and William S. Howell, *Persuasion* (Englewood Cliffs, N.J., 1952), pp. 244–245.

the speaker who seems worried about such things as his personal appearance, the dulcet quality of his voice, or the impression he is making on the big boss.

The speaker's manner when responding to questions, disagreements, agreements, supporting statements, challenges, and antagonism is also important. If the speaker responds nonverbally in a way that communicates to his listeners that he appreciates questions, respects the interrogator, and will answer to the best of his ability, he will build good will. If he responds in a way that nonverbally communicates that he feels the question was a waste of his valuable time, or that it was a stupid question, or that the questioner had no right to challenge his expertness, he will reduce his stature in the eyes of the audience.

If the speaker's manner under interrogation suggests that he has something to hide, or that he is wary of making a clear and complete response, or that he is unable to answer a question that a person in his position ought to be able to deal with, it will reduce his credibility.

Verbal suggestion to enhance speaker influence. What the speaker actually says verbally during the course of the presentation will also influence the trust he establishes, the feeling of competence he projects, and the likability of his image.

If the speaker is to be trusted, he will have to say things that give the impression that he is unselfish and guided by an acceptable code of ethics. Jack Gibb has discovered six message perceptions that are likely to cause defensive reactions in the listener. The six impressions that lead listeners to dislike and distrust a speaker are (1) the interpretation that the speaker is making an evaluation of the listener as a person rather than of the work under analysis, (2) the interpretation that the speaker is trying to exert control over the listener, (3) the interpretation that the speaker is trying to use strategy on the listener, (4) the interpretation that the speaker is not interested in the listener as a person, (5) the interpretation that the speaker feels superior to the listener, and (6) the interpretation that the speaker is being arbitrary and dogmatic.[12] The presentational speaker should phrase his speech in such a way as to guard against his listeners making any of these interpretations.

The speaker can build interpersonal trust by suggesting that he is absolutely fair, candid, and honest. "If I have made a mistake, I will be the first to admit it." "We may disagree but all I ask is for a fair hearing and I'm willing to listen to all sides on this question." "This is the way the thing looks to me now, but I'll be honest with you I have some serious doubts."

[12] Jack R. Gibb, "Defensive Communication," *Journal of Communication,* 11 (1961), 141–148.

The speaker working to establish a trusting relationship with the audience should not suggest that he is defensive about his status or expertness. If the speaker is perceived as resistant to any challenge of his authority, the audience will be distrustful of his statements. If the speaker uses technical jargon to cut down people who challenge him or if his analysis of the situation is filled with esoteric and technical language suitable only for an audience of experts, the audience will tend to not like or trust him.

The speaker can build trust by giving evidence that he is deeply involved and dedicated to the subject, the organization, and the audience. People rise to influence in groups and organizations partly because they communicate a deep concern for the enterprise. Someone who seems apathetic or uninterested, who communicates a "couldn't care less" attitude will not become trusted or influential.

We must be careful not to confuse high commitment and dedication to the good of the entire group with high bias. The speaker who suggests he is inflexibly committed to a highly biased position will be trusted only by his fellow true believers. Before hostile or apathetic listeners his bias will arouse distrust and cynicism.

The speaker can build interpersonal trust by volunteering to help others and the audience at a personal sacrifice. "I would be willing, if we can work it out, to come in a couple of Saturday afternoons on my own time to help with this."

In addition to trust, the speaker should suggest competence. Perhaps the most powerful suggestion of competence is a well-delivered, brilliantly conceived, and supported presentation. If the speaker does an extremely good job of analysis, proof, and clarification, the indirect suggestion of competence and ability is strong. But in addition to the over-all impression made by the entire speech certain other material can be added by the speaker to develop the image of an expert. Recall our discussion of the way a sophisticated listener tests the credibility of experts. The tests included such things as competence in the area, familiarity with the specific facts of the case, and ability and willingness to tell the truth.

The speaker may remind the audience of factors in his background, experience, and training that make him particularly competent to discuss the topic. Statements about the nature and extent of his preparation for the task if insinuated in an aside and tossed off rather than delivered in a boastful manner are useful.

The speaker may allude to his background. "As a psychiatrist I always have a tendency to look at the early childhood for influences on the personality." He may refer to his experience as an expert. "In my twenty-seven years of clinical practice I have never seen a more clear-cut case."

Quite often, a speaker can imply his status without undue boasting with asides like, "When I was in Washington recently I had an opportunity to discuss this matter with the President," or "On my recent trip to Hong Kong I spent quite a bit of time with a man who recently escaped from Communist China."

Finally, audiences tend to believe speakers they like. Showing a sincere interest in the audience, its hopes, fears, hobbies, and desires, is an excellent way to become liked.

The speaker may build good will by raising the status of the audience with compliments or flattery of the organization or of individuals in the audience by indicating their importance, by asking for their advice and help, and by attending to their questions, suggestions, and ideas. "We were pretty much stumped on the quality thing until Bill came up with a suggestion that really opened things up."

Finally humor can enhance the likability of a speaker. A person who is perceived to have a sense of humor, and who does not take himself too seriously, who can see the lighter side of the situation and his role in it, is likable. If the humor is a gentle kind turned back on oneself rather than irony, satire, or ridicule turned on someone else, so much the better.

The person who can amuse his audience at will is seldom perceived as insecure. The man who can relax and have fun in a formal speaking context is in command of the situation. A worried man seldom makes competent jokes. These stereotyped impressions help to explain why audiences characterize speakers who use humor effectively as confident and capable.

However, the speaker who comes to be known as a "funny man" accumulates a negative image when he wishes to make a serious and important suggestion. He is so much more successful as a jokester than as a serious speaker that listeners refuse to accept him in a serious role. When Hilarious Hugh confronts them, they automatically snicker, and unless he provides continuous "fun and games," they stop listening. Hugh is a clown and clowns are not highly respected as advisers on important matters.

Skill in the use of humor contributes to a speaker's prestige and likability but it must be of high quality and relevant for maximum effect. Unrelated jokes "dragged in" by the speaker may sharply lower his reputation with the audience. Listeners are often unimpressed with humor outside their interests. To work as positive suggestion in the presentation of the self, humor must be carefully selected according to high standards of relevance and economy. A free-flowing series of jokes and stories will not do the job today. Speaker influence is built by appropriate genuinely funny material that supplements a serious core of substantial content.

SUMMARY

Insufficient attention has been paid to the nonlogical dimension of presentational speaking. Systematic planning and execution of elements of suggestion in the presentation are as necessary as are careful preparation and delivery of its reasoned content.

Suggestion as a method of persuasion includes all factors that influence acceptance or rejection of a recommendation and that achieve their effect without being identified by the listener. The reasoning mechanism of the receiver is bypassed, and his responses are automatic, unthinking, the product of habit. In a successful presentation, suggestion clears the channels and readies the listener to respond favorably to the reasoned portion of the message.

The method of suggestion brings these tangible advantages and others: it gets past defenses; it can be colorful, memorable, and impressive; points established by suggestion are difficult to attack; and it has a universal "human interest" appeal.

Nonverbal suggestion includes *proxemic* elements, the factors in the environment and the production of the presentation that influence its outcome, and the *personal* elements, what the speaker does other than what he says to enhance or destroy his chances of success.

Verbal techniques of suggestion are *direct*, saying in so many words what the speaker wishes the audience to believe or to do, and *indirect*, implying the desired response in various ways, never revealing explicitly the point made. Much effective suggestion in the presentation is indirect. The presentational speaker should master its many forms. Humor is perhaps the most prevalent form of suggestion, one that must be studied seriously if its benefits are to be realized.

Among the more powerful methods of suggestion are five short cuts to acceptance: common ground, yes response, transfer, multiple options, and team play. These focus energies of listeners on the recommendation and are particularly effective in supplementing reasoned appeals.

Suggestion is extremely useful in establishing the speaker as a person of good and trustworthy character. Much recent research indicates that in the absence of other information and with variables controlled, the higher the prestige of the source the more credible the message. However, the results of attributing messages to high-prestige sources are relatively weak when compared to interpersonal influence developed by personal contact.

In addition to reputation established prior to a speech, a person can develop his credibility by nonverbal and verbal suggestion during the course of the speech. Important nonverbal techniques include cues that the speaker is in control of himself and his material and that he is audience-centered. Also useful are verbal suggestions that the person is unselfish and guided by an acceptable code of ethics. The speech will be more persuasive if the speaker is perceived as fair, candid, and honest, if he seems well-versed and expert in the subject, and if he reveals a sense of humor and uses humor wisely.

Elements of suggestion should never be left to chance, for they are responsible for most of the excitement, high interest, and enthusiasm generated by a presentation. Suggestion tends to be intimate and warm and involves the human personality. The ability of suggestion to touch the soul is illustrated by this gentle, graceful Chinese farewell:

> May the rain brush you lightly; may the sun shine on you; may your future path be through the stars.

QUESTIONS FOR DISCUSSION AND REVIEW

1. How does a symbol reaction differ from a signal reaction?
2. What sorts of items in a message may cause a signal response for one person but a symbol response for another?
3. What are some of the advantages of using suggestion as a method of presentation?
4. What are the important proxemic elements in a presentation?
5. What is meant by the formula $R = 1/D$?
6. How can the speaker decide when to use direct suggestion and when to use indirect suggestion?
7. What are appropriate and inappropriate uses of humor in the presentation?
8. How can the speaker control the use of suggestion in the presentation of himself, and what is beyond his control?
9. What interpersonal relationships can increase or detract from the influence of a speaker?
10. What are some ways in which a speaker can use nonverbal suggestion to enhance his personal influence?

REFERENCES AND SUGGESTED READINGS

BROWN, ROGER. *Words and Things.* New York: Free Press, 1958.

CAMPBELL, JAMES H., and HAL W. HEPLER, eds. *Dimensions in Communication.* Belmont, Calif.: Wadsworth, 1965.

CARPENTER, EDMUND, and MARSHALL MCLUHAN, eds. *Exploration in Communication.* Boston: Beacon Press, 1960.

MEYERHOFF, ARTHUR E. *The Strategy of Persuasion.* New York: Berkeley Publishing, 1965.

MONROE, ALAN H., and DOUGLAS EHRINGER. *Principles of Speech Communication.* 6th brief ed., Chicago: Scott, Foresman, 1969.

CHAPTER ELEVEN

MULTIMEDIA AIDS
TO THE
PRESENTATION

WHAT AUDIO-VISUAL AIDS CONTRIBUTE
TO THE PRESENTATION

Throughout the book we have stressed the theme that the meaning which shapes response is read into the message by the receiver, that in all communication, from a results-oriented point of view, *meaning is perception*. All senses contribute to the development of perceptions. Restricting the input of communication to hearing alone is an artificial limiting of the perceptual potential. Smell, taste, and touch are perhaps minor contributors to most acts of learning, and most information is acquired through hearing and vision. The eye registers incredible amounts of data, adapts to distances easily, and most important, while people can easily stop listening, they find it difficult to ignore happenings within their central or even peripheral range of vision.

One dominant reason speakers sometimes neglect the use of visual stimuli in person-to-person communication is their preoccupation with verbalism. Stuart Chase aptly labeled this tendency "The Tyranny of Words." Educators have intensified our commitment and dedication to the exclusive use of words to dispense information. The trend of the past three hundred years has been to package all knowledge in bundles of words. The trend continues despite the fact that linguistic symbols are more remote from reality than most alternative communication codes.

Research into the effectiveness of audio-visual components in communication has accumulated for three or four decades; as we describe various forms of audio-visual aids in this chapter, we will report pertinent results of that research. Here we will mention only a sweeping survey generalization: Across the board, in our elementary and high schools the proper use of available films alone would increase learning from 20 to 30 percent. Yet in elementary and secondary schools from 80 to 90 percent of the teachers are untrained in the use of films and other audio-visual materials. Realistic and understandably cynical educational innovators testify that it takes at least fifty years to bring about significant change in our educational system. Perhaps after another quarter of a century or so the proven results of using all senses in education may be translated into practice.

Business and the professions have advanced beyond the schools in the use of audio-visual materials, but progress has not been uniform. Fads and fashions, presentational gimmicks, come and go. Fragmentary use of visual devices is typical. Speakers tend to use a novel format or device where it is not needed, overuse it, or use it for purposes for which it is neither suited nor intended. Razzle-dazzle presentations with a bewildering but impressive flow of spectacular visuals utilizing several media have become popular beyond their effectiveness. What is needed is a systems approach to audio-visual adjuncts to task-oriented communication, derived from a comprehensive theoretical analysis of human and substantive elements involved.

The presentational speaker in business and the professions can derive much relevant theory from studies in audio-visual education. Many elements in a presentation are analogous to the teacher-pupil interaction. Like the classroom teacher, the presentational speaker confronts the central problem of communicating in such a manner that his auditors understand and remember. Both teacher and speaker must study the learning process to see how understanding and retention are accomplished. They must come to know what contributions to this process can be made by audible and visual supplements to language.

Edgar Dale made a substantial step toward understanding the place of audio-visual elements in the instructional process when he devised the "Cone of Experience."[1] We have modified his analysis of the educational implications of various levels of speaking to the more restricted communication typical of the presentation. Figure 11.1 presents our modification of the Cone of Experience.

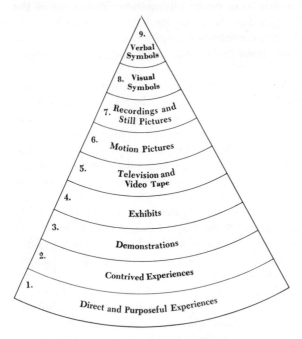

Figure 11.1   Cone of Learning Experiences

Three categories of quite different learning experiences emerge from the cone. Proceeding upward from the bottom, these are participative involvement (direct experience of events), passive involvement (observation, functioning as a witness to events), and symbolic involvement (learning patterns that do not resemble events they represent).

To relate these categories of learning more concretely to the layers comprising the cone, participative involvement or physically doing things (layers 1 and 2) provides maximum sensory stimulation; for example, driving a car, layer 1, and learning to fly by instruments in a Link Trainer, layer 2.

Hearing, sight, occasionally touch, seldom smell and taste are active in the levels of passive involvement (layers 3 through 7). Through

---

[1] Edgar Dale, *Audiovisual Methods in Teaching*, 3rd ed. (New York, 1969), chap. 4.

empathy, physical tensions produce covert participation, as in the experiment where seeing a short film on shooting free throws and practicing mentally each day improved skill in actually shooting free throws as much as daily physical practice.[2]

Visual symbols (e.g., European traffic signs) have a pictorial quality and suggest their meaning visually. Verbal symbols are completely artificial because they are arbitrary. Some patterned arrangement, as of letters in the alphabet, is arbitrarily assigned a connection to an event or to a class of events to establish verbal symbols.

Distinctions among layers in the cone are clarified by the dictionary definition of the word *abstract:* "conceived apart from matter and from special cases."[3] Since higher levels of the cone are further from reality, the cone can be said to represent activities ranging from the concrete to the abstract. As was noted in Chapter 10, the higher the level of abstraction, the greater the variability of meaning occurring in the minds of receivers of a message.

The area of each segment of the cone represents a varying amount of physical activity for the learner. In levels 1 and 2 the learner is very busy, physically. In layers 3, 4, 5, 6, and 7 he is selectively active, via empathy. In levels 8 and 9 the learner is inactive physically and engaged in making mental associations of arbitrary symbols and visual

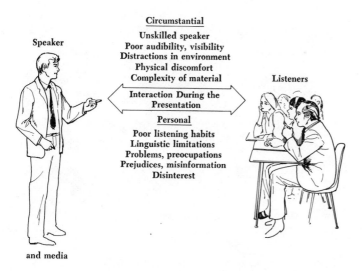

Figure 11.2   Obstacles to Listener Understanding

[2] S. F. Harby, "Comparison of Mental Practice and Physical Practice in the Learning of Physical Skills," Human Engineering Report SDC 269-7-27, Special Devices Center, 1952.

[3] *The American College Dictionary* (New York, 1955), p. 5.

Using the Overhead Projector

Trans World Airlines and Link Division, The Singer Co.

European Traffic
Signs

Training in a 747 Flight Simulator

General Mills, Inc.

Testing Cake Mix

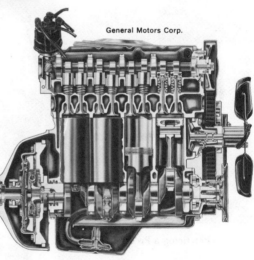

General Motors Corp.

Cutaway Model of 4-Cylinder Engine

American Museum of Natural History

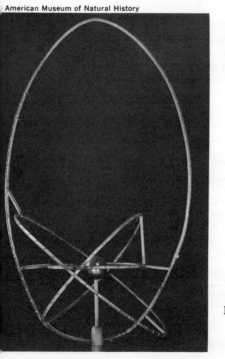

Model of an Atom

Mockup of an Auto
for Driver Testing and Training

Oravisual Co., Inc.

Link Division, The Singer Co.

Practicing a Presentation

Architect, John Andrews;
Photographer, Panda/Croyden Associates; Through **Architectural Record**

A Diorama to Show
Layout of a Community

3M Co., Visual Products Division

25-Minute Reel of 16mm Tape

General Mills, Inc.

Video Taping a Speaker

3M Co., Visual Products Division

Reel of 2-Inch Video Tape

Union Carbide Corp.

Filming a Lecture

RCA

Broadcast Video Tape Recorder

Sound Motion Picture Projector
(16mm) with Zoom Lens

Technicolor, Inc.

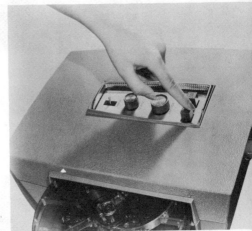

A Cartridge Film Projector

Oravisual Co., Inc.

Magnetic Chalkboard

Oravisual Co., Inc.

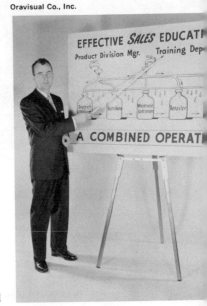

Demonstration Cards on Easel

Flip Chart

American Optical Corp.

Opaque Projector

Oravisual Co., Inc.

Flannel Board

**Automatic Slide Projector
with Remote Control**

Eastman Kodak Co.

DuKane Corp.

Filmstrip Projector with Remote Control

American Optical Corp.

Closeup of Overhead Projector

Overhead Transparency-
Making Machine

Charles Beseler Co.

Overhead Projector with
Acetate on Attached Rollers

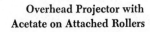

Using a Lavalier Microphone

Portable Stereophonic Tape Recorder

Bell & Howell

A Multimedia Room

images. Research findings substantiate the common-sense conclusion that the amount and vigor of physical activity in the act of learning profoundly influence understanding and recall.[4]

The social-psychological factors in the learning situation that are necessary to a successful presentation can be identified by locating the major barriers that reduce understanding and retention. Figure 11.2 presents a diagrammatic representation of the situational and interpersonal obstacles. Direct experience of events is intrinsically more likely to overcome both circumstantial and personal barriers to understanding than is perception of visual and verbal symbols.

The present chapter deals with the speaker's use of audio-visual experiences to overcome circumstantial and personal obstacles to understanding. Chapter 12 considers what the listener can do to help surmount these same barriers.

PARTICIPATIVE INVOLVEMENT EXPERIENCES

The most effective and the least used aids to presentation are those that provide an experience of active personal involvement. They are impressive and interesting because they are multisensory in their stimulation and have an actuality that pictorial or linguistic representations of events cannot approach. They are little used because they require more ingenuity and effort than the simpler devices such as pictures, charts, and words. Also, most speakers and audiences are unaccustomed to participative experiences in presentations. We tend to imitate our predecessors and to expect others to stay within the boundaries of the familiar.

Participative experience as an aid to communication can be classified as direct or contrived. In direct experiences the audience participates in an actual event, complete and undistorted. Contrived experiences result when the presentation incorporates imitations of actuality that are purposefully simplified to highlight important elements. Although the speaker manipulates and controls the participation of the audience, the experience still creates an effect very similar to direct experience.

Direct participative experiences. Actual participation in an activity is possible in two forms, either by the speaker taking the audience to the event in a field trip or by transporting the event to the audience. If a presentational speaker is proposing modification of a manufacturing operation, he can secure fullest understanding of the present method and of the nature of the change by taking his audience to the assembly line, showing them the old and new methods in action,

[4] *Report of the Activities of the Telemation Laboratory,* School of Education, University of Wisconsin, February, 1961–May, 1962; Clifford T. Morgan, *Introduction to Psychology* (New York, 1956), chap. 5; Bernard Berelson and Gary A. Steiner, *Human Behavior* (New York, 1964).

having them try their hand at the jobs to be done under current and under recommended procedures. If the presentation proposes a new cake mix to the Board of Control at Minnesota Mills, the members of the board might well go to the experimental kitchens and individually or in groups of two or three follow the directions on the box. Ideally, they would complete the baking process and taste their own final product, but if that plan takes too much time, they could mix the cakes, then sample others previously baked. The sales presentation frequently permits direct participation. The salesman trying to get a farm implement dealer to add a new corn picker to his line should take the dealer to a harvest field and have him operate the machine himself.

A speaker who has the audience manipulate, feel, see, hear, smell, and even taste "where the action is" creates involvement that cannot be duplicated in any other way. The maker of a presentation should aggressively seek out opportunities to build a field trip into his planned activities.

When the field trip is impractical, a speaker can sometimes transport devices and processes into the room where the audience is assembled. Instead of relying upon pictures and words to make his point, the speaker recommending the use of video-taped role-playing in the training of salesmen can set up a video-tape machine, have volunteer audience members play roles, and another member operate the recorder. Any demonstration of equipment becomes participatory involvement when operated by members of the audience.

If the purpose of the presentation is to sell a new product and if the product is sufficiently portable, the people planning the speech should have some samples in finished functioning form for audience members to study, handle, and operate. For example, if the speaker is presenting the advantages of a new machine for taking dictation, he might set up a typical secretarial installation of desk, chair, electric typewriter, and dictation machine and have one of the audience members dictate a memo. A secretary could then transcribe the memo to illustrate the way the new installation works. If the speaker takes some pains, he can develop a lively interchange among the observing members of the group, the performers, and himself, which will generate interest in the new device and its potential.

Admittedly, direct and realistic participative involvement is possible in only a minority of presentations. The important consideration is that the student of presentational speaking ought not overlook participative involvement whenever it *is* possible. Often, with a little ingenuity the speaker can discover ways to move the persons to the scene of action or the equipment to the people with gratifying, dynamic, and impressive consequences.

Contrived participative experiences. The person who contrives participation for the audience ordinarily uses objects that are three-dimensional, such as specimens, cutaway machines, models, and mockups. Less used but still valuable is the simulation of processes that are largely symbolic and two-dimensional.

Specimens are representative parts of a machine or process that can be isolated, handled, and inspected. A new valve that is the heart of an oil-pumping system can be used in the presentation about the complex system.

Cutaways are usually full-sized devices, modified by having parts eliminated and housings "cut away" to reveal the details of how some complex machine functions. The automatic transmission cutaway is typically mounted on a stand and driven at a slow speed by a small electric motor. As controls are adjusted, the operator can see precisely how neutral, reverse, and varied forward speeds are accomplished.

The models used as audio-visual aids may be classified as *theoretical* and *physical*. Theoretical models are usually two-dimensional drawings representing fairly abstract concepts in some structural relationship to provide an explanation for a complicated phenomenon. Typical of theoretical models are those explaining the process of communication. What we referred to as "paradigms" of man-to-man and man-to-machine communication in Chapter 3 are theoretical models, and Figures 3.1 and 3.2 in that chapter represent typical two-dimensional drawings of models in the theoretical sense. Occasionally, a model of theoretical relationships is three-dimensional, as in the instance when the structure of a molecule is represented by a rod-and-ball three-dimensional structure.

One kind of physical model is the person, usually female, who poses for pictures and displays of clothing and other merchandise. Human models are seldom used as aids to presentations. The physical model the presentational speaker finds most helpful is a literal simulation of reality, and quite often it is a physical representation to scale of another physical entity. When we speak of a "model" as an audio-visual aid in the remainder of the chapter we will be using the term to refer to physical models.

In this limited sense, models are,

> . . . *recognizable three-dimensional representations of real things.* The thing represented may be infinitely large, like the earth, or small as an atom. It may be an inanimate object such as a building, a monument, or a mine shaft; or it may be a living organism such as a paramecium, or the human heart. The model may represent something as intricate as a jet engine, a nuclear powered submarine, or a spacecraft, or as simple as a number of spools on a string. It may be complete in every detail or considerably more simplified than the original.[5]

[5] Walter A. Wittich and Charles F. Schuller, *Audiovisual Materials: Their Nature and Use* (New York, 1967), p. 173.

By a wide margin, models are the most flexible representations of physical relationships.

Advantages of using models are apparent in this list of characteristics supplied by Walter Wittich and Charles Schuller.

Models are three dimensional . . .
Models reduce or enlarge objects to an observable size . . .
Models provide interior views of objects . . .
Models eliminate the nonessentials of objects . . .
Models employ colors and texture to accent important features . . .
Many models can be disassembled and reassembled . . .
Models can be created. . . .[6]

A mockup is an elaborate, functioning model, often full size, designed to clarify complex interdependent processes or to train people in skills and techniques of operation, maintenance, and repair. The mockup of a telephone, for example, could consist of the essential components spread over a demonstration board with labels that identify parts and describe their functions. The speaker using such a mockup could easily measure voltages at all parts of the circuit and trace the voice signal with an oscilloscope. A presentation based on steps in a manufacturing process condensed and clarified in a mockup would be useful to the orientation of new employees. Devices that simulate an automobile moving through traffic to train and test drivers are complicated mockups, as are the famous Link Trainers used to sharpen the flying skills of military and airline pilots.

Mockups are useful in presentations whenever a dynamic, complex operation can be simplified and arranged so that the "how" of its operation becomes readily apparent. A danger is that the mockups may become unproductively elaborate. Often, restricting the mockups to an absolute minimum of essentials, and assembling them of cheap, disposable materials, will produce a working unit that is easy to operate and to understand.

The mockup is a *literal* simulation device. Often, more *symbolic* simulations are helpful to the presentational speaker. The planners of an important presentation might devise variations of computerized business games to check out the probable consequences of a proposed change in company policy, or to explore the market for a new product, or to predict the effect of a price change on profits. The speaker could use the computerized game to compare his recommendations to current practices in various hypothetical situations. He could involve the audience by having it play the game and try to outguess the machine.

Of course, development of the simulated situation does not require a computer or other data processing equipment. Realistic hypothetical situations that pose perplexing problems familiar to the participants

6 *Ibid.*, pp. 174–177.

will provide incentive for thoughtful evaluation of the related proposal.

Other techniques for audience participation. Although the direct and contrived audience participations that are designed to be the basic theme of the presentation are most closely related to the lower levels of the Cone of Learning Experiences and thus most effective in learning, the effectiveness of all audio-visual aids increases when the audience participates actively in the presentation. A rough rule-of-thumb is that the increase in audience interest and learning is roughly proportional to the amount of audience activity. The presentational speaker should know the ways and means of increasing the active involvement of his audience in audio-visual experiences. When appropriate, he should consciously "draw the audience in," converting passive participation into active participation by having its members do or say something.

Research into the uses of audio-visual materials in education supplies proven techniques for gaining audience participation.[7] If the audience is carefully prepared for a particular audio-visual experience, more will be learned than if its members are surprised by it. Preparing the audience consists of overviewing what is to come, telling what to watch and listen for, explaining what is nonessential or possibly confusing, defining strange vocabulary or unfamiliar processes, and answering questions. Only when the audience is informed of general procedure and specific purpose of the coming experience is it ready to benefit maximally from it.

Frequently, it is desirable to pause along the way to talk with the audience about what is going on. For example, stopping a film and letting people ask questions will increase learning. If a discussion develops over what has been seen and what is to come, learning will be considerably greater than if only questions are asked. A summary after using any audio-visual aid makes it more effective. When the speaker leads the audience to help him summarize, results are much superior to those from a summary done by the speaker alone.

A basic principle to help the speaker plan audience involvement is this: He should never do by himself what members of his audience can do as well. This applies particularly to demonstrations, when members

---

[7] *Ibid.*, chap. 2; *Technology in Learning*, Ontario Curriculum Institute, 1965; William H. Allen, "Research in Film Use; Student Participation," *Audio-Visual Communication*, R5 (1957), 423–450; Carl I. Hovland *et al.*, *Experiments in Mass Communication* (Princeton, N.J., 1949); Donald N. Michael, *Some Factors Influencing the Effects of Audience Participation on Learning from a Factual Film*, USAF Human Resources Laboratories, 1951; Kenneth H. Kurtz and Carl I. Hovland, "The Effect of Verbalization During Observation of Stimulus Objects upon Accuracy of Recognition and Recall," *Journal of Experimental Psychology*, 45 (1953), 157–164.

of the audience can aid the speaker, as volunteers from a magician's audience contribute to the show by assisting him.

Where there is no equipment to manipulate or materials for audience members to help arrange and manage, participation can take the form of *verbalizing content*. The skilled demonstrator can make his points by asking the right questions. Probably the best guarantee of high audience interest is to move the demonstration along with a series of thought-provoking and leading questions. The audience is encouraged to do some guessing and to call out answers. The developing presentation provides feedback to check each guess. Studies show that audiences like this feedback and that the process of making choices and finding that they are right or wrong increases learning. The questioning technique can be carried on into the final summary, with the audience being asked to recall the main points made and their significance.

Providing mental practice to aid understanding and recall is possible with audio-visual aids. Much reiteration is built into films and filmstrips and demonstrations repeat central points in various ways. Audience questions and discussion are certain to "hash over" familiar concepts and to focus upon their application. All of these reiterative activities constitute mental practice, the "covert" or inner verbalization of response that fixes words and ideas in memory and makes them more important to the learner.

Finally, involvement of the audience causes a much more animated interaction between speaker and listeners. The result is a two-way communication that is clearer and more pleasurable than a one-way sending of a message. A "team" spirit tends to emerge as speaker and receivers pool their efforts to make the presentation a success. The *quality* of the speaker-audience relationship may well be the decisive factor determining the outcome of many presentations. A warm, mutual respect is usually an outcome of vigorous two-way communication.

PASSIVE INVOLVEMENT EXPERIENCES

Most audio-visual aids to the presentation produce a passive involvement, casting the listener in the role of witness or observer. Even though the speaker involves the audience only passively, the audio-visual aids can help the communicative process by using direct sensory experiences to supplement the words in the message.

Demonstrations. The passive involvement device that most closely resembles the direct participative experience is that of the demonstration. Although the speaker manipulates the things in a demonstration as the audience watches, the idea, fact, or process can still be made vivid and concrete. Demonstrations can consist of films, still pictures, objects, models, mockups, easel pads, or chalkboards, alone or in any combination.

Much careful preparation is required for an effective demonstration. The speaker must keep the demonstration simple and yet pace it so interest does not lag. The wise speaker sets the stage for a demonstration with explanation, discusses each step as the demonstration develops, and frequently checks audience response to assure that every step is understood. Every element in the demonstration must be visible and audible to each receiver. Major points to be made must emerge as more prominent than other details. The demonstration should summarize from time to time and conclude with a skeletonized yet comprehensive crystal-clear final summary.

A good way to prepare a demonstration is to view it as a dramatic unit. The speaker should meticulously outline or script the sequence of events to be included in the demonstration. When the show goes on, everything must be in its place, for no interruptions or miscues should be tolerated. A rehearsal or two is mandatory. The best way to refine and "tighten up" a demonstration is to rehearse it with a perceptive critic. He can represent the intended audience and attempt to see the demonstration through their eyes. His reactions can help prevent the COIK fallacy that sabotages many demonstrations. COIK is translated "clear only if known," reminding us of the pitfall of assuming that the audience knows more than it does about our topic!

Written materials to supplement the demonstration are frequently helpful but their use often interferes with the communication. A safe procedure is to distribute written matter only after the demonstration is over. Earlier distribution guarantees that most people will attempt to read and look and listen at the same time, doing each ineffectively.

Exhibits.   Displays that are intended to accomplish the objectives of a demonstration without concurrent human assistance are called exhibits. An exhibit could show the products of the pastry division of Minnesota Mills in a way that would highlight the gap in the product line that a proposed new pie mix would fill. Such an exhibit might well create a frame of reference for an entire presentation.

Usually, one thinks of exhibits as belonging to store windows, fairs, museums, art galleries, bulletin boards in government agencies, and schools. However, relatively simple displays can often make the circumstances surrounding a presentation vivid and clear.

Ingredients of an exhibit are almost unlimited in variety and include posters, models, mockups, objects, chalkboards, voice narration, and still or motion-projected pictures. Interval projection of a series of 35 mm slides is often part of an exhibit. Animated exhibits are more attention compelling than a static display, so often a motorized process or changing lights justify added expense and effort by holding and directing a viewer's attention.

Exhibits, like demonstrations, can make clear complex relationships that cannot be adequately represented by two-dimensional graphs, diagrams, or pictures. The world-wide distribution of television by satellite can be quickly and accurately learned from a display. A diorama (a three-dimensional group of modeled objects) carefully scaled to give an impression of depth and blending into a painted background can be excitingly realistic. An audience can visualize a proposed new building in its setting by viewing a diorama more completely than by use of almost any other method of communication. An exhibit of this kind can be made highly artistic if talent is available.

The dominant principle governing the design and construction of an exhibit is to focus all elements upon a single central idea. Too often people prepare exhibits with multiple themes and the result is that the viewer becomes confused. As with the demonstration, the presentational speaker planning a display should remember: when in doubt, keep it single and simple.

Television and video tape.   Among the aids to the presentation that deserve thoughtful consideration are television and video tape. One striking result of extensive research into the effectiveness of television as an instructional device is that television is found to be as effective as a live teacher. Actually, the evidence of television's effectiveness covers not only school situations of a great variety and at all levels, but instruction of adults in the home and in the Armed Forces. Habits of TV viewing (most people spend about twenty hours a week watching their sets at home) cause members of an audience to spontaneously attend to and absorb televised messages.

CCTV, closed circuit television in which camera, video-tape recorder, and monitor receiver are connected by wires and operate without a broadcast signal, is the basic device usable in presentations. As is the case with the audio-tape recorder, the video-tape recorder doubles as playback device. Recorder and camera are reasonably portable, permitting taping of remote operations, events, and interviews for use in the presentation. No processing is necessary. After a fast rewind, a recorded scene can be played back as often as desired. When a person makes another recording, the tape is automatically erased, so by using the costly video tapes many times, the expense of video recording can be kept quite low.

When the organization wishes to keep video-taped segments, it is advisable to convert them to 16 mm sound movie film. A kinescope is a sound motion picture made from a TV monitor or video-tape recorder (VTR). With proper equipment, a technician can project the kinescope through a television set or through a standard motion picture projector. The kinescope is quite economical to make and is small and easy to store, in contrast to unwieldly reels of one-inch or two-inch video tape, each weighing several pounds. Small, private television systems in 1970 were limited to black and white images, but color is certain to become more popular in the future. Color kinescopes are as easy to make as those that are black and white and cost but little more.

Television as an an aid to the presentation can incorporate and consolidate very nearly all the other "passive involvement" gadgetry. Should the speaker wish to use a variety of aids without the trouble of managing them during the demonstration, he can put them on video tape. One roll of tape will carry everything he wishes to show and demonstrate, and all the speaker will have to do is start and stop the video-tape recorder. Photographs, diagrams, graphs, charts, filmstrips, slides, clips from motion pictures, models, mockups, actuality scenes recorded on the spot, posters, cartoons, interviews, excerpts from speeches, these and other elements can be planned in a scenario. Technicians can help the speaker record and edit the tape until it is properly paced and awkward junctures are eliminated. The persuasive impact of a well-produced variety of pertinent audio-visual aids on the television screen is considerable. The speaker can rehearse with his tape until he is letter perfect. Should he be operating in a well-equipped audio-visual room, his assistant in the control room can supply the television on signal, which might be given inconspicuously by pressing a button on the speaker's stand. His fringe benefits are improved timing and the likelihood of collecting more and better feedback from his listeners. CCTV has freed him from the distractions of handling multiple objects and operating several machines.

Not the least of the services rendered to the presentational speaker by the CCTV is the opportunity to look at and analyze his own presentation. As units of a presentation are assembled, they can be video-taped, polished, and perfected. Finally, the entire presentation may be taped and, preferably with the help of a friendly and knowledgeable critic, the speaker deliberately scrutinizes it, minute by minute. There is no better method of debugging a presentation. With the help of a few associates the speaker can stage a realistic question period so that all phases of the final event will have been experienced in advance. The speaker must take care not to memorize his message word for word, since his speaking will then lack spontaneity. Rather, he should vary his sentences, experimenting with different wordings during the rehearsals. The extemporaneous "run throughs" will result in the speaker's language steadily improving in clarity and efficiency.

Building a consolidated program of aids on video tape offers temptations to insert related or not-so-related drama and entertainment. Most of these opportunities should be resisted. Research into uses of instructional television indicates that accent upon the factual produces better results than stressing dramatic elements.[8] A touch of humor at occasional but unpredictable intervals is sufficient to produce the light touch that increases interest without interfering with the process of learning.

When television is viewed, the maximum number of people to watch a single home-type receiver is twenty. No viewer should be seated more than twelve screen lengths away. Television receivers for group use should have 21- or 24-inch screens, and they should be elevated from four and one-half to six feet above the floor. Television sets can be placed on movable stands and plugged into receptacles of built-in wiring rather than having them installed as a part of the basic structure of the auditorium.

Increasingly, organizations and enterprises of all sorts will be wired for TV. Of some use in presentations will be the ability to look at what is going on elsewhere at the moment. In the not too distant future televised materials will be stored in central video banks and the maker of the presentation will select his audio-visual materials from micro-filmed indexes. His selections will be transferred to his video tape by the world-wide satellite retrieval system. Television promises to make obsolete the firsthand use of objects, models, and exhibits by displaying them in full color on a wall-sized television screen.

Video tape will gradually replace motion pictures in presentations, but wherever large audiences are to be served, film will continue to be a much-used medium. Integrated uses of television and movies will continue to evolve. Already, motion picture makers find television a valuable aid. When they shoot a scene, they use a television camera simultaneously to record it on video tape. They can replay the tape immediately and detect any element in the scene that might require a "remake." If the episode passes the VTR inspection test, the motion picture director sends the film off to be printed and proceeds to the next scene.

Motion pictures.   The motion picture is probably the most expensive aid to communication. Producing a color film of professional quality costs a thousand or more dollars a minute. But because so many people see the same film, often over a period of several years, the per viewer cost may be the lowest of all audio-visual devices. Of course, the high initial costs make motion pictures prohibitive for presentations that reach a few people or for a one-shot situation.

Without doubt, also, the well-made sound motion picture in color is

[8] Clarence Carpenter and Leslie P. Greenhill, *An Investigation of Closed-Circuit Television for Teaching University Courses,* Pennsylvania State University, 1955; Leslie P. Greenhill *et al.,* "Further Studies of the Use of Television for University Teaching," *Audio-Visual Communication,* R4 (1956), 200–215; Percy H. Tannebaum, *Instruction Through Television: A Comparative Study,* Institution of Communications Research, University of Illinois, 1956.

one of the most impressive audio-visual devices. Where its use is appropriate, it is unexcelled in producing understanding and retention of learned material. Motion pictures lack the immediacy of TV but they benefit from better editing, and the bigger, more detailed, more brilliant pictures made possible by film will in all probability not be equaled by television for some time. Until they are, motion pictures will continue to be an important audio-visual tool.

No other audio-visual device can cope as well with the problems of motion, size, and time as can film. Film technique includes an almost unlimited magnification, zoom lenses, a nearly infinite range of speeding up and slowing down, the ability to re-create the past or explore the future, and integration of the arts of animation with all conventional audio-visual techniques. Because of its versatility, film can contribute significantly to the understanding of highly complex relationships and process. Perhaps because of positive transfer from commercial movies, good instructional films are also aesthetically satisfying.

In spite of the great potential of motion pictures, their use in presentations is specialized and restricted. Whenever a speaker is preparing a "how-to-do-it" demonstration, film becomes a possibility. Film loops and short films in cartridges make possible repeated viewing without delay and detailed comparison of alternative procedures. Cartridge film projectors and the short single-concept film coming into popular use may increase the utility of motion pictures in presentations.

Generally, homemade movies as aids to presentation have not been very helpful because 16 mm equipment is expensive and complicated and use of 8 mm film provides an insufficiently detailed picture. Currently improved films, cameras, and the Super 8 method of utilizing increased film area show some promise. But films made by the people who give the presentations usually look amateurish. Moviemaking is an exacting art requiring a mastery of many techniques and much knowledge of precise capabilities of the instruments used. Only a skilled cinematographer should attempt to create his own filmed aids. For the foreseeable future, needs of this sort can be met more successfully by use of video tape.

For some presentations, however, particularly those that have educational objectives, instructional films available from film libraries and audio-visual services may be useful. Careful previewing of these standard films will enable the speaker to build his presentation around the films and utilize the strengths of a professionally produced film by adapting it to his specific audience.

Perhaps the major problem in using sound motion picture aids to the presentation is finding what appropriate films are available and where to get them. Even small cities have film sources and information listed in the Yellow Pages of the telephone book under "Audio-visual Equipment and Supplies" or "Audio-visual Services." Most of the films one would consider using are listed as "instructional" or "educational" motion pictures, so lists of these should be requested. Public libraries, high schools, colleges, and universities keep these listings up-to-date and are usually glad to share them with members of their community.

Previewing a film before deciding to use all or part of it is an absolute necessity. Names and descriptions give only a vague impression of a film's content. Commonly, a library, school or audio-visual service can obtain a movie for preview purposes cost free or at small expense. Purchasing a sound motion picture for a single presentation or for even a few showings is expensive. Usually, rental is more economical and convenient.

Help in locating a film-producing agency can best be obtained from the above-mentioned sources of films and information about films. Frequently, a college or university will include a film production unit that will do a limited amount of custom production work to provide laboratory experience for its students and to generate income to amortize its overhead costs.

STILL PICTURES AND RECORDINGS

We classify still pictures and recordings together because they both appeal to only one of the senses and because they thus represent movement to a still higher level of the Cone of Learning Experiences. Looking at flat pictures and listening to sounds are, nonetheless, an important way to gain information.

A danger in the use of pictures is the "pitfall of projection," which in this instance is unrelated to malfunction of the projector. The speaker tends to assume without thinking that his listener will read into a picture the same meaning that he sees in it. The communicator "projects" his interpretation into the visual stimulus by assuming that other perceptions and reactions are identical to his own.

Suppose that a picture shows an automobile accident involving two cars that have had a glancing, head-on collision. Two apparently injured people are lying on the shoulder of the road near the heavily damaged cars. A policeman with a notebook is talking to two people, a man and a woman, who are neatly dressed.

A physician seeing the picture will likely note the appearance of the persons lying on the ground and by studying the damage to the cars will speculate concerning their injuries. He will also wonder about how long ago the accident happened and whether an ambulance is on the way. A mechanic will see the vehicles that have been damaged and think in terms of their repair. A lawyer might view the scene in the context of legal action, looking for evidence that one driver was at fault and wondering whether the people talking to the patrolman are eye witnesses who could testify. A policeman might find himself thinking about what is being written in the patrolman's notebook, whether traffic violation tickets had been issued, and whether the accident had been reported by radio and an ambulance requested. He will also wonder how he could record details of the accident, paths of vehicles, measurements made, and diagrams to be entered into his report of the accident. A highway engineer might observe the conditions of the road surface, look for traffic signs, intersections, obstructions, and attempt to ascertain the probability that highway conditions helped cause the collision.

The point of the above example is that pictures like words are subject to widely varied interpretations. What is obvious and important in a picture to one person may be unnoticed or disregarded by another. We tend to think that responses to pictures are uniform and we need to remind ourselves that with pictures as with language our interests and experiences shape our perceptions.

The "pitfall of projection" applies to other audio-visual aids as well as to still pictures. The uniformity of perception in an audience can be increased by appropriate setting-of-the-stage before and by concomitant commentary guiding responses along the way. With motion pictures careful preparation for the film in the form of telling the audience what to look for and a summary of the film and the points it made immediately after the projector is turned off are helpful in preventing misconceptions.

Nonprojected two-dimensional visual aids.   The chief nonprojected visual aid to the presentation in both amount and tradition of use is the chalkboard. Some years ago, all chalkboards were made of slate and were termed "blackboards." Now chalkboards come in varied colors, matching room décor and serving different purposes. They are made of slate, moss-surfaced glass, plastic, paint-coated wood, or vitreous-coated steel. The latter has magnetic properties that make possible considerably extended uses of the chalkboard. Here are a few techniques that exploit some of the potential of the modern chalkboard.

The speaker can prepare drawings and diagrams that are neat and accurate. Previously prepared visuals eliminate the major disadvantage of the chalkboard that comes from the necessity of drawing and talking at the same time, and may result in neither being done well. Here are several ways of preparing neat chalkboard displays.

1. Using slide, overhead, filmstrip, or opaque projector, project on the blackboard the picture, diagram, or chart and trace the desired outlines with chalk.

2. Make a pattern by tracing outlines of the drawing on heavy paper and punching ⅛-inch to ⅜-inch holes at ½-inch to 1-inch intervals along the lines. Rub an eraser bearing chalk dust over the pattern, leaving dots that can be easily connected to produce the finished drawing.

3. Hold template, or silhouette made of a stiff, lightweight material, against the chalkboard, while tracing its outline.

4. The grid method can enlarge a drawing accurately and easily. Draw the original on paper, perhaps 8½ × 11, which is blocked off into small squares. Lay off much larger squares on the chalkboard. Reproduce the drawing in enlarged form by duplicating the original, one square at a time.

5. With a magnetic chalkboard, two- and three-dimensional additions to the prepared visual can be attached to small magnets ready for use as the speaker talks about his drawing.

6. Any prepared chalkboard display can be covered until it is needed, thereby avoiding distracting the audience and permitting sequential development. Wrapping paper makes good cover material. It can be scotch-taped to the top frame of the chalkboard, held in place by "pinch clamps" used if the chalkboard has a map rail along the top, or with magnetic chalkboards covers of drawings can be secured by magnets.

Prepared chalkboard displays are helpful but will probably never replace concurrent lettering or drawing and speaking. For the speaker who is skillful at using the chalkboard to illustrate and develop his points along the way, simultaneous writing and speaking add movement and suspense to the presentation. Difficulties come because some people are inept at drawing or writing on the chalkboard, and from an inevitable loss of speaker contact with audience. When a person is drawing a diagram, he has difficulty watching his audience, and for at least some of the time his back may be turned to them. However, "along the way" lettering and drawing are essential to most presentations. Because this can be done on the overhead projector with less effort, greater visibility, and without turning from the audience, it may be wise for most speakers to use the chalkboard only for preprepared displays.

For major presentations speakers often use a series of prepared cards displayed on an easel stand. A popular size is 22 inches by 28 inches. The cards may carry lettering, drawings, graphs, diagrams, and so on, large enough to be easily seen by all. Cards are stacked in order on the easel, and as the speaker proceeds, he can reveal the next visual by taking away the previous one.

Once popular, the "large card on the easel" approach is giving way to the more convenient and economical transparency on the overhead projector, and to the flip chart. The flip chart consists of a pad of newsprint-sized paper, mounted on an easel, with its sheets attached only at the top, like a tablet of writing paper. Prepared visuals similar to those on cards can be drawn and lettered on consecutive flip chart pages. Instead of removing a card to reveal the next visual, the speaker "flips" a sheet back over the top of the easel. At the end of the presentation, turning back the pages preserves his visuals, intact.

For "along the way" use, the flip chart has certain advantages over the chalkboard. Instead of chalk, the speaker can use varicolored chemical markers, crayons, and wax pencils to draw and write on the pad. Instead of erasing, he flips the used sheet. If he wishes to keep a sheet for later reference or for use in his summary, it can be torn from the pad and taped to the wall or chalkboard. Sometimes it is possible to "paper the walls" of the room with the highlights of an entire presentation.

The flannel board, a rectangular surface as large as 4 feet by 8 feet, covered with a flannel-like fabric, is useful in situations where portability is not a factor. Display items, usually lettered or drawn on cardboard, are backed with a material that adheres to the flannel on the board. The speaker can build up a display, element by element, by simply touching the item to the board in the proper place at the right time. He can then pull off and relocate items, since the nature of the adhesion is such that neither of the surfaces involved is changed by the contact.

A great variety of photographs, drawings, charts, diagrams, graphs, posters, cartoons, and comics can be built into the uses of chalkboard, easel cards, flip charts, and flannel boards. Their use requires little explanation, with the exception of graphs and other quantitative representations of numerical data. The reader will find the design and construction of quantitative graphics treated in some detail in Chapter 7.

Projected still two-dimensional aids. Projection adds flexibility to the use of all varieties of pictorial material. Taking a picture of something is generally easier and cheaper than having it drawn or painted in a size usable as a direct visual. Projection enables an easy adjustment of picture size to the size of the audience, being accomplished by changing the size of the screen and the distance of the projector from the screen. With modern zoom lenses, some projectors can now fill screens of different sizes from a constant screen to projector distance.

Two basically different means of projection of still pictorial materials are in current use, the utilization of light reflected from the pictorial to produce the picture, known as *opaque projection,* and the use of light that passes through the picture, known as *transparency projection.* Opaque projection is accomplished by a machine called the opaque projector. It accepts any printed or written material up to approximately 10 inches by 10 inches and throws an enlarged image on the screen. It will also project images of three-dimensional objects, providing they are flat enough to present no great difficulties in achieving satisfactory focus. The major advantage of the opaque projector is that no processing is necessary; for example, a schematic in a book can be inserted directly into the machine, and its disadvantage is a picture lacking brilliance. Because the opaque projector puts relatively little light on the screen, the room must be darkened to the point where note taking becomes difficult or impossible. The low light level also limits the maximum size of an acceptable picture. A suggested rule of thumb is that opaque projection is not likely to be satisfactory for an audience of more than twenty-five people.

Transparency projection is accomplished by 35 mm filmstrips, by 35 mm, 2-inch by 2-inch, and 3¼-inch by 4-inch slides, and by the overhead projector. Filmstrips and slides require a relatively long "throw"; that is, the projector must be a considerable distance from the screen. For viewing slides and motion pictures the audience should sit no further from the screen than six screen widths, no closer than two and one-half screen widths, and no further to the side than 30 degrees from a line perpendicular to the screen. When movies and slides are shown, there should be no more than one-tenth of one foot candle of illumination on the screen. With a well-equipped audio-visual room, slides and filmstrips are normally projected from the control booth, thus avoiding distractions caused by mechanical devices being operated in the midst of the audience. All projection devices except the overhead projector require a substantially darkened room for satisfactory viewing.

Filmstrips are fixed sequences of still pictures on movie film, usually 35 mm, and they are projected by a simple, small machine that advances the film from one frame to the next. Filmstrips are black and white or in color, made with or without accompanying sound. If the filmstrip has an audio supplement, that is provided by either a disc or a magnetic tape recording. The sound filmstrip projector accepts either disc or tape playback "syncpulses," inaudible impulses that signal the projector to advance to the next picture. Sometimes the audio portion is supplied on disc or tape to be played on a separate player, in which case the film must be advanced by an operator at an audible signal on the recording, usually a "beep" of some sort.

Filmstrips are the most economical projected aids to presentations to produce or purchase. They are packaged in small cans that are easily stored and filed on racks. One can use the popular 35 mm camera to make a filmstrip for any particular purpose with a small fraction of the difficulties that attend the making of a movie. If the producers wish to add audio, they can record the tape or disc as the strip is projected, recording and rerecording until the result is satisfactory. Syncronizing pictures and voice is easy, because pictures are changed on signal and little critical timing is involved. As with the motion picture, all visual aids can be built into the filmstrip. Showing pictures of actual operations, models, mockups, and exhibits is effective and easy.

The results of research into the effectiveness of filmstrips as aids to instruction are impressive. Investigators have found that when compared to the sound motion picture, the most expensive aid, the filmstrip is equally effective. Silent filmstrips are as good as silent movies, and filmstrips with sound are as effective as sound movies. Again, considering results from hundreds of comparisons in many subject matter areas, the filmstrips have proved to be at least as effective as the lecture. Truly, the evidence suggests that filmstrip presentation of audio-visual materials ought to be considered as a possible option in many presentations.[9]

The fixed sequence of filmstrip pictures is both an advantage and a disadvantage. The pictures cannot get out of order or upside down, but the speaker has difficulty selecting a few pictures to be used from a strip, or making any change in the order in which they are shown. The added sound on tape or disc contributes further rigidity. The advantage of slides over filmstrips is flexibility. The speaker can select and rearrange properly labeled slides with ease. However, with proper equipment, cutting and splicing a filmstrip is not at all difficult. Consequently, portability and easy storage cause many people to prefer the filmstrip.

There is little advantage in prerecording explanation with a filmstrip or slides to be used in a presentation. On-the-spot adaptation to the audience and occasion are impossible when the spoken words are on disc or tape. The present speaker is more interesting to listen to than is the disembodied voice. And, of course, the important benefits of feedback can be realized only by the "live" lecturer. More effective communication usually results when the presentational speaker talks extemporaneously about his pictures to a responding audience.

The old 3¼-inch by 4-inch glass-mounted slide provided a magnificent picture but was expensive, fragile, and cumbersome. Where a great deal of detail in the picture is important, these large slides with their bulky projector are still in use. The popular tourist's friend, the adaptable 35 mm camera both for color and black and white, makes cheap high-quality cardboard or plastic mounted slides, which have

[9] H. E. Brown, "Motion Pictures or Film Slide," School Science Mathematics, 28 (1928), 217–526; David J. Goodman, "The Comparative Effectiveness of Pictorial Teaching Materials," Ph.D. Dissertation, New York University, 1942; Bernard Abrahamson, "A Comparison of Two Methods of Teaching Mechanics in High School," Science Education, 36 (March, 1952), 96–106; Anthony Stampolis and Lawrence Sewell, Jr., A Study of Film Strips Communicating Economic Concepts, Boston University School of Public Relations and Communications, 1952; John V. Zuckerman, "Predicting Film Learning by Pre-Release Testing," Audio-Visual Communication, R2 (1954), 49–56.

largely supplanted the larger glass mounted slides. An intermediate 2-inch by 2-inch cardboard- or plastic-mounted slide from a negative larger than 35 mm has achieved a limited use but with continued improvements in film may be unable to compete with the 35 mm which has become a world-wide standard for most still-picture, large-screen projection.

Slide projectors for 35 mm stills are available which are automated to a degree that makes an operator unnecessary. Magazines hold up to a hundred slides, remote controls permit the speaker to change pictures, to show again a picture shown before, to adjust focus, and to turn the projector on and off. Projectors that automatically correct the focus on each slide are an option. The presentational speaker can have his audio-visual aids on slides in his control booth projector, and with the room light control on his speaker's stand and his remote control for the projector he can produce the visual aids for his talk unassisted.

Displays and exhibits often make use of a rear projection device that shows slides on a translucent, frosted-glass screen. Also, attachments make possible the showing of 35 mm slides on a television monitor or home-type receiving set. The advantage of rear or television projection is that the room does not need to be darkened. Disadvantages are loss of picture detail and cumbersome, complex, heavy equipment that will serve only a few viewers at a time. However, if rear projection equipment is available, it may meet the needs of a presentation to groups from a half dozen to twelve or fifteen people in size.

More than any other projection device the overhead projector becomes an integral part of the presentation. The speaker has it with him at the front of the room, he turns it on and off, he writes and draws on it as he can on chalkboard or flip chart, he uses prepared visuals and adds to or modifies them on the spot, he uses the shadow of his pencil as a pointer, and all this takes place without breaking eye contact with the audience or changing the lighting in the room. The "overhead" is economical to purchase and operate. Its flexibility and utility have resulted in its becoming the most universally used projector in presentations and lectures.

Because the machine and its operator obstruct the view of the screen to some extent, optimum placement of the screen locates it slightly off-center and turned toward the projector, which is located toward the other side of the front of the room. A typical placement is illustrated in Figure 11.3. The overhead is close to the screen and because the picture is considerably above the level of the projector, a phenomenon known as "keystoning" takes place, causing the picture to be distorted in the fashion illustrated by Figure 11.4. Consequently, the screen should be equipped with a "keystone correcting device," simply a means by which the top of the screen can be moved toward

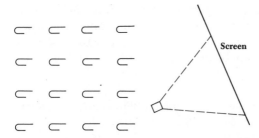

Figure 11.3 Proper Placement of an Overhead
Projector

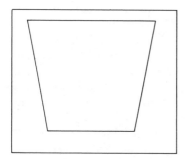

Figure 11.4 Keystoning Effect

the projector, or the bottom of the screen can be moved away until the
sides of the image are parallel to the edges of the screen.

The material of which transparencies are made is a thin, clear
acetate, slightly thicker than a sheet of paper, but fairly flexible. The
8½ × 11 plastic sheets can be prepared in advance by lettering and
drawing on them or by processing them in copying machines by which
typing, printing, and pictures can be transferred to the sheets. Prepared transparencies are often mounted in cardboard frames and it is
convenient for the speaker to write some of his notes on the cardboard
margins. Use of these notes is almost completely inconspicuous.

As a substitute for the chalkboard for "along the way" writing and
drawing, the speaker uses blank 8½ × 11 transparency sheets, or,
alternatively, an arrangement in which acetate is on rollers at the front
and back or on the sides of the machine, passing over the lighted surface. The speaker uses grease pencils or special markers with nylon or
felt tips to write on the strip of acetate, cranking it from one roller to
the other to provide a continuous supply of fresh surface. A soft cloth or
tissue will wipe drawing and writing from either sheet or roller of
acetate, and it can be reused.

Detailed instructions for use of any particular overhead projector can be obtained from makers of the machines but some general advice relating to problems and techniques of using the overhead projector should be mentioned here. Typing for transparencies should be done with oversize type, since regular office sizes are difficult to see. A good size type for projection purposes is either 6/32-inch or 8/32-inch. A convenient way to build up a diagram is by overlays, four or five of which can be used without excessive dimming of the picture. A sheet of paper can be used to cover part of a transparency, and moving the paper will achieve successive revelation of a series of items. Transparency film is obtainable in colors, and various pictographs, figures, and so on, can be purchased in silhouette or contrasting colors, as can letters and numerals to aid in preparing visuals. A motorized, polarized disk attachment can give a prepared picture an illusion of movement. Audience members can write and draw on transparency sheets, and these can be immediately projected. Many more variations in application of the versatile overhead projector exist and will be devised. The enterprising presentational speaker will thoughtfully exploit this valuable device.

Audio recording and playback. In most presentations sound is an adjunct to still or moving pictures. As such, it is produced by an audio channel added to the picture projector. The effective distribution of that sound is aided by good acoustics and by the proper placement of loudspeakers. The source of the actual sound waves, the loudspeakers, should be near the screen. People are not accustomed to seeing events and human interactions taking place at the front of the room while voices and accompanying sound effects come from the back. Loudspeakers can be in the ceiling at the front of the room for use with projected materials, or built into the front wall near the ceiling, or hung from the ceiling beside the screen.

When sound without pictures is appropriate in a presentation, it is almost always provided by a tape recorder. The modern high-fidelity tape recorder is reasonably inexpensive, it operates monophonically or stereophonically, and it can be operated with good results by a thoughtful layman.

Usually, the audible component of audio-visual aids consists of prerecorded sounds and voices. Making a good recording requires elimination of unwanted noises, freedom from echoes and reverberation, never permitting microphone and recorder to rest on the same surface (the microphone picks up the motor noise of the recorder), and getting the microphone as close to the source of sound as possible. The last item is crucial, and little understood. Sound energy diminishes as the square of the distance, so doubling the distance from the source results in the microphone getting one-fourth as much sound to record. Where people are recorded, the best possible microphone placement is to hang a lavalier mike around the neck of each, as is often the practice on radio and television panel programs.

The speaker can play tape recordings used in the presentation from the actual tape recorder on a table or stand beside him. Such direct playback is handicapped by the poor quality and low power of the playback-speaker circuit in the portable tape recorder. Much better results can be achieved if he connects or "patches in" the tape recorder to the sound system of the audio-visual room. The "patch" consists of an *electronic* connection from the recorder circuit to an input circuit of the room amplifier. *Never* play the tape recorder into a microphone, for the distortion introduced is substantial.

Spending time and effort to secure the highest fidelity audio possible, and the best possible distribution of that high-fidelity sound is a good investment. Audience reaction to "hi-fi" sound is usually appreciative, and reaction to distorted sound is almost always bitter and uncharitable.

The tape recorder can make a faithful record of events that has many uses. In a well-equipped audio-visual room a tape recorder in the control booth should be used to record every presentation. With several ceiling microphones, audience comments and questions can be picked up as well as the speaker-initiated segments. After the event, the speaker can review his effort and be sure of what he actually said, and listeners can borrow the tape to freshen their memory of certain points. Often misunderstandings develop that can be cleared up by reference to the audio record. And, of course, any portion of the tape can be transcribed and converted to a written record.

A MULTIMEDIA SETTING FOR EFFECTIVE PRESENTATIONS

The setting for the presentation includes fixed audio-visual elements that can be crucial to its outcome. Some ingredients of environmental suggestion were discussed briefly in Chapter 10. We turn our attention here to the problem of providing surroundings and equipment for the presentation that will maximize positive transfer and minimize negative transfer. Admittedly, we will emphasize the creation of ideal conditions while recognizing that practical limitations will in most instances necessitate a compromise. Perhaps few of our readers will ever be able to design and construct an optimum room for presentations, reports, and instruction. Nevertheless, by sketching the ideal conditions, we hope to indicate the full potential of audio-visual aids to presentational speakers.

What are the characteristics of a room suitable for presentations? The ideal setting is large enough to accommodate the listeners comfortably, and no larger. Its design creates an atmosphere of informality and fosters comfortable concentration directed to the front of the room. Considerable attention has been paid to acoustical characteristics. The room is soundproofed, so outside noises cannot be a distraction, and sound-treated, so very little reverberation is possible within it. All of the ceiling and part of the wall space is surfaced with sound absorbent material, and the floor is carpeted.

Lighting within the room is ample, glareless, and continuously controlled from darkness to maximum brilliance. Interior decoration has a variety of subdued colors. A tasteful harmony of furnishings, drapes, carpet, and wall treatment facilitates communication. Chairs are comfortable, movable, and provide a writing surface for each person. If more than twenty people are to be seated in the room, a low platform at the front is desirable, but the distance between listeners and speakers should be kept to a minimum.

Silent air conditioning is mandatory. Similarly, a built-in sound distribution system is an important part of the room. Loudspeakers, several of them, are flush with the ceiling, several microphones are suspended from the ceiling to permit recording of everyone in the room, and at the front of the room on the baseboard are plug-in connectors permitting use of lavalier, floor stand, hand-held and speaker's stand microphones, as well as television cameras, monitors, and receivers.

Magnetic chalkboards extend across the front wall of the room and halfway along the sidewalls. In the ceiling at the center of the front wall is a large pull-down projection screen, to be used with filmstrips, slides, and movies. To the side at the front another roll-up screen is suspended from the ceiling. This is angled slightly to permit locating the overhead projector a bit off center to the opposite side of the room, and it is equipped with a screen-tilting device to prevent "keystoning" of the projected picture.

The "nerve center" of the multimedia room is its combined recording-playback-projection booth. This separate enclosed space is located behind the center of the rear wall, and it lies entirely outside of the main room. Slots are cut into the main room's rear wall for projection of slides, filmstrips, and movies, and for television cameras used in videotaping. Inside the projection booth, which is more accurately referred to as a "control room," are located slide and motion picture projectors, sound recording and distributing equipment, television cameras, a television monitor, and one or two video taping machines. The control room is soundproofed and sound-treated. It is entered from the outside so activities connected with projection and recording will not affect events in the main area. All lights can be controlled from the booth.

The room described above includes the basic features and equipment that are part of its construction and are permanent. More exotic and highly useful integral equipment might well be added. A telephone speaker could be installed that would permit everyone in the room to overhear and participate in a call from a remote person or persons. Audio and television lines from other rooms and buildings could connect to the control room switchboard. Remote controls for lights, the sound system, and for booth-located projectors could be installed in the speaker's stand and at the rear of the room. Built into the rear wall one could have shelf space for coffee, soft drinks, and snacks, supplied from the outside. Extra screens and projectors make multiple comparisons easy, and may be justified. Every audio-visual room should be a product of particular requirements that are to some degree unique. The time to meet both general and specialized needs is when the room is being designed and built.

SUMMARY

Audio-visual aids to the presentation are necessary to provide a multisensory stimulus and to counter the influence of "verbalism," our tendency to place excessive reliance upon words. Research in schools, the military services and industry offers proof that concepts presented with audio-visual aids are more impressive and better remembered than when presented without.

The Cone of Learning Experiences classifies the way people can learn in the context of the presentation. Experiences in the cone range from the concrete to the abstract, from participative involvement through passive involvement, to symbolic involvement, which is the abstract level of language. Of nine levels in the cone, numbers 1 through 7 involve audio-visual aids, the major method of securing active and passive involvement.

Personal and circumstantial obstacles to listener understanding in a presentation are seen to be intrinsically vulnerable to appropriate use of audio-visual aids.

Participative involvement in a presentation is either direct and "on the scene" or contrived. Most presentations must rely upon contrived participation, but by use of specimens, models, and mockups contrived experiences can be highly effective.

The demonstration is the most elaborate of the passive involvement formats for using audio-visual aids. It makes use of all the audio-visual devices, providing a dynamic stimulus that is interesting and informative. The exhibit is relatively static but is useful in clarifying complex relationships.

Closed circuit television (CCTV) and video tapes are flexible aids to the presentational speaker. They have the advantages of being contemporary and capable of easy editing. Motion pictures serve large audiences better but cannot be adapted to the audience and the occasion as readily as the video tape–live television combination.

Chief among nonprojected visual aids are the chalkboard, easel cards, flip chart, and flannel board. Modern techniques have increased the utility of these familiar devices. Projected still visuals are obtained with opaque projection, silent and sound filmstrips, and slides. The filmstrip is probably the most economical and flexible of these visual supplements, with the 35 mm slide running a close second.

The overhead projector, the most popular projection aid to presentational speaking, can screen prepared visuals and can do equally well as a substitute for a chalkboard or flip chart for "along the way" drawing and writing. The overhead is operated by the speaker without the necessity of breaking eye contact with his audience.

Reproduction of sound without pictures is most conveniently done by using a modern portable tape recorder. Careful preparations are necessary in order to record high-fidelity sound. Playback is dramatically improved by "patching" the tape recorder into the amplifier that serves the sound distribution system in the audio-visual room.

Audience involvement is desirable to increase the learning and retention from all audio-visual experiences. Techniques of audience participation in use of films, filmstrips, and demonstrations are to be encouraged. Effectiveness of an audio-visual aid to presentation is proportional to the activity of the audience during its use.

The effectiveness of audio-visual aids depends not only upon their being easily seen and heard but upon the positive or negative transfer from the entire room in which the presentation occurs. A well-designed setting is comfortable and aesthetically pleasing. Screens, projectors, television and recording equipment are built in so as to make them both convenient and inconspicuous. Only when signs of amateurish improvisation are eliminated are listeners free to concentrate upon the factual and ideational content of the message.

QUESTIONS FOR DISCUSSION AND REVIEW

1. What can multi-media aids contribute to the presentation?
2. What is the relationship of the Cone of Learning Experience to the use of audio-visual aids?
3. What are the advantages of using direct rather than contrived participative experiences?
4. How are models used as audio-visual aids classified? Give examples of each type.
5. One form of audience participation is *verbalizing content*. In what ways can the speaker accomplish this?

6. What is the "COIK fallacy" and how can it be avoided in giving a demonstration?
7. How do sound motion picture and video tape compare as aids to the presentation?
8. How does the "pitfall of projection" cause misperceptions of visual aids and how can a speaker guard against it?
9. How do the modern chalkboard and the overhead projector compare as aids to the presentation?
10. What are the major design features of an ideal multimedia room for presentations?

REFERENCES AND SUGGESTED READINGS

BROWN, JAMES W., RICHARD B. LEWIS, and FRED F. HARCLEROAD. *A-V Instruction: Materials and Methods,* 2nd ed. New York: McGraw-Hill, 1964.

CONNOLLY, JAMES. *Effective Technical Presentations.* St. Paul, Minn.: 3M Business Press, 1968.

KEMP, JERROLD E. *Planning and Producing Audiovisual Materials.* San Francisco: Chandler Publishing, 1963.

SCHMID, CALVIN F. *Handbook of Graphic Presentation.* New York: Ronald, 1954.

WILCOX, ROGER P. *Oral Reporting in Business and Industry.* Englewood Cliffs, N.J.: Prentice-Hall, 1967.

CHAPTER TWELVE

RESPONDING TO THE PRESENTATION

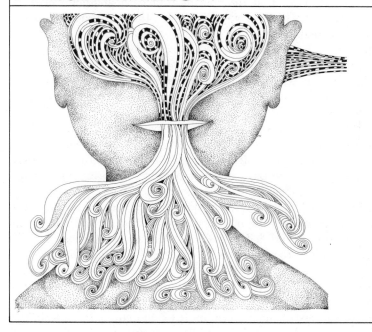

In Chapter 3 we developed the paradigm of the process of face-to-face communication. Recall that the main difference between man communicating with a machine, on the one hand, and with another person, on the other, was that the machine always accepted the role of receiver of the message. In the process of human communication, however, a person may try to achieve some goal by initiating a communication event and discover that the others refuse to accept the invitation to understanding and, instead, begin encoding messages designed to achieve their own goals. Certainly Cass Carlyle (in Chapter 3) discovered that to be the case in his interview with Albert Johnson that culminated in the hasty resignation. When the listeners to a presentation refuse to adopt a receiver orientation, they do not join the speaker in an interdependent relation aimed at mutual understanding.

In almost every communicative situation a person ought to willingly accept the duties of message receiver at appropriate points in the transaction. If the listener anticipates conflict, he certainly should allow the speaker to develop a complete message and should provide feedback until both parties are satisfied that they understand one another. Albert Johnson, disturbed by Cass Carlyle's opening moves, was unsure of what to expect and impetuously misunderstood almost all of Carlyle's statements. Johnson never accepted the role of listener. If the listener decides, after he understands the speaker's position, that he is not going to cooperate to achieve the speaker's intent, he ought clearly to assert himself in the role of source in another round of communication. The original speaker ought, then, assume a receiver orientation and play out the process until understanding is once again satisfactory to all parties. Johnson certainly asserted himself as a message source in his own right when he stood and began questioning Carlyle. At the crucial point when Carlyle might still have saved the situation by accepting the role of receiver, he became angry and stopped listening.

Understanding does not assure harmony and cooperation. The participants in the conference may still disagree, come into conflict, or grow to dislike one another after they achieve understanding, but they will do so on a realistic basis and not because of misunderstandings stemming from lack of communication skills.

For much of the book we have examined the process of communication from the point of view of the speaker. Since we are concerned with the preparation and delivery of presentations, we emphasized the skills and attitude required for successfully playing the role of message source. To restore a balance and assert once again the interdependent nature of face-to-face communication, we examine, in this chapter, the receiver's role in the process. The dynamic interplay required for successful communication is facilitated when those in the audience understand their role. In addition, people playing the role of listeners should possess the skills required to comprehend and to evaluate presentations and the abilities to creatively add deeper meanings to the messages they share with the speaker. The theory and practice of responding constructively to the presentation are the concern of the present chapter.

INTERDEPENDENCE OF SPEAKER AND LISTENER

The fundamental unit of communication is the *dyad*. A dyad consists of two persons. When John Jamison (in Chapter 1) prepared his recommendation to the Board of Control of Minnesota Mills, he planned dialogues with key members of the board. When he presented his talk, he literally conversed with one person, then another. His ultimate success rested upon favorable responses in a series of one-to-one transactions. No matter how large the audience, the impact of the speaker can be thought of as the sum of all the changes in individual listeners brought about by the interaction each experiences with the speaker. The critical variable in the effect the presentation has upon the listeners is the quality of the dyadic communication between the speaker and each listener rather than the quality of the speaker's "performance" per se.

Franklin B. Evans discovered the critical variable of the "quality of dyadic interaction" in a pioneering study of salesmanship. In a carefully controlled investigation Evans assessed the variables that predicted the success of life insurance sales interviews. He found that the factors that had always been thought to be crucial, such as the salesman's product knowledge and speaking ability and the prospective buyer's need and ability to pay for insurance, were not as important as the "tone" of the interpersonal relationship developed in the interview. If the two people liked each other, enjoyed the conversation, and were reluctant to terminate the interview, a sale tended to result. Evans summarizes: "The most important data are how the prospect perceives the particular agent and the similarities between agent and prospect that help the interaction situation to be free and pleasant."[1]

Because quality of dyadic interaction has come to be recognized as crucial to the outcomes of purposeful speech communication, we should examine further the interdependence of speaker and listener.

A simple action-reaction relationship. The speaker and his listeners can be present in the same room without interacting to a significant degree. Speakers do "talk at" audiences who refuse to receive their message. Lecturers in the classroom and outside achieve this triumph of noncommunication often enough for us to be concerned about it. The phenomenon that characterizes noninteractive speaking is almost total absence of feedback. Listeners are not responding to the message, so the speaker lacks data needed for his continuous adaptation to audience perceptions. In retaliation the speaker typically stops trying to communicate, centers his attention on the message, and purposefully ignores his audience. Because this nonreactive predicament guarantees failure for the presentation, we are dismissing it by simply noting that the speaker by trying to do something about the unresponsiveness of his audience can create an action-reaction relationship.

The simplest and most basic pattern of interaction of speaker and listener David Berlo labels "Action-Reaction Interdependence."[2] Feedback in this relationship is analogous to the thermostatic control of a furnace. When room temperature lowers, the thermostat sends the

---

[1] Franklin B. Evans, "Dyadic Interaction in Selling: A New Approach," an unpublished study done at the University of Chicago in 1964.

[2] David K. Berlo, *The Process of Communication* (New York, 1960), p. 109.

message "Turn on" and when a specified temperature is reached, it encodes "Turn off." Thermostat and furnace control each other, but in an unvarying stimulus-response sequence that may be termed "mechanical" because alternative possibilities are strictly limited. The action-reaction interdependence is similar to what we have previously referred to as a signal response to messages. Many of the communication events that operate at a habitual level or at the fringes of consciousness can be characterized as action-reaction events. The "give-me-a-cuppa-coffee" level of language usage or the typical "How are you this morning" action and the "I am fine today" reaction exemplify the most primitive level of communication.

If a speaker responds to audience laughter by telling more jokes or stops telling jokes when his listeners fail to laugh, he exhibits a furnacelike adaptability. This is not to be scorned, for keeping room temperature constant is a necessary and important achievement. Our point is that the productive use of feedback goes far beyond simple "thermostatic" action-reaction. In Berlo's words:

> People are not thermostats or furnaces. They have the capacity to make trial responses within the organism, to use symbols to anticipate how others will respond to their messages, to develop expectations about their own behavior and the behavior of others. The concept of *expectation* is crucial to human communication.[3]

Thus, advancing beyond the simple action-reaction relationship depends upon the extent to which audience and speaker are able to utilize *expectations*. This involves understanding, interpreting, and reacting to not only what the other is doing at the moment but what he is likely to do in the future. Instead of "Turn on" and "Turn off," hundreds of possible choices confront source and receiver. Potentialities of complex human communication feedback are sufficiently open-ended that no presentational speaker should content himself with a simple action-reaction relationship, useful as that may be. As we stressed in Chapter 10, symbol responses are often desirable in presentational speaking.

An empathic relationship.   The next level of interdependence between speaker and listener exhibits a considerably greater richness and complexity than the action-reaction situation. We will call the next higher level *empathic interdependence*.

In Chapter 10 we defined empathy as the tendency of human beings to imitate physically what they see and hear. We also indicated that empathy served the speaker in two ways: It enabled him to detect the nature of audience response from moment to moment, and it could

---

[3] *Ibid.*, p. 116.

be used by him to produce desired responses in the audience. We can now examine characteristics of the speaker-audience relationship that facilitate the productive uses of empathy.

Empathy supplies the speaker with muscle sets and tensions resulting from his miniaturized internal imitations of behavior of the audience. Without these he cannot adapt skillfully to varying listener perceptions, but unless he is able to understand and interpret his sensations *in an audience frame of reference* he cannot use them constructively. To benefit from empathy he must know a great deal about the responding individuals, and this knowledge encompasses their motives, habits, emotions, and feelings.

For example, if a speaker is to empathize with an audience, he must know the role it expects him to play, and how it is accustomed to behave. The present writer enjoys the challenge of giving high school commencement speeches. One year he had prepared a talk that he believed to be livelier than the average commencement address and indeed, at two commencements in suburban schools, audience response had been highly satisfactory. Parents and graduates showed the symptoms of attentive listening and chuckled happily at intended humor. It is easy to empathize with an appreciative audience, so that resulting circular responses quite exhilarated the speaker.

The third commencement was in a rural area some sixty miles from the city. The speaker arrived shortly before time for the ceremony to begin, and because there was considerable confusion about getting the graduates lined up in proper order and the band located out of the way of the graduation march, he omitted talking to the superintendent or to the local minister about the community and the audience. Perhaps he felt that his tried and tested speech was surefire, would work with any audience.

The opening of his speech featured a surprise "twist" that had previously produced a roar of laughter. With this audience, no one smiled or moved. He tried more vigorous delivery, adapted content to the occasion, with no response. The speaker's feedback was interpreted by him as totally negative. At the end of thirty minutes of desperate and frustrating effort, he could only conclude that his speech had been rejected by his listeners.,

After the graduates had received their diplomas and marched away, the local superintendent had a chance to talk with the speaker. He said, "I should have told you that in this community the only polite way an audience can treat a speaker is by sitting perfectly still. Never, to my knowledge, have they broken their standard pattern of being totally passive. But they listen well, and are very appreciative. I hope their lack of response didn't bother you!" Had the speaker known in advance the habits of his audience, he could have modified his interpretation of feedback and sensed many subtle indications of response.

An empathic interdependence *was* present in this commencement audience, but within the limits of particular social customs prevalent in that community. There was undoubtedly an intellectual identification and much vicarious experiencing of feelings, thoughts, and attitudes. Had the speaker understood the cultural conventions of audience reaction, his responses could have enhanced the empathic interaction rather than inhibited it. Our point is that a common understanding of appropriate behavior in a particular context by audience and speaker is necessary for optimum, constructive empathy.

The speaker needs to play the game of empathy within rules set by the audience, but members of the audience also have an opportunity to facilitate the productive uses of empathy. Liveliness in a group of listeners is contagious. Within the limits of accepted and appropriate behavior set by an audience and occasion there is a range of responsiveness possible. If you as a listener try to help the speaker by responding overtly in ways that reinforce him, others around you will begin to register similar behavior. An intra-audience empathy contributes more than is generally recognized to success or failure of a presentation. Just as being passive breeds passivity, listening actively produces more active listeners. Permitting yourself to be freely expressive in an audience may well be just as important as learning to be expressive as a speaker. Where people meet together frequently, passive patterns of audience behavior can be changed into lively audience-speaker interaction norms if a few people work at it patiently and persistently. Active auditors are happy participators, by and large, and the level of satisfaction relates to energy expended in getting the job done.

The level of interdependence of speaker and listener that we term the "empathic relationship" permits much and varied interaction but leaves the speaker in firm control. When the amount and nature of speaker-auditor interaction are sufficient to change the speaker-receiver relationship to a task-oriented small group, we say that their interdependence has reached the level of *involvement*.

Involvement.   When the purposes of the speaker become the purposes of his audience and vice versa, involvement occurs. Dialogue prevails. A member of the audience picks up the ball and runs with it. The speaker may be silent for sustained periods, often assuming the role of moderator directing participation rather than initiating. The involved audience lifts much of the load from the speaker's shoulders. The group becomes a working team, confronting obstacles and, together, overcoming them, as it modifies and implements the speaker's proposal. Typically, the involved audience develops great enthusiasm and generates tremendous momentum. Everyone acquires a stake in the enterprise, a vested interest that insures his dedication and effort.

Perhaps the best analogy to clarify the involvement interaction is the satisfactory sexual relationship. In good sex the roles of initiator and recipient shift unpredictably. Both parties contribute to the shaping of the experience, with a moment-to-moment spontaneity and creativity. Concentration is such that the task at hand crowds out all distractions. The joint effort becomes an end in itself and the ongoing process is as rewarding as the ultimate fulfillment.

Genuine speaker-audience involvement rests upon a foundation of openness and trust. Strangers find it difficult to participate in such an all-out unrestricted cooperation. People who are defensive, jealous, and hostile can seldom be helpful to or comfortable in an involved group. The warm interpersonal relationship which comes about when people who like each other work together often produces involvement. In the language of group process there must be a warm climate, permissiveness, and enjoyment of differences of opinion before there is the possibility that involvement may be achieved.

We are speaking of involvement as the most desirable form of speaker-listener interdependence. This is obvious, because shared purposes, knowledge, and desire to move together to the common goal release and coordinate human effort better than any known form of guidance from other persons. Only an involved group integrates and exploits these related factors while supplying its own impetus.

Just as an individual in an audience can encourage empathic reactions of his fellow auditors and the speaker, so can the audience member contribute to creating a state of involvement. When his activities and comments show not only high interest but trust and openness, when he lets others see the depth of his concern, their responses will become more open and concerned. The famous psychologist Carl Rogers once said, "It is safe to be transparently real." In our modern organizations this may seem to state a somewhat remote, impractical ideal, but to a participant in the audience of a presentation it represents a valuable guideline for responsive behavior.

The involvement of interpersonal communication may or may not include large amounts of what we have previously referred to as symbol response. When the task at hand is one that requires extensive analysis before decisions can be made or solutions recommended, involvement interdependence often does include careful reflection, the withholding of judgment, and the weighing of meanings. On the other hand, the group interaction may transcend reasoned discourse and lead to rare moments of almost mystical communion and insight. The utilization of all the participants' power of insight, reasoning, feeling, and creativity exemplifies the highest level of human interdependence and an ultimate in interpersonal communication. These rare moments of almost total understanding are never achieved without great effort, involvement, empathy, and creative contributions from the listener as well as from the speaker.

Speaker-listener interdependence ranges from practically none through simple action-reaction, to the empathic relationship and involvement. Responding to the presentation constructively implies purposeful efforts on the part of the listener to help the speaker increase interdependence as much as the situation permits. True involvement is not often possible but trying to approximate it contributes significantly to the success of the presentation.

LISTENING TO LEARN

Perhaps the most basic response to a presentation is comprehension of the message. This implies considerably more than simply hearing what is said, for hearing is not the same as listening. Hearing registers sound stimuli on a person's nervous system, while listening interprets them. Listening adds *perception* to auditory sensations, a process of attaching meaning to the signs and symbols one hears.

Most of the sounds that surround us are heard but not listened to. All of us are capable of concentrating on a task in a noisy room. We can refuse to let extraneous sounds distract us although they still agitate our ear drums and send impulses into our brains. We "tune out" unwanted sound by refusing to listen to or perceive it.

This ability to listen selectively suggests that listening is influenced by will power and practice. The training of Air Force radio operators provides abundant proof that this is true. The operator who can "read" Morse code practices listening to messages with increasing amounts of "white noise," a continuous roaring, rushing sound. With concentration and practice his skill in isolating code from noise becomes difficult to believe. A good operator can read a code message under noisy conditions such that the untrained person is unable to detect the presence of any code signals whatsoever!

The physical and mental distractions present in a presentation often create a situation analogous to the airborne operator striving to decode a distant signal in a thunderstorm. Self-discipline of a high order can force concentration and improve reception of the message, but unless the receiver has trained himself in the habits of good listening, his comprehension of the content presented is almost certain to be insufficient. Fortunately, the study of listening has advanced our understanding of the process substantially in recent years. We can now describe the behaviors associated with effective listening. Anyone who would improve his listening comprehension can systematically practice these techniques and establish habitual patterns of response that enable him to learn more from a spoken message and remember it longer.

HOW TO IMPROVE YOUR LISTENING COMPREHENSION

1. *Practice Listening to Difficult Material*

One of the causes of poor listening may be labeled the "recreation syndrome." We do a tremendous amount of "fun and games" listening throughout our lives. We select from the casual and inconsequential materials in our environment what gives us pleasure, what interests and amuses us. Our never-ending search for entertainment builds firm habits of attending to what is instantly comprehended without effort and resisting or avoiding entirely material requiring forced attention and thought. The result is a tendency to engage in entertainment-type listening to serious, task-oriented communication. When the presentational speaker explains the steps in a complicated process, we may "tune out" and wait for something more interesting to come along. When he asks us to remember some statistical information because he intends to use it later in his talk, we resent expending the necessary effort. At this point, we may rationalize and tell ourselves that it is the speaker's job to make listening easy, and if he does not do that for his audience, he deserves not to be remembered.

The fact is that much necessary and important listening is difficult. The person who stops comprehending at the first sign of perplexity or confusion will miss much that he needs to know and will suffer the penalties of not being informed. The skills of comprehending heard materials like most skills and abilities are acquired rather than inherited. They are developed only through use. Systematic practice in listening to challenging lectures, discussions, public service programs on radio and television at regular and frequent intervals, modifies the "recreation syndrome" and establishes habits of persistence and tenacity in wresting meaning from spoken verbal stimuli.

A frontal attack on the improvement of listening ability can be made with the help of commercially programmed and recorded exercise materials.[4] These can be used individually or in small groups, and with associated pretests and post-tests, supply the learner with evidence of the nature and extent of his improvement. Courses in listening are now offered by most educational institutions and in many business and professional organizations. Taking such a course gives one a sound base for later self-improvement, since specific learning techniques are taught and practiced under supervision.

Courses and commercial materials are helpful but not essential to

[4] An example of a self-help package to improve listening skills is the "Ralph G. Nichols' Complete Course in Listening" available from Dun and Bradstreet, Inc., Manager Development Division, 1290 Avenue of the Americas, New York, N.Y., 10019.

the improvement of listening skills. Simply listening to difficult material regularly and endeavoring to extract from it central ideas and
significant supporting evidence will benefit the listener a surprising
amount. The guiding principle to implement general self-practice in
listening is *be selective*. Selectivity must be in terms of an objective,
and for most materials the listener should ask himself, "What do I
want to remember, to meet my needs and interests?" With this question as a criterion, he identifies what seems central and necessary and
carefully discards most of the other facts and concepts. Such selective
listening forms habits useful in separating the wheat from the chaff in
a presentation.

2. Empathize with the Speaker

When a listener feels involved with a speaker, that is, has an ongoing
empathic relationship with him, comprehending what the speaker says
becomes effortless and efficient. What can the listener do to facilitate
the development of his empathy with the speaker? Mainly, he can play
the role of ideal auditor. He can tell himself, "I am going to be on the
speaker's side. I will ignore his mannerisms that might distract me. I
will figure out how he would like me to react, and respond that way.
In effect, I will function as his assistant." With this attitude the listener
can sense what the speaker is feeling and thinking, and empathy can
grow.

In the speaker-listener dyad we can identify two main components
that produce empathic interaction. One is natural, the automatic
tendency of one human being to participate in whatever goes on inside
the other. The second element is voluntary and purposeful. *Trying* to
be empathic increases empathy. When a listener is consciously attempting to sense the feelings in the speaker, when he is studying
nonverbal behavior and tones of voice and relating these to the content
of the message, his perceptions are other-than-self centered. Because
he can perceive more cues to speaker response when he is concentrating on the speaker, he collects more empathy-producing data and
becomes more empathic.

3. Work Hard at Listening

Techniques 1 and 2 above suggest that voluntary concentration in
listening accomplishes wonders. This leads to our third recommendation, since voluntary concentration implies work. But, why should
listening be hard work? Because the nature of human attention is such
that task-oriented listening violates its patterns severely.

Human attention is sporadic. It comes in short bursts rather than
persisting steadily. We listen to a speaker for fifteen to forty seconds,
typically, then turn him off for a while to think about something else.
We stay with the speaker for a longer or shorter period, depending on
how much he interests us, then turn him off again to pursue our other

mental activities. Often, the periods of attention to the speaker become shorter and shorter, and the periods during which we are occupied by other thoughts become longer and longer.

To break the pattern of sporadic attention requires "work" behavior. The listener must discipline himself by resisting attractive mental excursions and applying his energies to the task of listening. Such voluntary attention usually becomes nonvoluntary, for forcing attention to a speaker normally leads to becoming interested in what he is saying. Certainly, the only way such an intrinsic interest can come about is to compel attention through an act of will until perceptions generate favorable responses.

Three common-sense admonitions help "worked at" listening to be productive. The first points a finger at a barrier to communication everywhere, "Don't fake attention." All of us have learned to fool speakers by looking as though we are eager listeners, while we are actually woolgathering. Fake listening subverts any effort to work at unscrambling a difficult message.

The second advice is, "Overcome the bad news barrier." When a speaker states a fact that is contrary to our belief or distasteful to us, we often use the defense mechanism of ceasing to listen. To handle difficult material we must remove the barrier to hearing what we do not like, and learn to welcome differences. Many people have trained themselves to be more attentive to material they disagree with than to concepts conforming to their prejudices.

Finally, in working to generate an interest that does not come naturally, do not settle for a neutral and passive willingness to receive what you hear. Try to "pump up" a genuine interest, one with enthusiasm. While the "power of positive thinking" can be overestimated, the listener who tells himself that he is interested in and excited by the presentation often increases his comprehension. A positive attitude is needed to neutralize our natural skepticism, which keeps informing most of us that if an idea is new to us and contrary to our thinking, it can have little merit!

4. Review and Preview as You Listen

A hazard for the listener to overcome is the differential between thought speed and speech speed. The presentational speaker talks at a rate of 125 to 175 words per minute, while his audience can think 600 to 800 words per minute. Sporadic attention is encouraged by this differential. One problem confronting the well-intentioned listener is, "How can I keep busy?"

The first answer is, keep busy by thinking about the speaker's topic, not about other things. Selective listening, identifying central concepts and their support, is one excellent exercise. The game of anticipation is a constructive maneuver. Where is the speaker going next, and how will his talk develop from this point on? Once the listener has guessed what is coming, he is sure to listen carefully to check on his prediction. If he has guessed correctly, he is reinforced in his listening, and if he has predicted poorly, he will listen better to improve his batting average with his next prediction. Also, the listener can always utilize time while the speaker is repeating himself or adding an unnecessary illustration to review what has gone before. Recapitulation is a powerful aid to the memory, and recapping the parts of a presentation gives an improved grasp of the entire structure, as a unit.

The belief that spoken material is assimilated when received without the listener "chewing it over" and working at it seems to be universal. Research on the process of good listening contradicts this notion. Continuous review and preview contribute significantly to retention and understanding.

5. Suspend Judgment

We tend to be compulsive about decision-making. Confronted by a problem, we want to seize a solution and have it "over and done with." In listening, our compulsiveness often urges us to make up our minds early about the speaker's proposition. We await some significant statement or bit of factual information to help us make up our minds. If we find it and thereby prejudge the issue, we can relax and fake attention for the remainder of the speech. If we behave in this fashion, we are guilty of making an "inductive leap," jumping to a conclusion without the necessary evidence, a nasty hazard to the business of task-oriented listening.

To avoid hasty and unwarranted decisions a listener must "hear the man out," by consciously resisting the temptation to make tentative decisions along the way. Rather than listening for a decisive item, we suggest that the listeners arrange two columns, mentally or on paper, one of "pros" and one of "cons." At the end of the presentation, the columns will be complete and the pros and cons can be "added up" and compared. In this procedure clusters of variables can be kept in order and related. Without some such device important items will be overlooked and the more dramatic points, those in sharp conflict or in marked harmony with the views of the listener, will exert an excessive influence on the outcome.

6. Keep Calm

All listeners have tender areas easily irritated by hostile notions. If a person permits himself to respond emotionally to some content item in a speech, interesting distortions occur that unbalance his decision-making mechanism. Chapter 5 treated the effects of an emotional condition upon problem-solving ability, noting that the three concomitants of emotion (shock, diffusion, and transference) all function nonrationally. We can only conclude that if a listener becomes upset in any way, his ability to solve problems deteriorates and his decisions made in an emotional state are less wise than those formulated when he is calm.

Sometimes, keeping calm is no easy matter. One tested technique is to separate in one's mind the person and the concepts he is discussing. When a speaker says something that irritates a listener, the impulse of the receiver is to become angry at the speaker for saying it. This is entirely unproductive because it not only produces emotion but it also takes the listener's mind away from the topic. If the listener refuses to be diverted by his tendency toward such aggressive retaliation and instead analyzes the offensive item and how it fits into the case made by the speaker, he is much less likely to be emotionally disturbed.

The speaker's choice of words is often the factor that causes upsets in listeners. A defense against this irritant is the listener's ability to identify and classify what might be termed his "language of alienation." Each individual has long list of words that he responds to by overreacting. Here are some words and phrases that have been shown to upset the nervous systems of certain Americans: *dictator, Communistic, graduated income tax, national debt, hippie, Mary Jane, nigger, mother-in-law, abortion, data processing, computerization, motherfucker, sex education,* and so on, the compilation could be nearly endless. Probably the reader felt at least one twinge as he read through the list. We should identify the words to which we have become sensitized and, when one comes along, say to ourselves, "Oops, let's not get excited. The word is not the thing, and it would be foolish to become upset over a grouping of letters from the alphabet. Rather, what point was he trying to make?"

A final suggestion for maintaining self-possession is to resist identifying with a controversial position. Particularly when one is a member of the audience to a presentation, it is appropriate to assume an objective attitude. Deliberately detach yourself from your vested interests in the ongoing argument and become a disinterested observer, a collector and an interpreter of points made and support offered. Playing the observer role keeps your prejudices in check to some degree and increases your tendency to be reflective rather than impulsive in reacting to a message.

Perhaps you can maintain your personal stability by simply telling yourself, "Keep calm." However you do it, you will be a better and more useful listener to a presentation if you succeed in resisting the temptation to become upset.

7. Overcome Unfavorable Listening Conditions

A skilled listener will not tolerate an unfavorable listening condition that can be corrected. If he has difficulty seeing and hearing from a present location, he will move to a better seat. If the speaker is not talking loudly enough to be heard by all, our good listener will inform the speaker of that fact, not just once, but persistently until the deficiency is remedied. Should the public address system be malfunctioning or a visual aid be out of adjustment, the good listener will assume responsibility for bringing about proper functioning of those devices. He will not tolerate disturbances within the audience. If other listeners are carrying on a private conversation, he will "shh" them and do whatever is necessary to terminate the distraction.

Learning to attack, aggressively, unfavorable listening conditions is difficult for most of us. We have accustomed ourselves to accept, passively, not only boring speakers but circumstances that make comprehensive listening categorically impossible. The dull speaker may be something we can do nothing to improve, but the conditions of listening can be controlled. We can only conclude that the knowledgeable listener who identifies something in the environment that is restricting comprehension for himself and/or other listeners should overcome his passive auditor habits, and perhaps a natural shyness as well, and act boldly to remove the obstacle as soon as possible.

8. *Minimize Note Taking and Other Doodling*

Analysis of notes taken during speeches and of the use of those notes later might well lead us to the conclusion that note taking is a form of doodling. While some note taking may be necessary, most of it serves no useful purpose. Hence, we argue that note taking should be minimized in the interest of improving listening comprehension.

Serious note takers follow various unproductive systems. A favorite is the standard outline form, with heads, subheads, and sub-subheads, and for every "1" there must be a "2," for every "A," a "B." A difficulty is caused by the fact that most speakers do not follow standard outline forms. Consequently, the note taker tries to outline something that is not there. He rearranges the content into a basically different speech, and in so doing, misses much of what is said.

Another popular pattern for note taking is to list main points to be remembered on one page, important facts on another. When a main point is also an important fact, the classification dilemma is likely to divert the listener for some time. Then, too, facts separated from the points thus supported tend to lose meaning, and usually criteria for selecting the "important" facts are unclear and indefinite. If the note taker attempts to relate facts to main points by a number system, he soon confronts a complicated crisscrossing interlocking network sufficiently perplexing to discourage any later reference to those notes.

The pitfall common to all note taking is the compulsion to write more than is needed. Recording connectives, articles, most adjectives and adverbs, memorable phrases, and side comments is superfluous and amounts to verbal doodling. For the rare occasions when the taking of notes is essential, we recommend the following guidelines:

Be rigorously economical. Ask yourself, what will I almost certainly use later and will as certainly forget if I do not write it down?

Strip away all unnecessary verbiage. Avoid complete sentences and paragraphs. Simply list skeletonized items of content with no attempt to number or letter them or to show superior-subordinate relationships.

Within two hours after a presentation, review your notes and extract what you wish to keep in a coherent memo to yourself or to someone else. Throw away the remainder of the notes, for with the passage of time on-the-spot notes become less and less meaningful, and reading old, cold notes is both frustrating and deceptive.

More important, learn to gradually substitute the active listening techniques of review and preview for note taking. A trained and disciplined memory far outclasses any shorthand system of written symbols that must be later decoded and interpreted.

9. *Use the Key Active Listening Techniques*

When circumstances permit you as listener to participate in a dialogue with the speaker, use the key active listening techniques of *encouraging, restating, reflecting,* and *summarizing.*

The possibility of responding verbally to the speaker is often present in presentations and it can be exploited to improve listening comprehension dramatically. The four active listening techniques do not require prior knowledge of the topic on the part of the listener; yet through them he contributes interaction that converts a basically one-way talk into an effective dialogue. Figure 12.1 explains and exemplifies these techniques.[5]

The source of the key active listening techniques is nondirective counseling. The counselor participates by making statements like the examples cited that both stimulate and sharpen communication without influencing its content. Similarly, the listener to a presentation can achieve clarification and generally increase understanding of the speaker's message by making these four types of statements at appropriate times. Like the nondirective counselor, he does not introduce substantive materials but he can contribute significantly to improving the process of communication.

CRITICAL LISTENING

Listening to learn requires perception, understanding, and retention. To move toward decision from understood and remembered materials requires a further operation: *evaluation.* Critical listening is the process of adding systematic and valid evaluation to information already comprehended.

[5] The key active listening techniques and Figure 12.1 are adapted from Robert K. Burns, "The Listening Techniques," MS 155, 2–7, 2500, Industrial Relations Center, University of Chicago, 1958, pp. 4–25.

Type of Statement	Purpose	To Achieve Purpose	Examples
A. Encouraging	1. To convey interest.	Don't agree or disagree with man. Use noncommittal words with positive tone of voice.	1. "I see. . . ." 2. "Uh-huh. . . ." 3. "That's interesting. . . ."
B. Restating	1. To show that you are listening and understanding. 2. To let man know you grasp the *facts*.	Restate the man's basic ideas, emphasizing the facts.	1. "If I understand, your idea is . . ." 2. "In other words, this is the situation. . . ."
C. Reflecting	1. To show that you are listening and understanding 2. To let man know you understand *how he feels*.	Reflect the man's basic feelings.	1. "You feel that . . ." 2. "You were pretty disturbed by this . . ."
D. Summarizing	1. To pull important ideas, facts, etc., together 2. To establish basis for further discussion. 3. To review progress	Restate, reflect, and summarize ideas and feelings.	1. "These seem to be the key ideas you have expressed. . . ." 2. "If I understand you, you feel this way about the situation. . . ."

Figure 12.1 Key Active Listening Techniques

Much has been said in this book that can be used to achieve critical listening. Chapter 7 supplies standards for evaluating statistical support, Chapter 8 discusses sound uses of nonstatistical materials, and Chapter 9 presents information about reasoning as it is used to advance propositions in a presentation. The first and most basic technique of critical listening is to apply the criteria from these chapters to the message being received. We will summarize briefly the major questions to be answered in evaluating these three important aspects of the presentation and encourage the reader to refer back to the appropriate chapter for explication of any concept that is not completely clear.

Listening evaluation of statistical support. The first test of points based upon numerical information is twofold: Is there sufficient information, and is it clear and unambiguous? Clarity is achieved only when every item of data has an obvious purpose.

Is the relationship between support and the statement to be supported necessary and important? Often, statistical facts are "mixed up" with statements to be proved to provide the illusion of support, without an actual close relationship between the two.

Next, the critical listener scrutinizes the over-all patterns of statistical evidence. Do the statistics omit relevant areas of information? Is the most meaningful index of typicality used? What indices of variability are utilized and is the choice appropriate? Does the over-all use of statistics add to understanding of the problem?

A closer analysis of the speaker's statistical methodology raises these questions: Are his statistics descriptive or inferential? If inferential, are they representative? What were the sampling procedures? Is a confidence level computed, and is it satisfactory?

Statistically supported statements almost always yield comparisons and predictions, which suggest that these questions be answered: Are units in the statistics constant and comparable? Are they of the same magnitude or corrected? Are trends clearly presented quantitatively in tables and graphs? Do tables and graphs distort the data in any way?

While the above capsule summary of tests of statistical support is severely condensed, it provides guidelines for the critical listener. If a numerically based presentation is judged to be satisfactory on all the mentioned criteria, it will have some merit.

Listening evaluation of nonstatistical support.   Critical listening is facilitated if the receiver distinguishes between *evidence* and *clarification*. Evidence furnishes grounds for belief, or *proof*. Clarification contributes to understanding. These are different functions though they are often combined, and the distinction between them is important because different standards are applied to the ingredients of proof than to materials intended to increase understanding.

Proof is developed primarily through use of statistical evidence, real case studies, and testimony. Statistical support has been discussed, so we will turn to tests of case studies and testimony of witnesses used as proof.

Is the case study cited genuinely real? Often details are left out, or added, to make a more effective example. Is it representative or the exception? Are sufficient details supplied, and is assurance provided that necessary observation has been complete and accurate? Where several cases are used, are there enough of them to validate the claim? Are the cases, considered collectively, fairly representative? Where statistical evidence is also used, do the case or cases supplement the statistics and are they in harmony?

Testimony is the observation and/or judgment of a witness, and its first criterion is that of relevance: Does the testimony bear *directly* upon the point to be proved? Other tests are of the witness: Is he an expert in the subject on which he testifies? Did he have an opportunity to observe firsthand the events he reports? Is the witness respected by his peers? Is he known to be biased or to have related vested interests? When several witnesses are used, is their testimony in agreement or does it present contradictions?

Tests of clarification are less rigorous but perhaps just as important to the evaluation of a presentation. Hypothetical case studies are frequently useful: Are they reasonable in that available evidence indicates it would be possible for them to occur as described? Do they contribute significantly to the understanding of the problem? With analogies, literal and figurative, is there an identity of principle in the events related to each other by the analogy? Does the analogy make a truly pertinent point? Are narratives and anecdotes necessary? Is reiteration helpful? Do all the devices of clarification have a cumulative effect?

Evaluation of nonstatistical supporting material is accomplished in part by relating it to statistical supports. A final test is the extent to which they are integrated, the amount of weight each adds to the proof of the other by its supplementary function.

Listening evaluation of reasoning. Much of our advice on evaluating statistical and nonstatistical supports involves criticism of the reasoning process. But the critical listener will find it rewarding to make a judgment of the over-all quality of the thinking that was evidenced in the presentation. For this reason we isolate factors that are important to the constructive use of logical devices and relationships and suggest means of assessing them.

Can you as a listener readily perceive a comprehensive structure that relates all the parts of the speech in a systematic and sensible fashion? Does one point follow another in natural sequence, with a sense of progress and inevitability? Could you brief the talk as you listen, with relative ease?

Is the speaker's central purpose clear? Do all propositions contribute to that purpose directly? Is every proposition adequately supported? Are the propositions as concrete and specific as possible? Single? In report language? Worded positively? Not figurative or colloquial?

Viewing the speech as an attempt to solve a problem, does the speaker make clear how he follows an accepted problem-solving system? Does he omit any essential steps? Are exceptions and opposing arguments noted? Is appropriate documentation supplied? Are concealment and other deceptions avoided?

Since reasoning is effective with a particular audience only if it is adjusted to their expectations and abilities, is the reasoning used by the speaker adapted to the knowledge, interests, and motives of his audience? And, since thoughtful materials are communicated more effectively when worded concretely rather than abstractly, is the factual and reasoned content of the presentation worded as concretely, specifically, and simply as possible?

To be effective as reasoned discourse, a speech must be delivered in a manner that encourages a deliberative, thoughtful response. A final criterion of reasonableness deals with speaker-audience interaction:

Does the speaker by his style and tone of speaking make clear to the members of his audience that he intends them to think through a problem with him, step by step, and reach a solution through the exercise of their best judgment?

RECURRING FALLACIES OF PRESENTATION

Advancing proposals involves the matters examined above, and careful attention paid to the listed items will be rewarded by a sound objective evaluation in which the listener can place his confidence. In addition to considering relevant specifics of particular supports and the qualitative dimension of critical thinking we should pay special attention to three persistent fallacies that flaw many a presentation. The *post hoc* fallacy, the hasty generalization, and "either-or" analysis occur so frequently and their effects are so devastating to thoughtful response that we will explain and comment upon each in turn.

Post hoc fallacy. The complete Latin name for this classic fallacy explains its nature: *post hoc, ergo propter hoc;* after this, therefore because of this. Its deceptive effect is a result of the unwarranted assumption that because two events are related in time sequence, the first is the cause of the second. Since causes precede consequences, it is easy to believe that an earlier related happening brought about modification of present circumstances, that a causal "connection" indeed exists.

Republican administrations are associated with depressions and Democratic administrations with wars in the United States because of *post hoc* thinking. Republicans took office and a severe recession followed, leading to the instant conclusion that the new regime is responsible. Wars were begun or declared in Democratic administrations. Therefore, Democratic leadership causes wars. Other variables that functioned as partial causes, many of them in the nature of trends over long periods of years, are ignored.

Post hoc interpretations are attractive because of their simplicity. A somewhat dramatic incident is followed by a significant, atypical event. The human mind, perpetually in search of explanations, makes an inductive leap to account for the event by assuming that the prior incident was responsible. The fallacy is abetted by our loose use of the language of causal relation. We talk of single causes when multiple causes are necessarily operating, as: "What was the cause of World War II?" Similarly, we are careless in using words to predict effects: "If we automate that operation in the assembly line, the union will strike the plant." Our habitual thinking is undisciplined in accepting oversimplified explanations of phenomena and in taking for granted causal relationships for which there is little or no proof.

Post hoc thinking often results from a failure to note that the apparent cause and effect may both be effects of a more remote causation. A sensible challenge to the belief that smoking cigarettes causes cancer of the lungs is the hypothesis that the heavy smoker has a neurophysiological make-up that predisposes him to both smoking and cancer. Reorganization of an enterprise frequently involves a change in leadership. If, subsequently, the organizational machinery runs more smoothly, the almost universal interpretation will be that the new leader caused the improvement. In most cases among the many variables, organizational changes probably influence the shape of the new order more than do the actions of the person who is imported or promoted. Generally, the higher the status of the office holder, the more he is credited with influencing people and events. Sometimes it seems that the President of the United States is considered to be the cause of everything that happens during and immediately after his administration.

To avoid the *post hoc* fallacy a speaker must distinguish cause and effect from another important logical operation, reasoning from concomitant variation. To make the point that two variables are associated in a concomitant variation is simply to show that they occur together, reliably. This is useful knowledge. Not long ago in medical research when a drug was found to relieve the symptoms of a disease, the drug was not released for use until cause-and-effect actions had been discovered. Tracing cause-and-effect connections through the human body often consumed years of labor. Now to a significant degree concomitant variation has replaced causation as a laboratory research method. If administration of a drug reliably accompanies relief of symptoms of a disease, after a check to make sure there are no serious, undesirable side effects the drug can be marketed and distress can be alleviated.

The critical listener is ever alert to the possibility that the speaker may confuse time sequence with a cause-and-effect relationship. He knows that sound cause-to-effect or effect-to-cause arguments are rare, because of multiple variables present in all human interactions. When a speaker uses the language of concomitant variation and resists the temptation to talk loosely about causes and results, the listener can be assured that the speaker appreciates the deceptiveness of *post hoc* thinking.

The fallacy of hasty generalization. A lay definition of the hasty generalization fallacy is "jumping to conclusions." While this is a figurative rather than an operational definition, it suggests very nicely the essence of hasty generalization: making a premature statement of definite and sweeping character that goes far beyond available supporting materials. The *post hoc* fallacy may be considered a special instance of hasty generalization, one in which the cause is assumed.

Typically, however, *no* evidence of causation exists in *post hoc,* and hasty generalizations are made from some, but inadequate evidence.

We will list several types of hasty generalization, and our readers can discover other categories. A popular form generalizes about a class of phenomena from a single instance. "Adapt this plan of participative management? We tried it five years ago, but it didn't work." The implication, not often stated in so many words is, "If one attempt to implement participative management failed, all other such attempts are doomed to failure." Here, as is often the case with fallacious reasoning, stating the implied assumption reveals the absurdity of the argument.

Another much used and abused hasty generalization makes statements about groups of people or phenomena, asserting similarities without factual evidence. Usually, the sources of these statements are legend or folklore. Strangely, because the base of such a generalization is a well-known belief or stereotype, many accept it as soundly reasoned. Here are current examples: "Bosses are not interested in the welfare of their employees." "Members of a labor union will attempt to restrict production." "Companies with extensive data processing equipment are cold and impersonal places to work." "Colleges are Ivory Towers that fail to teach people how to make a living." "Salesmen have to be supervised or they won't do their work." "Policemen mistreat their prisoners." "Ministers cheat on their income tax." Hasty generalizations like these resemble mottos or maxims that people persist in believing in spite of their contradictory nature, as is the case with "A stitch in time saves nine" and "Haste makes waste."

When hasty generalizations about people and events occur in a presentation, they usually fill the role of a basic assumption. "Since this is known to be true" reasons the speaker, "it should guide our decision, and we should do thus and so." Attention is thus turned away from the generalization, and the critical listener must remind himself to ask, "Is there any proof for that sweeping statement?"

A third kind of hasty generalization "loads the dice" by concluding from a collection of unrepresentative instances. You can make any kind of generalization about the interests, personalities, or abilities of college professors or executives that you wish to make—providing you control your sample. If I study five professors who are homosexual, artistic, and impractical, I can conclude logically that my sample is homosexual, artistic, and impractical, but I cannot logically say anything about "college professors" from my research. But people tend to conclude concerning an entire population from samples as biased as this one. The distortion is made palatable by suppression of the clearly implied word "all"; instead of "all college professors are thus and so" we say "college professors are—." A confusing ambiguity is introduced and the speaker, if challenged, can reply "I didn't say *all*," a weasel way to avoid responsibility for his claim. The listener will be aided in his search for suspect generalizations if he supplies the word "all" when he feels it has been omitted.

Another fallacy of hasty generalization is the application of a sound normative conclusion to an individual instance. Practically all sound generalizations are statements of central tendency; that is, they imply the words "by and large" rather than "each and every." Consequently, they admit of occasional exceptions, and any single case may be one of those exceptions. "Executives are more intelligent than their employees" is a sound generalization, but it would be fallacious to say, "Therefore, boss Simpson is smarter than electrician Voltsman." Attributing a trait of a group to a member is similarly unjustified. "Baggage handlers are brawny so Muscles O'Donovan must be brawny" is bad reasoning, for Muscles may be an exception, a ninety-pound weakling. Dealing with operations rather than people is still more tricky: "Chrome-plating parts in our machines has been more successful than nickel-plating, so we should chrome-plate this pipe" may be a hasty and invalid conclusion because of particular chemical agents in the vicinity that attack chrome.

Thoughtful speakers seldom if ever apply a normative generalization to an individual instance, and the critical listener will discount heavily any attempts to make such an application.

A speaker's use of generalizations is a major indicator of the quality of his reasoning. Conservative, precise, and meticulous generalizing is reliably associated with clear and logical thinking. We might class this relationship as an example of concomitant variation.

The fallacy of "either-or" analysis. Deeply rooted in our habitual thought patterns is the tendency to maximize differences. We strive for contrasts and push toward extremes. We like to make clean-cut and definite decisions. We tend to classify people and events in mutually exclusive categories. By so doing, we simplify the world so we can feel we understand it. If we emphasize similarities instead of differences, things and people seem very much like each other, and sorting them out for purposes of reacting to them becomes very complicated indeed.

Semanticists refer to our preference for extremes as "two-valued orientation." We like to classify our surroundings as black or white rather than in shades of gray, to phrase it metaphorically. We refer to a movie as "exciting" or "boring," seldom as "mildly interesting." Personalities we classify as "outgoing" or "introverted." Human abilities are similarly dichotomized: A musician is "talented" or "talentless," a design engineer is "imaginative" or "without imagination," and a student is either "bright" or "stupid." In reality, most musicians are probably talented to some degree, design engineers are reasonably imaginative, and the average student is part bright and part stupid.

When a speaker in a presentation indulges in either-or analysis of a problem, he distorts it severely because, to hear him tell it, the favorable features have no disadvantages and the unfavored aspects have nothing worthwhile in them. Thoughtful confrontation of pros and cons is ordinarily a balancing process with much to be said on both sides. All solutions have advantages and disadvantages. Only by the "shades of gray" kind of analysis can the small but important differences be isolated. The speaker who habitually analyzes his issues and evidence on a continuum rather than into a dichotomy will be contributing to the realistic appraisal of the situation that his audience wishes to accomplish.

CREATIVE LISTENING

Our earlier discussion of speaker-audience interdependence suggests that in situations of empathic relationship and involvement the listener has opportunities to contribute to the ongoing communication by initiating changes in events. Members of the audience possess knowledge and abilities to interpret information that, added to the speaker's, can increase productivity of the presentation. We term participation of this sort by people in an audience *creative listening*.

Being creative in listening requires the making of personal decisions to attempt to change the course of the presentation in some way. Usually, this is accomplished by addition of a bit of information or an idea, or by selecting a concept and interpreting or elaborating it, or by advancing new integrations of materials previously mentioned. But we must note a rare and occasionally appropriate act of creative listening, the decision to "turn off" the speaker.

There are instances when the good judgment of the critical listener tells him that the present speaker-audience interaction is impossible. Given the task, the speaker, this audience and situation, nothing significant *can* result. Once a listener has arrived at this decision, the sensible thing to do is sit quietly and direct his mental energies to some other problem. Too often we behave in a ritualistic fashion as though progress is being made and everything is going well when it is not. The creative listener can help most by refusing to cooperate in this group self-deception.

In potentially productive speaker-audience interactions a developing empathy and involvement set the stage for increasing listener participation. If this is to advance the thinking of the group and improve its attack upon a common problem, it must be creative rather than redundant. In Chapter 6 we discussed the way a person can go about making a creative analysis for a presentation and the way creative thinking usually takes place in a purposive daydream. Often the images tumbling through the consciousness are fragmentary, and sometimes, ridiculous or farfetched, but many times important insights come in a flash of illumination during such "mulling over" while driving a car or before dropping off to sleep at night.

On occasion, people talking with one another find themselves caught up in a chain of fantasizing similar to the creative moments that individuals experience.[6] Someone suggests an idea that is picked up by another, and soon a number of the participants are excitedly adding to the dialogue. Under the pressure of the fantasy the constraints that often operate in group discussion are released and people feel free to experiment with ideas, to play with concepts, and to be ridiculous. More and more members of the conference are drawn into active involvement in the communication and the level of excitement and cohesion among the participants rises. Like the abstract picture or the ambiguous modern poem the original message serves as a stimulus for the others to interpret or "read in" additional meanings or feelings of their own. If the speaker accepts the additions, gains from them, and encourages them, the speaker and listeners can help one another to greater insight and understanding.

The total creative involvement of the listener in the communication thus creates a situation in which the flow of meaning is no longer from source to receiver, as in the paradigm of man talking to machine, but rather both source and receiver add to a common reservoir of meaning until the result is greater than either could have produced alone. Thus, the final growth in learning and insight takes place in the source as well as in the receiver. In the highest level of communication, involvement interdependence, the listener responds to the original message by testing, adding, and modifying the meaning. If the listener's contributions stimulate the speaker to see more in the idea than he originally had in mind and he resists the temptation to criticize the modification, his next suggestion may stimulate the listener to still further creative additions. Ideally, the speaker and listener, source and receiver, take turns shaping the original message, adding meanings until the final outcome of the communication is much more complex and exciting than the original meaning intended by the source when he initiated the first message.

Basic to creative listening and involvement is an attitude termed "dialogistical." People with a dialogistical attitude coming into involvement interdependence create what modern communication theory calls a *dialogue*. The dialogistical attitude is one of not being defensive, of being subject-centered. The dialogistical person is always independent, a free agent. He is *open*, willing to reveal himself and his convictions. He is equally willing to hear others, and conveys to them an

[6] For a full discussion of fantasy themes and their function in small groups, see Robert F. Bales, *Personality and Interpersonal Behavior* (New York, 1970).

eagerness to learn their opinions. His speaking shows trust in all other individuals and the group by its frankness and sincerity.

The dialogistical person is disciplined, assuming responsibility for himself and others. He gives himself freely and openly in dialogue but restricts himself to guard against infringing upon the freedom of others. He sees to it that others are free to initiate as they will, and reinforces their attempts to be creative. He shapes his own contribution in the context of the statements of others, being always careful that his openness generates complementary openness. He shows that he not only welcomes differences, but that he enjoys them.

The dialogistical person tends to approach each new idea with the attitude that it is worth considering, modifying, and adopting. How can the idea be used, or improved, or encouraged? When the speaker has a dialogistical attitude, he does not immediately go on the defensive when a listener suggests a modification of his original ideas. When the listener has a dialogistical attitude, he does not immediately search for flaws in the ideas, but rather he searches for strengths as well as weaknesses.

The dialogue we are describing shows a delicate balance of freedom and restraint. It is far from the chaos of "saying whatever you feel at the moment," yet impulsive response is necessary as is a playful attitude at times. The limitations come from group considerations. A person striving to create dialogue subordinates his self-interest to the group's welfare. In dialogistical interactions we cannot be individuals going our separate ways but must be individuals working together.

The process of presentational speaking has become less formal and more "interactive" in recent years. The trend to dialogue will continue. Listeners will initiate idea modifications with greater frequency. The ideal of dialogue, admittedly unattainable, furnishes guidelines to insure productivity in the implementation of the new freedom. Resources of the group become available through disciplined creative listening, directed toward achievement of dialogue among the speaker and members of his audience.

John Jamison had barely finished his twenty-minute presentation to the Board of Control of Minnesota Mills when Homer Lydgate, who had become restless and eager as John built his presentation to the close, broke in. Lydgate excitedly accepted the idea of the new product but suggested a production modification to meet a developing consumer trend in flavoring. John felt a wave of anxiety, but recalling his coaching with Paul Osterhus he repressed his urge to respond with rebuttal arguments and instead concentrated on listening to what Lydgate was saying. Lydgate's excitement was contagious, and as John developments, he saw the potential in Homer's suggestion. He also realized that the required modification in production plans would be listened to new information about latest advertising and marketing slight. He picked up the idea and suggested the possibility of revisions without undue delay in production. John was delighted when Joe Perkins broke in bringing all of his production talent to the problem of modification. When even Marshall Everding grew excited and involved in the financing of the new modifications, the board meeting became an involved, task-oriented conference approaching the ideal of dialogue. The end result was not only approval of John's basic proposition but modifications and improvements that assured the success of the new venture.

Not all presentations move as smoothly through the stages from planning to fruition as did John Jamison's speech at Minnesota Mills. Nor are all communication events as crucial and successful. Yet, in tracing the development of the case of the new product we have seen the necessity, complexity, and satisfactions inherent in making presentations in business and the professions. The mixed or multimedia communication event is the basic way that important information and persuasion will be presented to the decision makers of the future.

SUMMARY

Responding to the presentation depends upon the nature of the interdependence of speaker and audience. This ranges from a negligible interaction through a simple action-reaction, to an empathic interaction, and to the most highly interdependent relationship, that of involvement. In "involvement," listeners are most active and contribute most to the presentation.

Listening is a critical variable in the presentation. The most basic listening ability is to understand and remember the message. It is known as listening comprehension. "Listening to learn" can be improved by several procedures: (1) practice listening to difficult material, (2) empathize with the speaker, (3) work hard at listening, (4) review and preview as you listen, (5) suspend judgment, (6) keep calm, (7) overcome unfavorable listening conditions, (8) minimize note taking and other doodling, and (9) utilize four key active listening techniques.

Critical listening adds evaluation to understanding and remembering and is a separate listening ability. To evaluate parts of a message the listener applies appropriate criteria. In particular, he needs to know and apply the tests of statistical support, of nonstatistical supporting materials, and of the reasoning process used in the presentation. In addition, he should understand and be alert to three recurring fallacies of presentation: (1) the *post hoc* fallacy, (2) the fallacy of hasty generalization, and (3) the fallacy of "either-or" analysis.

A third listening skill that has recently been recognized is that of creative listening. This ability increases contributions of the individual listener to group thinking and problem solution. The ideal pattern of speaker-listener and listener-listener interaction for creativity in listening is the communicative relationship known as *dialogue*. When listeners work to achieve dialogue, their opportunities to be constructively creative increase.

QUESTIONS FOR DISCUSSION AND REVIEW

1. What is the reasoning that justifies the conclusion: "All communication is dyadic"?
2. What are the differences among these patterns of speaker-audience interdependence: simple action-reaction, empathic relationship, and involvement?
3. How does listening differ from hearing?
4. What is the "recreation syndrome" and how does it interfere with listening comprehension?
5. Which of the nine techniques of improving listening comprehension seem to you to be most important? Why?
6. What are the elements that enter into critical listening?
7. What are the three "recurring fallacies"? Give an example of each.
8. How is creative listening influenced by the nature of speaker-listener interdependence?
9. What are the characteristics of the kind of communication we call "dialogue"? How does this relate to creative listening?
10. What are several ways in which an audience can respond constructively to a presentation?

REFERENCES AND SUGGESTED READINGS

BORMANN, ERNEST G., WILLIAM S. HOWELL, RALPH G. NICHOLS, and GEORGE L. SHAPIRO. *Interpersonal Communication in the Modern Organization.* Englewood Cliffs, N.J.: Prentice-Hall, 1969.

DUKER, SAM. *Listening: Reading.* Metuchen, N.J.: Scarecrow Press, 1966.

DUKER, SAM. *Listening Bibliography*, 2nd ed. Metuchin, N.J.: Scarecrow Press, 1968.

NICHOLS, RALPH G., and LEONARD STEVENS. *Are You Listening?* New York: McGraw-Hill, 1957.

WAGNER, GEY, *et al. Classroom Instruction Through Listening Games.* Darien, Conn.: Teachers Publishing, 1962.

INDEX

Ability to predict response, 17, 18
Abstractness, *see* Proposition
Acronym, 184
Addiction to routine continuum, 97–98
Ad hoc, 75–76; committee, 76; meeting, 75–80, 81, 85, 86
Agenda, 69–70, 72–73
Ah hah experience, 114
Ambiguity, 225–226
Amplification, 135–136
Analogy, 176–178
Anecdote, 179
Aphorism, 183
Aristotle, 125, 234
Armstrong, Neil, 225
Arrangement, 117
Attention, 228–229, 290–291; gaining and maintaining, 228–229; voluntary and involuntary, 229
Audience, 63, 64
Audience participation, 260–261
Audio recording and playback, 275–276
Authority, defined, 27
Autosuggestion, 222

Bar graphs, 158–163
Barrier to understanding, 31–32
Begging the question, 198
Berlo, David, 234, 283, 284
Bob Gibson case, 127–129
Boomerang effect, 224
Brief, briefing, 193
Brigance, William Norwood, 207
Burden of proof, 16, 17, 199
Business meeting, functions of, 64

Case study, 169–170
CCTV, *see* Television and video tape

Cerf, Bennett, 227
Chairman, 77–78, 79
Chalkboards, uses of, 268–269
Change agent, 16–18
Channels, 47
Channels of persuasion, 214
Characterization, 178
Chase, Stuart, 245
Circular response, 220
Claim, *see* Proposition
Clarification, 168–169; tests of, 298
Coercion, 92, 93
Coherence, 112
Cohesiveness, 80, 84
COIK fallacy, 262
Commitment to contribution, 102, 103
Common ground, 230–231
Communication, man-to-machine, 44–49; man-to-man, 49–53; objectives of source, 49–50
Comprehensiveness, 112, 113
Conciseness, 112
Concomitant variation, 300
Concreteness, *see* Proposition
Conferences, 55–59; conduct of, 57–59; directive techniques for, 57; environment of, 56–57; nondirective techniques for, 57–58; planning, 55–56; timing, 56
Confidence level, 146–147
Confidence limits, 147
Conformity, 85–86
Core of learning experiences, 246
Countersuggestion, 224
Creature of habit, 96–99
Critical thinking, 187, 207
Cutaways, 258

Dale, Edgar, 246
Deficit motives, 99–102
Delivery techniques, 220–221; empathic, 221; kinetic, 220–221
Demonstrations, 261–262
Descriptive statistics, 145
Dewey, John, 122, 123
Dialogue, 304–305
Diffusion, 94, 95
Dog and pony show, 11
Dominant deficit motive, 102
Drucker, Peter, 102, 103
Dyadic interaction, 282–283

Easel stand, uses of, 269–270
Elements of the presentation, 18–20; adaptation to human obstacles, 19; to circumstances, 19; to motives, 19, 20; the recommendation, 18; of self, 18, 19
Emotion, 94, 95, 292–293
Empathy, 221, 284–286; interdependent, 286; in listening, 286
Encoding, 47
Esteem, 35, 67–68, 71; needs, 100–102
Ethos, *see* Source credibility
Evans, Bergen, 227
Evans, Franklin B., 283
Evidence, 168–169, 174–175
Exhibits, 262–263
Expectations, utilizing, 284

Fables, 180
Fallacies of presentation, 299–303; either-or analysis, 302–303; hasty generalization, 300–302; *post hoc,* 299–300
Fantasy in creativity, 304
Fear response, 93

Feedback, 48–49, 52, 58–59, 66
Feelings, 94, 95
Figurative analogy, 176–178
Figurative language, 225
Filmstrip projection, 271–272
Fisher, B. Aubrey, 123
Flannel board, 270
Flexibility-rigidity, 97–99
Flip chart, 270
Formal communication channels, 23
Formal status, and ad hoc meeting, 77
Fortran, 47

Galbraith, John K., 13, 64
Gibb, Jack R, 238
Giffin, Kim, 234
Gobbledegook, 226
Gould, C. R., 11, 154, 155
Gove, Bill, 227–228, 229
Graphs, 156–164; bar, 158–163; line, 156–158; pictograph, 164; pie chart, 163; semilogarithmic, 158; use in presentations, 164
Graham, Billy, 215, 216
Group attention span, 70–71
Group decision-making, 73–75
Group norms, 84–85

Habit, defined, 98
Habits as motive, 96–99
Herzberg, Frederick, 91, 92
Hovland, C. I., 235
Humor, 227–230
Hyperbole, 216
Hypnosis, 214
Hypothetical cases, 175–176

Implication, simple, 223–224
Impromptu 1 pattern, 126–129
Inductive leap, 292, 299
Inferential statistics, 145
Intent of a message, 195
Interorganizational presentations, 14
Interpercentile range, 143
Interpersonal presentations, 15
Interpreting evidence, 187
Intraorganizational presentations, 12–14
Involvement, 286–288

Janis, I. L., 235
John Jamison case, 3–7
Johnson, Lyndon B., 225

Kelley, H. D., 235
Kepner, Charles, 98
Key active listening techniques, 295–296

Kinescope, 263–264

Ladder of abstraction, 209; of deficit motives, 100
Language of alienation, 293
Leader, 77–78
Leaders, successful and unsuccessful, 109, 110
Leadership, in ad hoc meeting, 77; emergence, 83
Lemert, James, 234
Likert, Rensis, 93
Line graph, 156–158
Listening, 52–53, 288–306; creative, 303–306; critical, 295–303; comprehension, 288–295, and improvement of, 289–295; recreation syndrome, 289
Literal analogy, 176–178
Loaded language, 124, 192

McGregor, Douglas, 91, 103
Management, and authority, 27; duties of, 26; and responsibility, 26
Maslow, A. H., 99, 100
Mean, 141, 143
Meaning as perception, 244–245
Median, 141–142
Meetings, official organization, 28
Mertz, Robert, 234
Message, 48
Message preparation, 113–115; analysis stage, 113, 114; audience adaptation stage, 115
Mockups, 259–260
Mode, 141–142
Models, 258
Moderator, 77, 79
Monroe, Alan H., 130
Motion pictures, 265–267
Motivation, 90–106; misuse of, 91
Motive analysis, defined, 92; Jamison case, 105, 106
Mulling over, 113, 114, 205, 304
Multimedia room, 276–278
Multiple options, 233

Narratives, 178–180
Negative suggestion, 222
Newtonian physics, 65
Newton's law of gravity, 65–66
Nichols, Ralph G., 188
Nonverbal dimension, 217, 237–238
Nonverbal feedback, 58, 72–73
Normative generalization, 302

Note taking, 294–295
Notes, speaker's use of, 131, 132

Obstacles to listener understanding, 247
Official communication, 23
Opaque projection, 270–271
Opener, the, 128, 129
Optimum environment for presentation, 218
Oral reports, 12
Organization, 22–36; cultural context, 23; formal aspects of, 23–24; informal aspects of, 34–36
Organizational position, 28–32; barriers to understanding, 31–32; and message receiver, 30; and status, 28–32
Organizing materials, 115–119
Other-than-self centered motives, 102–105; preoccupation with people, 104, and with processes, 104
Overhead projector, 273–275

Parables, 179–180
Paradigm, defined, 43; group dynamics, 81; man-to-machine communication, 46; man-to-man communication, 51, 65
Participant, ad hoc meeting, 77–78
Participative involvement experiences, 256–261
Passive involvement experiences, 261–276
Patterns of organization, 120–131; psychological-progression, 130, 131; scientific problem-solving, 122–124; state the case and prove it, 125–129
Percentile, 142–143
Perception of message, and status, 29–30
Persuasion, defined, 91–93
Persuasiveness, and message source, 29–30
Physiological needs, 100–102
Pictograph, 164
Pie chart, 163
Piggy-back phenomenon, 230
Pitfall of projection, 4, 267–268
Planning reasoned content, 200–203
Position authority, and receiver, 33–34; and source, 32–33

Positive suggestion, 199, 222

Power, 34–35, 67–68

Power of positive thinking, 222, 291

Presentational speaking, described, 9–15; style of, 134–135

Presentations and oral reports, 12

Primary tensions, 81–82

Problem analysis, 203–206

Problem-solving, plan for, 204–206

Process, defined, 45–46

Proof, 168; tests of, 297

Proportioning, 117

Proposition, 116–117, 194–199; abstraction-concreteness of, 194; effective wording of, 195–199; moral and, 195; purpose and, 194, 195

Proxemics, 217–220

Proximity, 219

Quality of interaction, 17

Questions, 58–59

Quotations, 183

Random sampling, 145–147

Range, 143; of presentations, 11, 12

Rapport, building, 227–228

Reasoned appeals, criteria of, 208–210; absolute, 208–210; contingent, 208

Reasoned elements, evaluating, 188–193

Reasoning, 188–211, 296–303; cultural differences in, 207; and motivation, 207–208; tests of, 298–299

Recap with a twist, 126, 128, 129

Receiver, 48, 58

Reiteration, 181–182

Relevance, 112

Report language, 124, 192

Resistance to change, 16, 97–99

Response criterion, 137–139

Restatement, 181–183

Reuther, Walter, 216

Rigidity-flexibility, 97–99

Rise of presentational speaking, 7–9

Ritualistic presentations, 219

Rogers, Carl R., 97, 287

Role emergence, 83–84

Sampling, random and systematic, 145–147

Schuller, Charles F., 259

Secondary tensions, 82

Security needs, 100–102

Selecting material, 116, 117

Semilogarithmic graphs, 158

Sherman, John K., 216

Shock, 94, 95

Signal reaction, 214–216, 284

Slanting, 197–198

Slide projection, 271–273

Slogan, 183

Slope of abstraction-concreteness, 196

Small group, 62–70; complexity of, 65–68; optimum size for, 63

Social needs, 100–102

Source, 48, 71

Source credibility, 29–34, 174, 234–240; and formal position, 29; and personal characteristics, 29

Source-receiver interdependence, 281–288

Speaker-audience relationship, 219–220

Speaker-listener relationships, 282–288; action-reaction, 283–284; empathic, 284–286; involvement, 286–288; noninteractive, 283

Specialization, and formal status, 25–26; in organizations, 24–25

Specimens, 258

Speech speed, 291

Standard deviation, 143–144

Standard measures, 149

Statistical information, 136–137

Statistics, 139–166; and case studies, 169–170; and counting, 149–150; descriptive, 145; expressing relationships, 148–149; indexes of typicality, 141–144; indexes of variability, 142–144; inferential, 145–148; oversimplification of, 148; summary table of, 151–155

Status, 71

Stereotype of the speaker, 228, 235–237

Stereotypes, 99

Stereotyping, 77, 85

Still pictures as aids, 267–274

Strategy of selection, 4

Suggestion, 138; advantages of, 215–217; basic concept, 213–215; elements of, 192; example of, 215; and group norms, 85; nonverbal techniques, 217–221; verbal techniques, 221–234

Supporting material, 136; absolute tests, 137–138; response criterion, 137–138

Symbol reaction, 214–215, 284

Symbolic simulations, 259–260

Systematic sampling, 145–146

Table of organization, 27

Tables, 151–155

Tape recorder, see Audio recording and playback

Team play, 233–234

Television and video tape, 263–265

Terror threshold, 93

Testimony, 170–174; of authorities, 172–174; eyewitness, 171–172; hearsay, 171

Theory A and Theory B, 227–228

Theory X and Theory Y, 103, 104

Thought speed, 291

Threat persuasion, 92, 93

Together device, 230–231

Transfer, 219, 231–233

Transference, 94, 95

Transitions, 117–119; nonverbal, 117, 118; verbal, 118, 119

Tregoe, Benjamin, 98

Trust, 239–240, 287, 305

Truth, 137–138, 209–210

Twist, the, 126, 127

Two-valued orientation, 302–303

U2 spy plane case, 188–193

Understatement, 225

Unit plan for rational presentation, 200–203; basic structure, 200; sample unit, 203

Unity, 111

Vagueness, 225–226

Validity, 137–138, 209–210

Verbalism, preoccupation with, 245

Video tape, see Television and video tape

Weaver, Andrew T., 130

Wittich, Walter A., 259

Woods, David, 7, 9

Woolbert, Charles H., 130

Word manipulation, 224–225

Wording of propositions, 195–199

Yes response, 231

Zero-history group, 76, 77, 80, 81, 85

Printer and Binder: The Murray Printing Company

81 82 83 84 85   10 9 8 7

DATE DUE